D0824926

The CIVIC CULTURE

The Little, Brown Series
in Comparative Politics

Under the Editorship of

GABRIEL A. ALMOND

JAMES S. COLEMAN

LUCIAN W. PYE

AN ANALYTIC STUDY

The CIVIC CULTURE

POLITICAL ATTITUDES AND DEMOCRACY IN FIVE NATIONS

Gabriel A. Almond
Stanford University

Sidney Verba
Stanford University

Boston
LITTLE, BROWN AND COMPANY

LIBRARY OF CONGRESS CATALOG CARD NO. 65–12525

ELEVENTH PRINTING

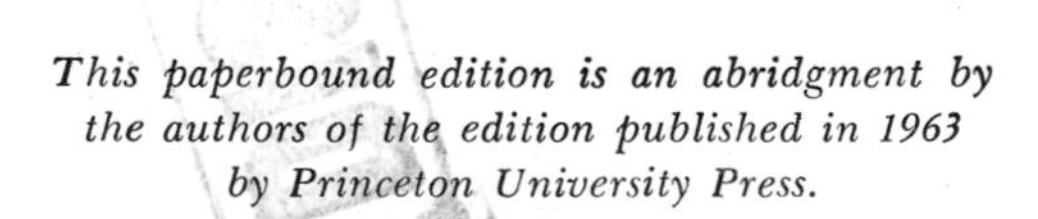

This paperbound edition is an abridgment by the authors of the edition published in 1963 by Princeton University Press.

Published simultaneously in Canada by Little, Brown & Company (Canada) Limited

PRINTED IN THE UNITED STATES OF AMERICA

TO RICHARD, PETER, AND SUSAN;

MARGARET AND ERICA:

CITIZENS AND FUTURE CITIZENS

. . . And this our form, as committed not to the few, but to the whole body of the people, is called a democracy . . . . The offices of the State we go through without obstructions from one another; and live together in the mutual endearments of private life without suspicions; not angry with a neighbor for following the bent of his own humor, nor putting on that countenance of discontent, which pains though it cannot punish — so that in private life we converse without diffidence or damage, while we dare not on any account offend against the public, through the reverence we bear to the magistrates and the laws . . . . There is visible in the same persons an attention to their own private concerns and those of the public; and in others engaged in the labor of life there is a competent skill in the affairs of government. For we are the only people who think him that does not meddle in state affairs — not indolent, but good for nothing.

— PERICLES, *On the Causes of Athenian Greatness*

Foreword

The Little, Brown Series in Comparative Politics has three main objectives. First, it will meet the need of teachers to deal with both western and non-western countries in their introductory course offerings. Second, by following a common approach in the analysis of individual political systems, it will make it possible for teachers to compare these countries systematically and cumulatively. And third, it will contribute toward re-establishing the classic relationship between comparative politics and political theory, a relationship which has been neglected in recent decades. In brief, the series seeks to be global in scope, genuinely introductory and comparative in character, and concerned with broadening and deepening our understanding of the nature and variety of political systems.

The series has two parts: the Country Studies and the Analytical Studies. The country studies deal with a set of problems and processes deriving from a functional, as against a purely structural, approach to the study of political systems. We are gratified that the participants, all of them mature scholars with original insights of their own, were willing to organize their discussions around a common set of functional topics in the interest of furthering comparisons. At the same time, each author has been urged to adapt the common framework to the special problems of the country he is discussing and to express his own theoretical point of view.

An introductory book, *Comparative Politics: A Developmental Approach,* written by Gabriel Almond and G. Bingham Powell, Jr., provides an analytical supplement to the Country Studies. It also opens our set of Analytical Studies, which offer basic discussions of such topics as political change in the emerging nations, comparative analyses of interest groups, political socialization, political communication, political culture, and the like. We hope these books will prove to be useful and stimulating supplements to the country series as well as points of departure in more advanced courses.

In *The Civic Culture* Gabriel A. Almond and Sidney Verba apply the modern techniques of social research to some of the classic problems of comparative politics. It is a study of the political culture of democracy. It describes the political beliefs, aspirations, emotions, and actual participation in politics of citizens in five countries — Germany, Italy, Mexico, Great Britain, and the United States. Their purpose in presenting this book is to give an understanding of the relationship between the attitudes of citizens and the functioning of modern democratic states. *The Civic Culture* is based on one of the largest cross-national surveys ever attempted in the field of comparative politics. Over 5,000 interviews were conducted as a basis for the book.

This abridgment of *The Civic Culture* contains the substantive portions of the clothbound edition published by the Princeton University Press in 1963. It is essentially a condensation and no material changes have been made. Some of the data reproduced in the larger edition are not reported here. The principal difference lies in the absence of description and discussion of the methodological apparatus of the study. For a fuller discussion of the methodological problems of cross-national survey research, of the sample used in this study, and for a full report of the questionnaires used, the reader is invited to consult the clothbound edition.

Gabriel A. Almond
James S. Coleman
Lucian W. Pye

Preface

THIS STUDY of the political culture of democracy had its inspiration about thirty years ago in the Social Science Division of the University of Chicago. Much of what now goes under the name of the behavioral approach to the study of politics originated there in the period between the wars. It is a tribute to the vision of the men who created this leaven that it has taken three or four decades for their conception of political science to become a common possession. In particular, this study owes its inspiration to the work of Charles E. Merriam. His *Civic Training* series formulated many of the problems with which this study is concerned, and his *New Aspects of Politics* suggested the methods that have been used in its execution.

We are concerned in this book with a number of classic themes of political science: with what the Greeks called "civic virtue" and its consequences for the effectiveness and stability of the democratic polity; and with the kind of community life, social organization, and upbringing of children that fosters civic virtue. In using survey research to study these classic themes, we are also following the traditional practice of relying on the most precise methods available to us for the investigation of these problems. Perhaps Tocqueville and Bryce, were they living today, would have relied somewhat on the cross-section survey in their comparative studies of democratic attitudes.

Our study will suggest that there exists in Britain and the United States a pattern of political attitudes and an underlying set of social attitudes that is supportive of a stable democratic process. In the other three nations studied — Germany, Italy, and Mexico — these patterns are less evident. But this conclusion ought not to lead the reader to despair about the prospects for democracy in the latter three nations. Our study is but a snapshot in a rapidly changing world, and though we can specify some serious problems these nations may have to overcome to achieve a more stable and democratic polity, we cannot and do not conclude that these problems are impossible of solution. Even more important, our conclusions ought not to lead the reader to complacency about democracy in Britain and the United States. As long as full participation in the political system and access to the channels of social betterment are denied to significant segments of their populations, their democratic promise remains unfulfilled.

Five thousand people — Britons, Germans, Italians, Mexicans, and Americans — were interviewed to provide us with our data. We asked our respondents in the cities, towns, and villages of these five countries to cooperate with us in a scientific study, under university auspices, of problems of democracy and political participation. In a very real sense, this is their book, and we as authors hope we have kept faith with them.

Five years transpired from the planning of this study to its completion, and our debts are many. We are pleased first to acknowledge the strong support given by the late Frederick S. Dunn, Director of the Center of International Studies at Princeton University when the study was begun, and by Klaus Knorr, Director of the Center during the later phases of the project. In the development of the research design and survey instrument, as well as in the administration of the project, we had the help of International Research Associates of New York; we acknowledge especially the collaboration of Elmo Wilson, Helen Dinerman, and Frank Bonilla. Morris Rosenberg of the National Institute of Mental Health made important contributions in the planning stage, in the construction of the research instrument, and in the analysis of the pretests. Herbert

Hyman helped us greatly in the planning and pretesting stages of the study. Maurice and Ruth Farber and Robert E. Lane made original contributions to the construction of the survey instrument.

During the course of the study we benefited from the research assistance of a number of people. Louise K. Comfort took a major role in the planning and pretesting of the interview schedules and in the gathering of comparable material from other surveys. Anne Munholland provided general statistical assistance and performed the exacting task of rechecking our data for publication. Morris Davis contributed to our analysis of other survey material and prepared a memorandum on theories of citizenship. Annelisa Kelley helped with the gathering of other survey data and aided in the translation of the research instrument. Annette Ducey and William Flanagan supervised and carried out much of the statistical analysis of the data; Lotte Doverman and Peter Almond helped in the statistical analysis. We are grateful also for the aid of Robert Scott in the analysis of the Mexican life-history interviews.

For secretarial assistance we are grateful to Gail Ahlgren, Barbara Jacobs, and Sarah Bondy. The Center for Advanced Study in the Behavioral Sciences provided the facilities for the final preparation of the manuscript.

We are happy to acknowledge our collaboration with the interviewing agencies in each of the nations studied. In the United States our survey was conducted by the National Opinion Research Center of the University of Chicago, and it was under the supervision of Selma Monsky and Jacob Feldman; in Great Britain, Research Services Ltd. of London conducted the survey under the supervision of Mark Abrams and A. E. S. Ehrenberg; in Germany the DIVO Institut, Frankfort, carried out the interviewing program under the direction of Gerhart Baumert and Peter Schmidt; in Italy the work was done by the Istituto Italiano Dell'Opinione Pubblica, Milan, under the direction of Ernesto Norbedo. The Mexican survey was carried out by International Research Associates of Mexico, Mexico City, under the supervision of George Gaither and Alfred Wilson.

An earlier draft of the manuscript benefited from the careful reading and valuable comments of Harry Eckstein, Herbert Hyman, Robert Scott, and Alex Inkeles.

This study was generously supported by the Carnegie Corporation of New York. We have many reasons to express our gratitude to its officers, in particular to John Gardner, William Marvel, and James Perkins. Needless to say, responsibility for the substance and the conclusions of the study is ours.

Gabriel A. Almond
Sidney Verba

Table of Contents

The CIVIC CULTURE

CHAPTER I

An Approach to Political Culture

THIS IS A STUDY of the political culture of democracy and of the social structures and processes that sustain it. The faith of the Enlightenment in the inevitable triumph of human reason and liberty has been twice shaken in recent decades. The development of Fascism and Communism after World War I raised serious doubts about the inevitability of democracy in the West; and we still cannot be certain that the continental European nations will discover a stable form of democratic process suitable to their particular cultures and social institutions; nor can we more than hope that together they will discover a European democracy.

Without having first resolved these doubts, the events since World War II have raised questions of the future of democracy on a world scale. The "national explosions" in Asia and Africa and the almost universal pressure by previously subjected and isolated peoples for admission into the modern world put this more special political question into the broader context of the future character of the world's culture. Culture change has acquired a new significance in world history. The groping toward enlightenment and control over nature that acquired momentum three or four centuries ago in the West has become a world-wide process, and its tempo has shifted from centuries to decades.

The central question of public policy in the next decades is what content this emerging world culture will have. We already have a partial answer to this question and could have predicted it from our knowledge of the processes of cultural diffusion.[1] Physical goods and their mode of production seem to present the least difficulties in diffusion. It is apparent that these aspects of Western culture are diffusing rapidly, along with the technology upon which they depend. Since economic modernization and national unification require a large social overhead investment in transportation, communication, and education, and since these in turn call for taxation, regulation, and administration, the model of a rational bureaucracy also diffuses relatively easily. The idea of an efficient bureaucracy has much in common with the idea of a rational technology. Lucian Pye refers to modern social organization as being based on an organizational technology.[2] It has in common with engineering and technology a mixture of rationality and authority. Engineering is the application of rationality and authority to material things; modern social organization is their application to human beings and social groups. Though the non-Western world is far from having successfully developed an industrial technology and an efficient bureaucracy, there can be little question that it wants these institutions and has some understanding of them.

What is problematical about the content of the emerging world culture is its political character. Although the movement toward technology and rationality of organization appears with great uniformity throughout the world, the direction of political change is less clear. But one aspect of this new world political culture is discernible: it will be a political culture of participation. If there is a political revolution going on throughout the world, it is what might be called the participation explosion. In all the new nations of the world the belief that the ordinary man is politically relevant — that he ought to be an involved participant in the political system — is widespread. Large groups of people who

[1] Ralph Linton, *The Study of Man: An Introduction,* New York, 1936, pp. 324-46.

[2] Committee on Comparative Politics, Social Science Research Council, *Memorandum on the Concept of Modernization,* November 1961.

have been outside of politics are demanding entrance into the political system. And the political elites are rare who do not profess commitment to this goal.

Though this coming world political culture appears to be dominated by the participation explosion, what the mode of participation will be is uncertain. The emerging nations are presented with two different models of the modern participatory state, the democratic and the totalitarian. The democratic state offers the ordinary man the opportunity to take part in the political decision-making process as an influential citizen; the totalitarian offers him the role of the "participant subject." [3] Both modes have appeal to the new nations, and which will win out — if indeed some amalgam of the two does not emerge — cannot be foretold.

If the democratic model of the participatory state is to develop in these new nations, it will require more than the formal institutions of democracy — universal suffrage, the political party, the elective legislature. These in fact are also part of the totalitarian participation pattern, in a formal if not functional sense. A democratic form of participatory political system requires as well a political culture consistent with it. But the transfer of the political culture of the Western democratic states to the emerging nations encounters serious difficulties. There are two principal reasons. The first of these concerns the nature of the democratic culture itself. The great ideas of democracy — the freedoms and dignities of the individual, the principle of government by consent of the governed — are elevating and inspiring. They capture the imaginations of many of the leaders of the new states and of the modernizing older ones. But the working principles of the democratic polity and its civic culture — the ways in which political elites make decisions, their norms and attitudes, as well as the norms and attitudes of the ordinary citizen, his relation to government and to his fellow citizens — are subtler cultural components. They have the more diffuse proper-

[3] See Frederick C. Barghoorn, "Soviet Political Culture," a paper prepared for the Summer Institute on Political Culture, sponsored by the Committee on Comparative Politics, Social Science Research Council, Summer 1962.

ties of belief systems or of codes of personal relations, which the anthropologists tell us spread only with great difficulty, undergoing substantial change in the process.

Actually, Western social science has only begun to codify the operating characteristics of the democratic polity itself. The doctrine and practice of a rational bureaucracy as an instrument of the democratic political powers are less than a century old. Doubts about the possibility of a neutral bureaucracy were expressed in England as recently as the 1930's, and on the European continent such doubt is widespread today. The complex infrastructure of the democratic polity — political parties, interest groups, and the media of communications — and the understanding of their inner workings, operating norms, and social-psychological preconditions are only now being realized in the West. Thus the image of the democratic polity that is conveyed to the elites of the new nations is obscure and incomplete and heavily stresses ideology and legal norms. What must be learned about democracy is a matter of attitude and feeling, and this is harder to learn.

The second principal reason why the diffusion of democracy encounters difficulties among the new nations concerns the objective problems confronting these nations. They are entering history with archaic technologies and social systems, drawn toward the gleam and power of the technological and scientific revolutions. It is not difficult to see why they should be drawn toward a technocratic image of the polity: a polity in which authoritarian bureaucracy predominates and political organization becomes a device for human and social engineering.

In almost every instance, however, though in differing measure, the leaders of the modernizing nations appreciate the distortions and the risks in adopting an authoritarian form of polity. Though they cannot fully understand the subtle balances of the democratic polity and the nuances of the civic culture, they tend to acknowledge their legitimacy as the expression of an impulse toward the humane polity. In characterizing their situation, we have left out a significant element. For though it is true that they are fascinated by science and technology and are drawn to an impatient technocratic polity as a means of attaining the new things of this world, they are also the creatures of their own traditional cultures and would prefer to deal gently with these cultures if this choice were available.

THE CIVIC CULTURE

It is as an answer to this ambivalence that the civic culture recommends itself. For the civic culture is not a modern culture, but one that combines modernity with tradition. Britain offers an example of how such a culture can develop. The development of the civic culture in Britain may be understood as the product of a series of encounters between modernization and traditionalism — encounters sharp enough to effect significant change but not so sharp or so concentrated in time as to create disintegration or polarization. Partly because of her insular security, Britain came into the era of national unification and of absolutism able to tolerate a greater measure of aristocratic, local, and corporate autonomy than could continental Europe. A first step toward secularization was the separation from the Church of Rome and the beginnings of toleration of religious diversity. A second step was the emergence of a thriving and self-confident merchant class, and the involvement of court and aristocracy in the risks and calculations of trade and commerce.

Independent aristocrats with secure local power in the countryside, courageous nonconformists, rich and self-confident merchants — these were the forces that transformed the tradition of the feudal estates into the parliamentary tradition and enabled Britain to pass through the era of absolutism without destroying her pluralism. Britain thus entered the industrial revolution with a political culture among its elites which made it possible to assimilate the gross and rapid changes in social structure in the eighteenth and nineteenth centuries without sharp discontinuities. The aristocratic Whigs found it possible to enter a coalition with nonconformist merchants and industrialists, to establish securely the principles of parliamentary supremacy and representation. The traditional aristocratic and monarchic forces assimilated enough of this civic culture to compete with the secularist tendencies for popular support and, indeed, to mitigate their rationalism and impart to them a love and respect for the sacredness of the nation and its ancient institutions.

What emerged was a third culture, neither traditional nor modern but partaking of both; a pluralistic culture based on communication and persuasion, a culture of consensus and diversity, a culture that permitted change but moderated it. This was the civic culture. With this civic culture already consolidated, the working classes could enter into politics and, in a process of trial and error, find the language in which to couch their demands and the means to make them effective. It was in this culture of diversity and consensualism, rationalism and traditionalism, that the structure of British democracy could develop: parliamentarism and representation, the aggregative political party and the responsible and neutral bureaucracy, the associational and bargaining interest groups, and the autonomous and neutral media of communication. English parliamentarism included the traditional and modern forces; the party system aggregated and combined them; the bureaucracy became responsible to the new political forces; and the political parties, interest groups, and neutral media of communication meshed continuously with the diffuse interest groupings of the community and with its primary communications networks.

We have concentrated on British experience because the whole story of the emergence of the civic culture is told in British history, whereas developments in the United States and the countries of the "Old Commonwealth" began after some of the major battles had been won. Actually, in the course of the nineteenth century the development of the democratic culture and infrastructure was more rapid and more unequivocal in the United States than in Britain, since the United States was a new and rapidly expanding society and relatively unimpeded by traditional institutions. Though their basic patterns are similar, the civic cultures of Britain and the United States have somewhat different contents, reflecting these differences in national histories and social structures.

On the European continent the record is more mixed.

Though their patterns differ in many respects from those of Britain and America, the Scandinavian countries, Low Countries, and Switzerland appear to have worked out their own version of a political culture and practice of accommodation and compromise. In France, Germany, and Italy the encounters between modernizing tendencies and the traditional powers seem to have been too massive and too uncompromising to permit the emergence of a shared culture of political accommodation. The civic culture is present in the form of aspiration, and the democratic infrastructure is still far from being attained.

The civic culture and the open polity, then, represent the great and problematic gifts of the West. The technology and science of the West have now already passed out of her unique possession and everywhere are destroying and transforming traditional societies and cultures. Can the open polity and the civic culture — man's discovery of a humane and conservative way to handle social change and participation — spread as well?

As we consider the origin of the open polity and the civic culture — indeed, as we consider the areas in the West where their emergence is still in doubt — we may fall victim to one or both of two moods. The first is one of mystery or awe over a process whereby mankind on only a small part of the earth's surface muddled toward a humane and reasoned taming of violence and groped toward its transformation into a constructive instrument available to all interests. As mystery, it becomes a unique cultural heritage unavailable to foreigners. The second mood is one of pessimism, which seems to have replaced the mood of democratic optimism that existed before World War I. How can a set of arrangements and attitudes so fragile, so intricate, and so subtle be transplanted out of historical and cultural context? Or, how can these subtleties and these humane etiquettes survive even among ourselves in a world caught in the grip of a science and technology run wild, destructive of tradition and of community and possibly of life itself?

No one can provide definitive answers to these questions. But as social scientists we can put the questions in such a way as to get useful answers. Though we may share the mood of wonder and awe at the intricacy of the democratic mechanisms and the unique historical experience out of which they emerged, we are confronted with a contemporary historical challenge for which mood by itself is an inadequate response. If we are to come closer to understanding the problems of the diffusion of democratic culture, we have to be able to specify the content of *what* has to be diffused, to develop appropriate measures for it, to discover its quantitative incidence and demographic distribution in countries with a wide range of experience with democracy. With such knowledge we can speculate intelligently about "how much of what" must be present in a country before democratic institutions take root in congruent attitudes and expectations.

Efforts to deal with this problem have usually been based on impressions and inferences from history, on inferences from democratic ideology, on certain kinds of sociological analysis, or on psychological insights. Thus in our efforts to estimate the prospects of democracy in countries such as Germany and Italy, or in the developing areas of the non-Western world, we frequently try to draw "lessons" from British and American history. It has been argued, for example, that the long continuity of British and American political experience and the gradual process of change have both contributed to effective democratization. Similarly, the growth of a vigorous and numerous middle class, the development of Protestantism, and in particular the nonconformist sects, have been considered vital to the development of stable democratic institutions in Britain, the Old Commonwealth, and the United States. There have been efforts to derive from these experiences some standards as to what attitudes and behavior must be present in other countries if they are to become democratic.

Even more common than drawing inferences from history has been our tendency to derive criteria of what has to be diffused from the institutional and ideological norms of democracy itself. It is argued that if a democratic system is based on the sharing of influence among the adult population as a whole, then, if the system is not to be subverted, the individual must use his power intelligently for the good of the polity. Theorists of democracy from Aristotle to Bryce have stressed that democracies are maintained by active citizen participation in civic affairs, by a high level of information about public affairs, and by a widespread sense of civic responsibility. These doctrines tell us what a democratic citizen ought to be like if he is to behave according to the requirements of the system.

Still a third type of investigation of the conditions favoring the development of stable democracy are studies of the economic and social conditions associated with democratic systems. Both Lipset and Coleman find a strong correlation between indices of modernization and democratization.[4] The main problem presented by these studies is that the cultural and psychological consequences of "modern" technologies and processes are left to inference. We know that democracies, in comparison to other political systems, tend to have more literate and educated people, that their per capita income and wealth are higher, and that they enjoy in greater proportions the amenities of modern civilization. But this type of analysis not only omits the psychological basis of democratization, it also cannot explain the significant deviant cases. Thus Germany and France, which rank high on the indices of modernization, are classified by Lipset as unstable democracies. Cuba and Venezuela, both of which rank high in economic development in Latin America, have long histories of dictatorship and instability. This kind of study is suggestive of hypotheses but does not tell us directly what kind of cluster of attitudes is associated with democracy.

Another type of approach to the culture and psychology of democracy is based on the insights of psychoanalysis. Harold Lasswell has gone furthest in specifying the personality characteristics of the "democrat."[5] In his list of democratic character qualities he includes (1) an "open ego," by which he means a warm and inclusive attitude toward other human be-

[4] Seymour M. Lipset, *Political Man,* New York, 1960, pp. 45ff.; Gabriel A. Almond and James Coleman, *The Politics of the Developing Areas,* Princeton, N.J., 1960, pp. 538ff.

[5] *The Political Writings of Harold D. Lasswell,* Glencoe, Ill., 1951, pp. 495ff.; Lasswell, *Power and Personality,* New York, 1946, pp. 148ff.

ings; (2) a capacity for sharing values with others; (3) a multivalued rather than a single-valued orientation; (4) trust and confidence in the human environment, and (5) relative freedom from anxiety. Though the relationship between these characteristics and democratic behavior seems to be clear, Lasswell's democratic qualities are not specifically *political* attitudes and feelings, and they may actually be encountered in great frequency in societies that are not democratic in structure.

Our study grows out of this body of theory about the characteristics and preconditions of the culture of democracy. What we have done amounts to a series of experiments intended to test some of these hypotheses. Rather than inferring the properties of democratic culture from political institutions or social conditions, we have attempted to specify its content by examining attitudes in a number of operating democratic systems. And rather than deriving the social-psychological preconditions of democracy from psychological theory, we have sought to determine whether and to what extent these relations actually exist in functioning democratic systems. We do not argue that our study will shut off speculation and provide the precise and tested propositions of a complete theory of democracy, but, rather, that some of these propositions will survive the test of empirical-quantitative analysis and some will not. This stage of experiment should focus and direct inquiry by providing some answers to old questions and suggesting some new questions.

In still another respect we hope to contribute to the development of a scientific theory of democracy. By far the greatest amount of empirical research on democratic attitudes has been done in the United States. In our study we have included, in addition to our own country, Britain, Germany, Italy, and Mexico. Why we selected these particular countries is discussed below. Our five-country study offers us the opportunity to escape from this American parochialism and to discover whether or not relations found in the American data are also encountered in democratic countries whose historical experiences and political and social structures differ from one another.

TYPES OF POLITICAL CULTURE

In our comparison of the political cultures of five contemporary democracies, we employ a number of concepts and classifications which it will be useful to specify and define. We speak of the "political culture" of a nation rather than the "national character" or "modal personality," and of "political socialization" rather than of child development or child rearing in general terms, not because we reject the psychological and anthropological theories that relate political attitudes to other components of personality, or because we reject those theories which stress the relationship between child development in general terms and the induction of the child into his adult political roles and attitudes. Indeed, this study could not have been made without the prior work of those historians, social philosophers, anthropologists, sociologists, psychologists, and psychiatrists who have been concerned with the relationships between the psychological and political characteristics of nations. In particular, this study has been greatly influenced by the "culture-personality" or "psychocultural approach" to the study of political phenomena. This approach has developed a substantial theoretical and monographic literature in the past twenty-five years.[6]

[6] General theoretical statements of this approach are to be found *inter alia* in Ruth Benedict, *Patterns of Culture,* New York, 1934; Alex Inkeles and Daniel Levinson, "National Character: The Study of Modal Personality and Socio-Cultural Systems," in Gardner Lindzey (ed.), *Handbook of Social Psychology,* Cambridge, Mass., 1954, Vol. II; Bert Kaplan (ed.), *Studying Personality Cross-Culturally,* Evanston, Ill., 1961; Abram Kardiner, *The Psychological Frontiers of Society,* New York, 1939; Kardiner, *The Individual and His Society,* New York, 1945; Clyde Kluckhohn, Henry Murray, and David Schneider, *Personality in Nature, Society, and Culture,* New York, 1955; Harold D. Lasswell, *Psychopathology and Politics* in *Political Writings, op. cit.;* Nathan Leites, "Psychocultural Hypotheses About Political Acts," in *World Politics,* Vol. I, 1948; Ralph Linton, *The Cultural Background of Personality,* New York, 1945; Margaret Mead, "The Study of National Character," in Daniel Lerner and Harold D. Lasswell, *The Policy Sciences,* Stanford, 1951. Particularly relevant to our work is Alex Inkeles, "National Character and Modern Political Systems," in Francis L. K. Hsu (ed.), *Psychological Anthropology,* Homewood, Ill., 1961. And one of the most important recent contributions to the theory of national charac-

We employ the term "political culture" for two reasons. First, if we are to ascertain the relationships between political and nonpolitical attitudes and developmental patterns, we have to separate the former from the latter even though the boundary between them is not as sharp as our terminology would suggest. The term "political culture" thus refers to the specifically political orientations — attitudes toward the political system and its various parts, and attitudes toward the role of the self in the system. We speak of a political culture just as we can speak of an economic culture or a religious culture. It is a set of orientations toward a special set of social objects and processes.

But we also choose political *culture,* rather than some other special concept, because it enables us to utilize the conceptual frameworks and approaches of anthropology, sociology, and psychology. Our thinking is enriched when we employ, for example, such categories of anthropology and psy-

---

ter and political culture is Lucian W. Pye's *Politics, Personality, and Nation Building,* New Haven, 1962, which both develops a general theory of personality and political attitudes and applies this to a study of Burmese patterns.

Studies of Germany include: R. Brickner, *Is Germany Incurable?* Philadelphia, 1943; H. V. Dicks, "Personality Traits and National Socialist Ideology," *Human Relations,* Vol. III, 1950; David Rodnick, *Postwar Germans,* New Haven, 1948, and Bertram Schaffner, *Fatherland. A Study of Authoritarianism in the German Family,* New York, 1948.

Studies of the United States include: Geoffrey Gorer, *The American People,* New York, 1948; Margaret Mead, *And Keep Your Powder Dry,* New York, 1942, and David Riesman, *The Lonely Crowd,* New Haven, 1950.

Studies of Russia include: H. V. Dicks, "Observations on Contemporary Russian Behavior," *Human Relations,* Vol. V, 1952; Geoffrey Gorer and John Rickman, *The People of Great Russia,* London, 1949; Nathan Leites, *A Study of Bolshevism,* Glencoe, Ill., 1953; Margaret Mead, *Soviet Attitudes Toward Authority,* New York, 1951, and Dinko Tomasic, *The Impact of Russian Culture on Soviet Communism,* Glencoe, 1953.

For England, see Geoffrey Gorer, *Exploring English Character,* New York, 1955. For France, see Nathan Leites, *On the Game of Politics in France,* Stanford, 1959; Rhoda Metraux and Margaret Mead, *Themes in French Culture,* Stanford, 1954, and Lawrence Wylie, *Village in The Vaucluse,* Cambridge, Mass., 1957. And for Japan, see Ruth F. Benedict, *The Chrysanthemum and The Sword,* Boston, 1946.

chology as socialization, culture conflict, and acculturation. Similarly, our capacity to understand the emergence and transformation of political systems grows when we draw upon the body of theory and speculation concerned with the general phenomena of social structure and process.

We appreciate the fact that anthropologists use the term culture in a variety of ways, and that by bringing it into the conceptual vocabulary of political science we are in danger of importing its ambiguities as well as its advantages. Here we can only stress that we employ the concept of culture in only one of its many meanings: that of *psychological orientation toward social objects*. When we speak of the political culture of a society, we refer to the political system as internalized in the cognitions, feelings, and evaluations of its population. People are inducted into it just as they are socialized into nonpolitical roles and social systems. Conflicts of political cultures have much in common with other culture conflicts, and political acculturative processes are more understandable if we view them in the light of the resistances and the fusional and incorporative tendencies of cultural change in general.

Thus the concept of political culture helps us to escape from the diffuseness of such general anthropological terms as cultural ethos and from the assumption of homogeneity that the concept implies. It enables us to formulate hypotheses about relationships among the different components of culture and to test these hypotheses empirically. With the concept of political socialization we can go beyond the rather simple assumptions of the psychocultural school regarding relationships between general child development patterns and adult political attitudes. We can relate specific adult political attitudes and behavioral propensities to the manifest and latent political socialization experiences of childhood.

The political culture of a nation is the particular distribution of patterns of orientation toward political objects among the members of the nation. Before we can arrive at such distributions, we need to have some way of systematically tapping individual orientations toward political objects. In other words, we need to define and specify modes of political orientation and classes of political objects. Our definition and classification of types of political orientation follow Parsons and Shils, as has been suggested elsewhere.[7] "Orientation" refers to the internalized aspects of objects and relationships. It includes (1) "cognitive orientation," that is, knowledge of and belief about the political system, its roles and the incumbents of these roles, its inputs, and its outputs; (2) "affective orientation," or feelings about the political system, its roles, personnel, and performance, and (3) "evaluational orientation," the judgments and opinions about political objects that typically involve the combination of value standards and criteria with information and feelings.

In classifying objects of political orientation, we start with the "general" political system. We deal here with the system as a whole and include such feelings as patriotism or alienation, such cognitions and evaluations of the nation as "large" or "small," "strong" or "weak," and of the polity as "democratic," "constitutional," or "socialistic." At the other extreme we distinguish orientations toward the "self" as political actor; the content and quality of norms of personal political obligation, and the content and quality of the sense of personal competence vis-à-vis the political system. In treating the component parts of the political system we distinguish, first, three broad classes of objects: (1) specific *roles* or *structures,* such as legislative bodies, executives, or bureaucracies; (2) *incumbents* of roles, such as particular monarchs, legislators, and administrators, and (3) particular public *policies, decisions,* or *enforcements* of decisions. These structures, incumbents, and decisions may in turn be classified broadly by whether they are involved either in the political or "input" process or in the administrative or "output" process. By "political" or "input" process we refer to the flow of demands from the society into the polity and the conversion of these demands into authoritative policies. Some structures that are predominantly involved in the input process are political parties, interest groups, and the media of communication. By the administrative or output process we refer to that process

[7] Gabriel A. Almond, "Comparative Political Systems," *Journal of Politics,* Vol. XVIII, 1956; Talcott Parsons and Edward A. Shils, *Toward a General Theory of Action,* Cambridge, Mass., 1951, pp. 53ff.

by which authoritative policies are applied or enforced. Structures predominantly involved in this process would include bureaucracies and courts.

We realize that any such distinction does violence to the actual continuity of the political process and to the multifunctionality of political structures. Much broad policy is made in bureaucracies and by courts; and structures that we label as input, such as interest groups and political parties, are often concerned with the details of administration and enforcement. What we are referring to is a difference in emphasis, and one that is of great importance in the classification of political cultures. The distinction we draw between participant and subject political cultures turns in part on the presence or absence of orientation toward specialized input structures. For our classification of political cultures it is not of great importance that these specialized input structures are also involved in the performance of enforcement functions and that the specialized administrative ones are involved in the performance of input functions. The important thing for our classification is what political objects individuals are oriented to, how they are oriented to them, and whether these objects are predominantly involved in the "upward" flow of policy making or in the "downward" flow of policy enforcement. We shall treat this problem in greater detail when we define the major classes of political culture.

TABLE I.1 *Dimensions of political orientation*

	1. System as general object	*2. Input objects*	*3. Output objects*	*4. Self as object*
Cognition				
Affect				
Evaluation				

We can consolidate what we have thus far said about individual orientations toward the polity in a simple 3 x 4 matrix. Table I.1 tells us that the political orientation of an individual can be tapped systematically if we explore the following:

1. What knowledge does he have of his nation and of his political system in general terms, its history, size, location, power, "constitutional" characteristics, and the like? What are his feelings toward these systemic characteristics? What are his more or less considered opinions and judgments of them?

2. What knowledge does he have of the structures and roles, the various political elites, and the policy proposals that are involved in the upward flow of policy making? What are his feelings and opinions about these structures, leaders, and policy proposals?

3. What knowledge does he have of the downward flow of policy enforcement, the structures, individuals, and decisions involved in these processes? What are his feelings and opinions of them?

TABLE I.2 *Types of political culture*

	System as general object	*Input objects*	*Output objects*	*Self as active participant*
Parochial	0	0	0	0
Subject	1	0	1	0
Participant	1	1	1	1

4. How does he perceive of himself as a member of his political system? What knowledge does he have of his rights, powers, obligations, and of strategies of access to influence? How does he feel about his capabilities? What norms of participation or of performance does he acknowledge and employ in formulating political judgments, or in arriving at opinions?

Characterizing the political culture of a nation means, in effect, filling in such a matrix for a valid sample of its population. The political culture becomes the frequency of different kinds of cognitive, affective, and evaluative orientations toward the political system in general, its input and output aspects, and the self as political actor.

Parochial Political Culture. When this frequency of orientations to specialized political objects of the four kinds specified in Table I.2 approaches zero, we can speak of the political culture as a parochial one. The political cultures of African tribal societies and autonomous local communities referred to by Coleman[8] would fall into this category. In these societies there are no specialized political roles: headmanship, chieftainship, "shamanship" are diffuse political–economic–religious roles, and for members of these societies the political orientations to these roles are not separated from their religious and social orientations. A parochial orientation also implies the comparative absence of expectations of change initiated by the political system. The parochial expects nothing from the political system. Similarly, in the centralized African chiefdoms and kingdoms to which Coleman refers, the political cultures would be predominantly parochial, although the development of somewhat more specialized roles in these societies might mean the beginnings of more differentiated political orientations. Even larger-scale and more differentiated polities, however, may have predominantly parochial cultures. But relatively pure parochialism is likely to occur in simpler traditional systems where political specialization is minimal. Parochialism in more differentiated political systems is likely to be affective and normative rather than cognitive. That is to say, the remote tribesmen in Nigeria or Ghana may be aware in a dim sort of way of the existence of a central political regime. But his feelings toward it are uncertain or negative, and he has not internalized any norms to regulate his relations to it.

The Subject Political Culture. The second major type of political culture listed in Table I.2 is the subject culture. Here there is a high frequency of orientations toward a differentiated political system and toward the output aspects of the system, but orientations toward specifically input objects, and toward the self as an active participant, approach zero. The subject is aware of specialized governmental authority; he is affectively oriented to it, perhaps taking pride in it, perhaps disliking it; and he evaluates it either as legitimate or as not. But the relationship is toward the system on the general level, and toward the output, administrative, or "downward flow" side of the political system; it is essentially a pas-

[8] Almond and Coleman, *Politics of the Developing Areas,* p. 254.

sive relationship, although there is, as we shall show below, a limited form of competence that is appropriate in a subject culture.

Again we are speaking of the pure subject orientation that is likely to exist in a society in which there is no differentiated input structure. The subject orientation in political systems that have developed democratic institutions is likely to be affective and normative rather than cognitive. Thus a French royalist is aware of democratic institutions; he simply does not accord legitimacy to them.

The Participant Political Culture. The third major type of political culture, the participant culture, is one in which the members of the society tend to be explicitly oriented to the system as a whole and to both the political and adminstrative structures and processes: in other words, to both the input and output aspects of the political system. Individual members of the participant polity may be favorably or unfavorably oriented to the various classes of political objects. They tend to be oriented toward an "activist" role of the self in the polity, though their feelings and evaluations of such a role may vary from acceptance to rejection, as we shall show below.

This threefold classification of political cultures does not assume that one orientation replaces the others. The subject culture does not eliminate diffuse orientations to the primary and intimate structures of community. To the diffuse orientations to lineage groups, religious community, and village it adds a specialized subject orientation to the governmental institutions. Similarly, the participant culture does not supplant the subject and parochial patterns of orientation. The participant culture is an additional stratum that may be added to and combined with the subject and parochial cultures. Thus the citizen of a participant polity is not only oriented toward active participation in politics, but is also subject to law and authority and is a member of more diffuse primary groups.

To be sure, adding participant orientations to subject and parochial orientations does not leave these "earlier" orientations unchanged. The parochial orientations must adapt when new and more specialized orientations enter into the picture, just as both parochial and subject orientations change when participant orientations are acquired. Actually, some of the most significant differences in the political cultures of the five democracies included in our study turn on the extent and the way in which parochial, subject, and participant orientations have combined, fused, or meshed together within the individuals of the polity.[9]

Another caution is necessary. Our classification does not imply homogeneity or uniformity of political cultures. Thus political systems with predominantly participant cultures will, even in the limiting case, include both subjects and parochials. The imperfections of the processes of political socialization, personal preferences, and limitations in intelligence or in opportunities to learn will continue to produce subjects and parochials, even in well-established and stable democracies. Similarly, parochials will continue to exist even in "high" subject cultures.

Thus there are two aspects of cultural heterogeneity or cultural "mix." The "citizen" is a particular mix of participant, subject, and parochial orientations, and the civic culture is a particular mix of citizens, subjects, and parochials. For the citizen we need concepts of proportions, thresholds, and congruence to handle the ways in which his constellation of participant, subject, and parochial attitudes is related to effective performance. For the civic culture, which we shall treat in detail below, we need the same concepts of proportions, thresholds, and congruence to handle the problem of what "mix" of citizens, subjects, and parochials is related to the effective performance of democratic systems. When we compare the political cultures of our five countries we shall have the occasion to discuss these questions again.

Our threefold classification of participant, subject, and parochial is only the beginning of a classification of political cultures. Each one of these major classes has its subclasses, and our classification has left out entirely the dimension of political development and cultural change. Let us look into this latter question first, since it will enable us to handle the problem of subclassification with a better set of conceptual tools.

[9] See below, chaps. VIII and IX.

Political cultures may or may not be congruent with the structures of the political system. A congruent political structure would be one appropriate for the culture: in other words, where political cognition in the population would tend to be accurate and where affect and evaluation would tend to be favorable. In general, a parochial, subject, or participant culture would be most congruent with, respectively, a traditional political structure, a centralized authoritarian structure, and a democratic political structure. A parochial political culture that was congruent with its structure would have a high rate of cognitive orientations and high rates of positive affective and evaluative orientations to the diffuse structures of the tribal or village community. A subject political culture congruent with its system would have a high rate of cognition and high positive rates of the other two types of orientation to the specialized political system as a whole, and to its administrative or output aspects; whereas the congruent participant culture would be characterized by high and positive rates of orientation to all four classes of political objects.

Political systems change, and we are justified in assuming that culture and structure are often incongruent with each other. Particularly in these decades of rapid cultural change, the most numerous political systems may be those that have failed to attain congruence, or are moving from one form of polity to another.

To represent schematically these relations of congruence/incongruence between political structure and culture, we present Table I.3.

Any one of the three major types of political cultures may be located on the matrix in Table I.3. Thus we may speak of "allegiant"[10] parochial, subject, and participant cultures when cognitive, affective, and evaluative orientations to the appropriate objects of the polity approach unity, or perfect congruence between culture and structure. But congruence between culture and structure may be best represented in the form of a scale. The limits of congruence between culture and structure are established in columns 1 and 2 of the table. The

[10] We have borrowed the concept "Allegiant" from Robert E. Lane's book, *Political Ideology,* New York, 1962, pp. 170ff.

congruence is strong when the frequencies of positive orientations approach unity (+); the congruence is weak when the political structure is cognized but the frequency of positive feeling and evaluation approaches indifference or zero. Incongruence between political culture and structure begins when the indifference point is passed and negative affect and

TABLE I.3 *Congruence/incongruence between political culture and structure**

	Allegiance	*Apathy*	*Alienation*
Cognitive orientation	+	+	+
Affective orientation	+	0	–
Evaluative orientation	+	0	–

* A (+) sign means a high frequency of awareness, or of positive feeling, or of evaluation toward political objects. A (–) sign means a high frequency of negative evaluations or feelings. A (0) means a high frequency of indifference.

evaluation grow in frequency (–). We may also think of this scale as one of stability/instability. As we move toward the first column in the figure, we are moving toward an allegiant situation: one in which attitudes and institutions match; as we move toward the third column, we are moving toward alienation: where attitudes tend to reject political institutions or structures.

But this scale is only a beginning, since the incongruence may take the form of a simple rejection of a particular set of role incumbents (e.g., a particular dynasty and its bureaucracy); or it may be an aspect of a systemic change, that is, a shift from a simpler pattern of political culture to a more complex one. We have already suggested that all political cultures (with the exception of the simple parochial ones) are mixed. Thus a participant culture contains individuals who are oriented as subjects and parochials; and a subject culture will contain some parochials. We use the term "systemically mixed" political cultures to refer to those in which there are significant proportions of both the simpler and more complex patterns of orientations. When we say these cultures are systemically mixed, we do not intend to suggest that there is an inevitable tendency for the development to complete itself. The process of political culture change may stabilize at a point that falls short of congruence with a centralized authoritarian structure or a democratic one; or the development may take a course such as in Britain, where a slow, continuous pattern of cultural change was accompanied by correspondingly continuous changes in structure. Political cultures may remain systemically mixed for a very long time indeed, as witnessed by the experience of France, Germany, and Italy in the nineteenth and present centuries. When they do remain mixed, however, there are inevitable strains between culture and structure, and a characteristic tendency toward structural instability.

If the three types of political culture represented in Table I.2 are the pure forms of political culture, we may distinguish three types of systemically mixed political cultures: (1) the parochial-subject culture, (2) the subject-participant culture, and (3) the parochial-participant culture.

The Parochial-Subject Culture. This is a type of political culture in which a substantial portion of the population has rejected the exclusive claims of diffuse tribal, village, or feudal authority and has developed allegiance toward a more complex political system with specialized central governmental structures. This is the classic case of kingdom building out of relatively undifferentiated units. The chronicles and histories of most nations include this early stage of shift from local parochialism to centralized authority. But the shift may stabilize at a point that falls short of a fully developed subject culture. The loosely articulated African kingdoms, and even the Ottoman Empire, are examples of stable, mixed subject-parochial cultures where the latter predominates and central authority takes the form of a primarily extractive, dimly cognized set of political objects. The problem of cultural change from parochial to subject patterns is a difficult one, and unstable moves back and forth are common in the early history of nations.[11]

[11] The classic case is that of the succession to King Solomon in the kingdom of Israel. When Solomon died, the parochial (tribal and lineage) leaders of Israel came to his son Rehoboam, saying, "Thy father made our

What we are suggesting is that the composition of this class may be viewed as subvarieties arranged on a continuum. At one extreme we might place the political culture under Prussian absolutism, which went rather far in suppressing parochial orientations; at the other, the political culture in the Ottoman Empire, which never went further than an extractive external relationship to its constituent, more or less parochial units. The contrast between Prussian and British absolutism is an interesting one from this point of view. We have already made the point that even "high" political cultures are mixes, and that the individual orientations comprising them are also mixes. In Prussia, in the typical individual case, we may assume that the intensity of the subject orientation was much stronger than that of the parochial, while in Britain we suggest there was greater balance, and, furthermore, the parochial and subject strata were more congruent. These *psychological* mixes may explain the contrast between the eighteenth century Prussian and British authority images: the first, of *kadavergehorsam*; the second, of the self-confident, if deferential, country squire, merchant, and yeoman. Similarly, the *cultural* mix in Prussia probably involved more of a polarization between a persisting parochial sub-culture — exemplified in the extreme case by the peasantry on the East German estates — and a subject subculture among those groups most affected by the impact of Prussian absolutism: the bureaucracy down to the lowest levels and the increas-

---

yoke hard; but do thou now make lighter the hard service of thy father, and his heavy yoke which he put upon us and we will serve thee." Rehoboam's older counselors advised him to lighten the yoke and pay more respect to the autonomy of the persisting parochial tribal and lineage groups. His younger men — fanatical modernizers — offered him the celebrated advice to tell the traditional leaders of the people, "My little finger is thicker than my father's loins. . . . If my father hath burdened you with a heavy yoke, I will add to your yoke; if my father hath chastised you with whips, then will I chastise you with scorpion thorns" (I Kings 12:4-11). The consequences of Rehoboam's acceptance of the advice of the young modernizers, as told in the rest of *Kings,* suggest that too violent an attack on parochialism may cause both parochial and subject orientations to decline to apathy and alienation. The results are political fragmentation and national destruction.

ingly large proportion of Prussian manpower undergoing the Prussian army experience.

Thus change from a parochial to a subject political culture may stabilize at a number of points on the continuum and produce different political, psychological, and cultural mixes. We also suggest that the kind of mix that results has great significance for the stability and performance of the political system.

The Subject-Participant Culture. The way in which the shift from a parochial to a subject culture is solved greatly affects the way in which the shift from a subject to a participant culture takes place. As Pye points out, the inculcation of a sense of national loyalty and identification, and of a propensity to obey the regulations of central authority, is the first priority problem in the emerging nations.[12] In the shift from a subject to a participant culture, the parochial and local autonomies, if they survive, may contribute to the development of a democratic infrastructure. Certainly this is what happened in the British case. Local authorities, municipal corporations, religious communities, and merchant groups in which the tradition of guild freedoms still persisted became the first interest groups in the developing British democracy. The lesson is a significant one. Precisely because the development of a subject culture in England stopped short of destroying local and parochial structures and cultures, these could become available at a later time and in modified form as an influence network that could relate Britons as competent citizens to their government. The more massive impact of the Prussian state authority drove parochial institutions into privacy, or assimilated them to state authority. Thus the era of democratization in Germany began with a great gap between the private and public spheres, and the infrastructure that emerged failed to arc across from individual, family, and community to the institutions of governmental authority.

In the mixed subject-participant culture a substantial part of the population has acquired specialized input orientations and an activist set of self-orientations, while most of the re-

[12] Pye, *Politics, Personality, and Nation Building,* pp. 3ff.

mainder of the population continue to be oriented toward an authoritarian governmental structure and have a relatively passive set of self-orientations. In the Western European examples of this type of political culture — France, Germany, and Italy in the nineteenth and present centuries — there was a characteristic pattern of structural instability with an alternation of authoritarian and democratic governments. But more than structural instability results from this kind of cultural mix. The cultural patterns themselves are influenced by the structural instability and the cultural stalemate. Because participant orientations have spread among only a part of the population, and because their legitimacy is challenged by the persisting subject subculture and suspended during authoritarian interludes, the participant-oriented stratum of the population cannot become a competent, self-confident, experienced body of citizens. They tend to remain democratic aspirants. That is, they accept the norms of a participant culture, but their sense of competence is not based on experience or on a confident sense of legitimacy. Furthermore, the structural instabilities that frequently accompany the mixed subject-participant culture, the frequent ineffectiveness of the democratic infrastructure and of the governmental system, tend to produce alienative tendencies among the democratically oriented elements of the population. Taken together, this kind of a political cultural stalemate may produce a syndrome with components of idealist-aspiration and alienation from the political system, including the infrastructure of parties, interest groups, and press.

The mixed subject-participant culture, if it persists over a long period of time, also changes the character of the subject subculture. During the democratic interludes the authoritarian-oriented groups must compete with the democratic ones within a formally democratic framework. In other words, they must develop a defensive political infrastructure of their own. Although this does not transform the subject subculture into a democratic one, it certainly changes it, often to a significant degree. It is not accidental that authoritarian regimes that arise in political systems with mixed subject-participant cultures tend to have populistic overtones, and in the more recent period of totalitarianism these regimes have even adopted the democratic infrastructure in a grossly distorted form.

The Parochial-Participant Culture. In the parochial-participant culture we have the contemporary problem of cultural development in many of the emerging nations. In most of these countries the political culture is predominantly parochial. The structural norms that have been introduced are usually participant; for congruence, therefore, they require a participant culture. Thus the problem is to develop specialized output and input orientations simultaneously. It is not surprising that most of these political systems, always threatened by parochial fragmentation, teeter like acrobats on tightropes, leaning precariously at one time toward authoritarianism, at another toward democracy. There is no structure on either side to lean on, neither a bureaucracy resting upon loyal subjects, nor an infrastructure arising from responsible and competent citizens. The problem of development from parochial to participant culture seems, on first look, to be a hopeless one; but if we remember that most parochial autonomies and loyalties survive, we may at least say that the development of participant cultures in some of the emerging nations has not yet been precluded. The problems are to penetrate the parochial systems without destroying them on the output side, and to transform them into interest groups on the input side.

POLITICAL SUBCULTURE

We have already made the point that most political cultures are heterogeneous. Even the most fully developed participant cultures will contain surviving strata of subjects and parochials. And even within that part of the culture that is oriented toward participation there will be persistent and significant differences in political orientation. Adapting the terminology of Ralph Linton to our purposes, we use the term "subculture" to refer to these component parts of political cultures.[13] But we have to distinguish at least two types of subcultural cleavage. First, the term may be used to refer

[13] Ralph Linton, *The Cultural Background of Personality.*

to population strata that are persistently oriented in one way toward policy inputs and outputs, but are "allegiantly" oriented toward the political structure. Thus in the United States the left wing of the Democratic party and the right wing of the Republican party accept as legitimate the structures of American politics and government, but differ persistently from each other on a whole range of domestic and foreign policy issues. We refer to these as policy subcultures.

But the kind of cleavage we are most interested in is that which occurs in systemically mixed systems. Thus in a mixed parochial-subject culture one part of the population would be oriented toward diffuse traditional authorities, and another toward the specialized structure of the central authoritarian system. A mixed parochial-subject culture may actually be characterized by a "vertical" as well as a horizontal cleavage. Thus if the polity includes two or more traditional components, then there will be, in addition to the emerging subject subculture, the persisting separate cultures of the formally merged traditional units.

The mixed subject-participant culture is a more familiar and even more contemporary problem in the West. A successful shift from a subject to a participant culture involves the diffusion of positive orientations toward a democratic infrastructure, the acceptance of norms of civic obligation, and the development of a sense of civic competence among a substantial proportion of the population. These orientations may combine with subject and parochial orientations, or they may conflict. England in the nineteenth and present centuries moved toward and attained a political culture that combined these orientations. It is true, of course, that the Radicals in the first part of the nineteenth century and the Socialist and Labour left-wing groups at a later time were opposed to the monarchy and the House of Lords. But these tendencies resulted in the transformation, not the elimination, of these institutions. Political subcultures in England, consequently, are examples of our first type of cleavage, the one based on persistent policy differences rather than upon fundamentally different orientations toward political structure.

France is the classic case of the second type of political-cultural heterogeneity. The French Revolution did not result in a homogeneous orientation toward a republican political structure; instead, it polarized the French population into two subcultures, one of participant aspiration and one dominated by subject and parochial orientations. The structure of the French political system has been at issue ever since that time, and what was at first a bipolarization of political culture was followed by further fragmentations, as the Socialists followed the Jacobins, and the Communists the Socialists, and as the right wing divided into a "rallied" and an "unrallied" part. In many other European countries the failure of the dominant elites to respond to the moderate demands for structural and policy changes put forward by the left in the first half of the nineteenth century led to the development of the structurally alienated, revolutionary socialist, syndicalist, and anarchist left of the second half of the nineteenth century.

In England, the Old Commonwealth, the United States, and the Scandinavian countries, the issues of political structure were resolved in the course of the nineteenth and early twentieth centuries: what emerged were homogeneous political cultures, in the sense of structural orientation. The subcultural phenomena in these countries turn on persistent policy differences. Left and right both tend to accept the existing political structure and differ only on the substance of policy and political personnel. What is most interesting is that in this group of countries in the last decades, the policy differences have tended to become less sharp, and there is a larger common body of agreement. In other words, subcultural cleavage has attenuated and cultural homogeneity has extended from structural orientation into policy orientation.

This brief discussion of political subculture serves only to introduce the concept. Some of its implications and consequences will be considered at later points in the book. But we would mislead the reader if we were to suggest that our study treats proportionally each aspect of political culture. Our study stresses orientation to political structure and process, not orientation to the substance of political demands and outputs. We need not apologize for this emphasis, but must point out how this choice may tend to obscure significant dimensions of political culture, and significant relationships between general psychocultural patterns and the substance of politics and public policy. A study that stressed orientation to public policy would require at least as much of a major effort as the present one. It would have to relate systematically types of public policy orientations to types of social structure and cultural values, as well as to the socialization processes with which they are related. A similarly rigorous separation of public policy orientation, general culture orientation, and socialization patterns would also be necessary, in order for us to discover the real character and direction of relationships among these phenomena.

THE CIVIC CULTURE: A MIXED POLITICAL CULTURE

At an earlier point we discussed the historical origins of the civic culture and the functions of that culture in the process of social change. Much of this book will offer an analysis and description of the culture and of the role it plays in the maintenance of a democratic political system. It will be useful therefore to spell out, if only briefly, some of its main characteristics.

The civic culture is not the political culture that one finds described in civics textbooks, which prescribe the way in which citizens ought to act in a democracy. The norms of citizen behavior found in these texts stress the participant aspects of political culture. The democratic citizen is expected to be active in politics and to be involved. Furthermore, he is supposed to be rational in his approach to politics, guided by reason, not by emotion. He is supposed to be well informed and to make decisions — for instance, his decision on how to vote — on the basis of careful calculation as to the interests and the principles he would like to see furthered. This culture, with its stress on rational participation within the input structures of politics, we can label the "rationality-activist" model of political culture. The civic culture shares much with this rationality-activist model; it is, in fact, such a culture *plus something else*. It does stress the participation of individuals in the political input process. In the civic cultures described in this volume we shall find high frequencies of political activity, of exposure to political communications, of political discussion, of concern with political affairs. But there is *something else.*

In the first place, the civic culture is an allegiant participant culture. Individuals are not only oriented to political input, they also are oriented positively to the input structures and the input process. In other words, to use the terms introduced earlier, the civic culture is a participant political culture in which the political culture and political structure are congruent.

More important, in the civic culture participant political orientations combine with and do not replace subject and parochial political orientations. Individuals become participants in the political process, but they do not give up their orientations as subjects or as parochials. Furthermore, not only are these earlier orientations maintained, alongside the participant political orientations, but the subject and parochial orientations are also congruent with the participant political orientations. The nonparticipant, more traditional political orientations tend to limit the individual's commitment to politics and to make that commitment milder. In a sense, the subject and parochial orientations "manage" or keep in place the participant political orientations. Thus attitudes favorable to participation within the political system play a major role in the civic culture, but so do such nonpolitical attitudes as trust in other people and social participation in general. The maintenance of these more traditional attitudes *and their fusion* with the participant orientations lead to a balanced political culture in which political activity, involvement, and rationality exist but are balanced by passivity, traditionality, and commitment to parochial values.

MICRO- AND MACROPOLITICS: POLITICAL CULTURE AS THE CONNECTING LINK

Developments in social science methods in recent decades have enabled us to penetrate more deeply into the motivational basis of the political attitudes and behavior of individuals and groups. A substantial literature has accumulated, which includes studies of electoral attitudes and behavior, analyses of the relations between ideological and public policy tendencies and deeper attitude or personality characteristics, psychopolitical biographies of political leaders, studies of political attitudes in particular social groupings, and the like. Rokkan and Campbell refer to this focus on the individual, his political attitudes and motivations, whether as individual or as a member of a sample of a larger population, as "micropolitics," distinguishing it as a research approach from "macropolitics," or the more traditional concern of the student of politics with the structure and function of political systems, institutions, and agencies, and their effects on public policy.[14]

Although the relationship between individual political psychology and the behavior of political systems and subsystems is clear in principle, much of the micropolitical literature is content to assert this relationship in general terms. The implication is given that since political systems are made up of individuals, it may be taken for granted that particular psychological tendencies in individuals or among social groups are important for the functioning of political systems and their outputs. This may indeed be the case when the researcher is concerned with the psychological conditions affecting the behavior of a particular role incumbent or incumbents, such as a particular political decision-maker at one extreme, or an electorate at the other. On the other hand, much of this literature fails to make the connection between the psychological tendencies of individuals and groups, and political structure and process. In other words, the currency of political psychology, though it has undoubted value, is not made exchangeable in terms of political process and performance.[15]

[14] Stein Rokkan and Angus Campbell, "Norway and the United States of America," in *International Social Science Journal,* Vol. XII, No. 1, 1960, pp. 69ff.

[15] For a valuable analysis of the problem of "linkage" between public opinion and governmental action, see V. O. Key, *Public Opinion and American Democracy,* New York, 1961, chaps. XVI ff.

We would like to suggest that this relationship between the attitudes and motivations of the discrete individuals who make up political systems and the character and performance of political systems may be discovered systematically through the concepts of political culture that we have sketched out above. In other words, the connecting link between micro- and macropolitics is political culture. At an earlier point we stressed that individual political orientations must be separated analytically from other kinds of psychological orientations, in order for us to test hypotheses about the relationship between political and other attitudes. We also defined the political culture as the particular incidence of patterns of political orientation in the population of a political system. Now, through the concepts of political subculture and role culture, we can locate special attitudes and propensities for political behavior among parts of the population, or in particular roles, structures, or subsystems of the political system. These concepts of political culture allow us to establish what propensities for political behavior exist in the political system as a whole, and in its various parts, among special orientation groupings (i.e., subcultures), or at key points of initiative or decision in the political structure (i.e., role cultures). In other words, we can relate political psychology to political system performance by locating attitudinal and behavioral propensities in the political structure of the system.

Thus any polity may be described and compared with other polities in terms of (1) its structural-functional characteristics, and (2) its cultural, subcultural, and role-cultural characteristics. Our analysis of types of political culture is a first effort at treating the phenomena of individual political orientation in such a way as to relate them systematically to the phenomena of political structure. It enables us to escape from the oversimplifications of the psychocultural literature in two significant ways. By separating political orientation from general psychological orientation, we can avoid the assumption of the homogeneity of orientation, and look at this instead as a researchable relationship. And by examining the relationship between political cultural tendencies and political structural patterns, we can avoid the assumption of congruence between political culture and political structure. The relationship between political culture and political structure becomes one of the most significant researchable aspects of the problem of political stability and change. Rather than assuming congruence, we must ascertain the extent and character of the congruence or incongruence, and the trends in political cultural and structural development that may affect the "fit" between culture and structure.

We suggest that this research strategy will enable us to realize the full creative potentialities of the great insights of the psychocultural approach to the study of political phenomena. It is our own hypothesis that such research will show that *the importance of specific learning of orientations to politics and of experience with the political system* has been seriously underemphasized. Such learning is not only cognitive in character, but also involves political feelings, expectations, and evaluations that result largely from political experiences rather than from the simple projection into political orientation of basic needs and attitudes that are the product of childhood socialization.

In still another respect our theory of political culture may serve to make the psychocultural approach more directly relevant to the study of the political system. In our discussion of types of political culture and the problem of congruence between culture and structure, we have pointed out that congruence is a relationship of affective and evaluative allegiance between culture and structure. Each kind of polity — traditional, authoritarian, and democratic — has one form of culture that is congruent with its own structure. Starting from the orientation and psychological requirements of different types of political structure, we are in a better position to formulate hypotheses about the kinds of personality tendencies and socialization practices that are likely to produce congruent political cultures and stable polities. Thus in the case of the civic culture, we may say that a pattern of socialization which enables the individual to manage the inevitable dissonances among his diffuse primary, his obedient output, and activist input roles supports a democratic polity. We can then look at socialization patterns and personality tendencies and ask just which of these qualities are crucial, to what extent they must be present, and what kinds of experience are most likely to produce this capacity for dissonant political role management. Our findings will show that the civic orientation is widespread in Britain and the United States and relatively infrequent in the other three countries, but we would be most hesitant to attribute these gross differences in political culture to the relatively slight differences in childhood socialization brought to light in our findings. They seem more clearly to be related to characteristics of the social environment and patterns of social interaction, to specifically political memories, and to differences in experience with political structure and performance. The most productive research on political psychology in the future will treat childhood socialization, modal personality tendencies, political orientation, and political structure and process as separate variables in a complex, multidirectional system of causality.

In one class of political contexts, however, the relations between political structure and culture, on the one hand, and character and personality, on the other, are relatively clear and dramatic. This is in our category of mixed political cultures. Here, in the parochial-subject, the subject-participant, and the parochial-participant cultures, we are dealing with societies that are either undergoing rapid systemic cultural-structural change or else have stabilized in a condition of subcultural fragmentation and structural instability. Fragmentation of political culture is also associated with general cultural fragmentation (e.g., the sharp division between the modernizing urban society and the traditional countryside; between the industrial economy and the traditional agrarian economy). We may assume that in these rapidly changing and fragmented societies, cultural heterogeneity and the high incidence of discontinuity in socialization produce a high incidence of psychological confusion and instability. Nowhere would this be more marked than in the parochial-participant cultures of the emerging nations of Asia and Africa. Lucian Pye, *in Politics, Personality, and Nation-Building,* has provided us with a dramatic study of this kind of discontinuity in culture and socialization, its consequences for personality development and for the characteristics and performance of the Burmese political system.[16]

THE COUNTRIES INCLUDED IN THE STUDY

Our comparative study of political culture includes five democracies — the United States, Great Britain, Germany, Italy, and Mexico — selected because they represent a wide range of political-historical experience. At one extreme we selected the United States and Britain, both representing relatively successful experiments in democratic government. An analysis of these two cases will tell us what kinds of attitudes are associated with stably functioning democratic systems, the quantitative incidence of these attitudes, and their distribution among different groups in the population.

At the same time, a comparison of Britain and the United States might be useful as a test of some of the speculation about the differences between these two often-compared countries. Two recent writers on British politics comment on the persistence of traditional attitudes toward authority in that country. Brogan points out that in the historical development of Britain the culture of democratic citizenship, with its emphasis on initiative and participation, was amalgamated with an older political culture that stressed the obligations and rights of the subject.[17] Eckstein points out that the British political culture combines deference toward authority with a lively sense of the rights of citizen initiative.[18]

In the United States, on the other hand, independent government began with republican institutions, in a mood that rejected the majesty and sacredness of traditional institutions, and without a privileged aristocratic class. The functions of government tended to be relatively limited, and bureaucratic authority was the object of distrust. The American populist ideology rejected the conception of a professional, authoritative governmental service and the corresponding role of the obedient subject. The spoils system and political corruption

[16] *Op cit.*, pp. 52-53 and 287ff.

[17] D. W. Brogan, *Citizenship Today,* Chapel Hill, N.C., 1960, pp. 9ff.

[18] Harry Eckstein, "The British Political System," in S. Beer and A. Ulam, *The Major Political Systems of Europe,* New York, 1958, pp. 59ff.

further undermined the prestige of governmental authority. In an even broader sense, and for reasons we cannot deal with here, the general pattern of authority in American social systems, including the family, tended to stress political competence and participation rather than obedience to legitimate authority.

In our comparison of the British and American political cultures, then, can we establish that Englishmen are more likely than Americans to have incorporated allegiant subject orientations as well as participant ones? And are they better able than Americans to manage the dissonances between democratic activism and "subject obedience"?

Several considerations led us to select Germany in our comparative study. Prussia, like Britain, had a relatively long period of effective, legitimate government before the introduction of democratic institutions. During the German unification in the nineteenth century, the Prussian bureaucratic authoritarian pattern was imposed more or less successfully on the other German states included in the nation. It has been argued that while Germany developed both a *Rechtsstaat* and a subject political culture, the experiments with democratic participation in the late nineteenth century and in the Weimar period never developed a participant political culture necessary to sustain these democratic institutions and give them force and legitimacy. Much of the speculation about the stability of contemporary democratic institutions in Germany turns on the question of the extent to which a sense of the responsibilities and opportunities of citizenship and mutual trust among political groupings have actually taken root among the German people.

One might conclude from an examination of their histories that Britain and Germany have in common deferential attitudes toward authority, growing out of their long predemocratic experiences with authoritarian control. But examination of history brings out one most significant difference. British government control in its predemocratic period never became as complete or as exhaustive of initiative as did the German. Brogan points out that even in the centuries when Englishmen were "subjects" there was a broad area of autonomy, freedom to form societies and engage in limited self-government.[19] In other words, even in the long centuries of British authoritarian government there was a limited participant component in the British political culture. Thus the amalgamation of citizen attitudes with subject attitudes is a centuries-old process, long predating the parliamentary and suffrage reforms of the seventeenth, eighteenth, and nineteenth centuries. These reforms did not founder on a hard and unyielding subject culture, but could root themselves on a long-existent culture of pluralism and initiative.

As Krieger points out in his penetrating analysis of the development of German political ideas and movements, the German conception of liberty — from the days of the struggle of the princes against the imperial authority to the attainment of nationhood in the nineteenth century — was identified with the freedom of the state from external limitations rather than with the initiative and participation of individuals.[20] However, democratic political culture tendencies have been, and are, present in German society. They were present in the nineteenth century, in the Weimar period, and are to be observed today. Our study will enable us to establish which elements of a participant culture are present in the German population and which are lacking.

We have included Italy and Mexico in our study as examples of less well-developed societies with transitional political systems. Italy, at least in the South and the islands, has a premodern social and political structure. If we consider Italian political history for a moment, it is evident that Italy never really developed an allegiant national political culture in modern times. The Italian monarchy of the pre-World War I period was denied legitimacy by the Church. The rule of *non expedit* required that the faithful refuse to accord legitimacy to the new state, refuse to participate in its processes.[21] During the Fascist interlude an effective state appa-

[19] Brogan, *op. cit.,* pp. 14ff.

[20] Leonard Krieger, *The German Idea of Freedom,* Boston, 1957, *passim* and pp. 458ff.

[21] D. A. Binchy, *Church and State in Fascist Italy,* London, 1941.

ratus developed, but it was more the external control of a society by a coercive authority than a relatively free according of legitimacy to an established political system. In this respect Italy is unlike Britain and Germany, both of which had integrated and legitimate authoritarian systems before the introduction of democratic institutions.

In his study of a village in the southern Italian province of Lucania, Banfield characterizes the political culture of this area as "amoral familism," according legitimacy neither to the bureaucratic authoritarian organs of the state, nor to the civic-political organs of party, interest group, or local community.[22] It would be incorrect to view all of Italy in these terms, but our own data will tend to support Banfield's claim that the Italian political culture contains unusually strong parochial, alienative subject, and alienative participant components. Democratic aspirational tendencies are also present, primarily concentrated on the left, but these are relatively weak in comparison with the widespread mood of rejection that affects the attitudes of the great majority of Italians toward their political system in all its aspects.

We selected Mexico as our fifth country in order to have at least one "non-Atlantic community" democracy. Mexico can hardly be viewed as representing the emerging nations of Asia and Africa, yet no single country could possibly represent the variety of socio-political structures and historical experiences of the emerging nations. It has in common with many of these nations a high rate of industrialization, urbanization, and increased literacy and education. Before the revolution, Mexican government and politics were essentially alien, extractive, and exploitative structures resting uneasily on a society made up essentially of kinsmen, villagers, and ethnic and status groups. In the last thirty or forty years, however, the Mexican Revolution has deeply affected the social and political structure and has stimulated modern and democratic aspirations and expectations.[23]

[22] Edward C. Banfield, *The Moral Basis of a Backward Society*, Glencoe, Ill., 1958, pp. 7ff.

[23] Robert E. Scott, *Mexican Government in Transition*, Urbana, Ill., 1959, pp. 56ff.

In contrast to Italy, where a large portion of the population tends to view the political system as an alien, exploitative force, many Mexicans tend to view their revolution as an instrument of ultimate democratization and economic and social modernization. At the same time, the Mexican democratic infrastructure is relatively new. Freedom of political organization is more formal than real, and corruption is widespread throughout the whole political system. These conditions may explain the interesting ambivalence in Mexican political culture: many Mexicans lack political experience and skill, yet their hope and confidence are high; combined with these widespread participant aspirational tendencies, however, are cynicism about and alienation from the political infrastructure and bureaucracy. In addition, Mexico is the least "modern" of our five countries; that is, there is still a relatively large tradition-oriented village population and a high illiteracy rate. Perhaps the Mexican case will provide useful leads about the characteristics of political culture in non-Western countries undergoing similar experiences in modernization and democratization.

In this brief comparison of the political-historical experience of our five countries, we have been formulating hypotheses about the differences in political culture we might expect to find among them. However, inferences about political culture drawn from history leave unanswered the question of how much of a country's historical experience lives on in the memories, feelings, and expectations of its population, in what form it can be said to live on, which elements of the population are the bearers of which historical memories, and with what intensity. Here newer scientific methods can combine with the more traditional approaches, in our search for living history in the political cultures of peoples. Our survey will translate the rather simple and massive expectations inferred from history into quantities, demographic distributions, and regularities or relations. There is no necessary conflict between the methods of history and those of the behavioral sciences; they are actually supplemental and mutually supportive.

THE FIVE-NATION SURVEY

The present work attempts to apply some of the methods developed in the field of systematic survey research to the study of comparative politics. Unlike most other studies of political attitudes, ours is cross-national. Most survey studies of voting behavior or of other political attitudes have taken place within a single nation, the bulk of them in the United States.[24] Our study is multicontextual — a study of five nations. Throughout this book we shall concentrate on those nations — on their similarities and their differences. Because of our comparative approach, we must regretfully bypass interesting problems within the individual countries.

The present book is based upon about one thousand interviews carried on in each of five nations (about five thousand interviews in all). In each case an attempt was made to obtain a national cross-section sample.[25] The interviews ranged in length from about forty minutes to somewhat over an hour, though in some cases they lasted much longer. The interviews were largely structured, with about ten per cent of the questions open-ended in form. In each nation a small proportion of the respondents interviewed as part of the national cross-section were reinterviewed with a longer and less structured interview, which attempted to elicit more material of the sort dealt with in the cross-section interview, as well as to obtain a description of what we call an individual's "political life history." [26]

The cross-section interviews were carried on in June and

[24] Some exceptions are: William Buchanan and Hadley Cantril, *How Nations See Each Other,* Urbana, Ill., 1953; The International Teacher's Study, reported in Eugene Jacobson and Stanley Schachter (eds.), "Cross-National Research: A Case Study," *Journal of Social Issues,* X (1954). See also Stein Rokkan, "Comparative Cross National Research: II Bibliography," *International Social Science Bulletin,* VII (1955), pp. 622-41.

[25] In Mexico the sample is of cities of 10,000 or more population.

[26] The original plan was to obtain 125 such interviews in each country. For a variety of reasons it was impossible to reinterview that many. The number of reinterviews actually completed were: United States, 49; United Kingdom, 114; Germany, 135; Italy, 121, and Mexico, 120.

July of 1959 in all of the nations except the United States; the interviews in the United States were carried on in March, 1960. In most cases the follow-up interviews took place about six months to a year after the first interviews.[27]

SURVEY DATA AND POLITICAL SYSTEMS

The present work is partly a study in what has been called "micropolitics." It deals with the political orientations and behavior of a cross-section sample. The one thousand or so respondents in each country are viewed in the first instance as individuals. They have no relationship to one another; one respondent has no knowledge of the other respondents and no interaction with them — certainly none that is explored in our study. Yet we are interested in the respondents, not as individuals, but as members of complex social systems. We wish to make statements, based on those separate interviews, about the general state of attitudes in these nations. And we wish to make statements about the relationship between these attitudes and the way in which the political systems operate. In particular, we are interested in understanding democratic political systems; and these systems consist of much more than the individual or collective attitudes of their members. They consist as well of formal structures of government, political parties, structures of power and influence, shared norms, patterns of policy, communication, interaction, and so forth. The major problem of analysis is, therefore, how to use responses from one thousand individuals who have never met to answer questions about the characteristics of a political system. It is as if that system were a large map on the wall of a darkened room, and all we know of it is what is revealed by one thousand separate pinpoints of light. These points of light (our interviews) illuminate the spots on the map that they touch. But they light up only a small part of the map

27 We cannot go into the many technical problems associated with the design and analysis of the research. For a fuller account, the reader is referred to the unabridged version of this book published by the Princeton University Press. See in particular Chapter 2 and Appendix A of that version.

and leave the areas between the dots completely dark. We want to say something, not merely about the points that are illuminated, but about the entire map itself.

There are a number of ways in which one may use the individual pinpoints of light to illuminate the territory between them. In the first place, one assumes that the results of interviews with one thousand individuals can be generalized to the entire population — with, of course, the usual allowances made for errors. Second, though we only talk to individuals and do not observe them interacting with others or engaged in political activity, we do ask them about their attitudes toward others, their relations with others, their social activities, their organizational memberships, and their political activities. If we can generalize about the respondents' answers, we can make statements about the number of people in each nation who hold to certain attitudes and engage in certain behavior; we can also describe the network of relations among people: the frequencies of such behavior as organizational membership, informal social contact, and political activity, and the frequencies of such attitudes as interpersonal trust and cooperativeness that refer, not merely to single individuals, but to the relations among individuals.

The third and crucial point is that one must assume that the attitudes we report have some significant relationship to the way the political system operates — to its stability, effectiveness, and so forth. The distribution in a society of such attitudes as the belief that the political system is legitimate, that it operates effectively, that it is amenable to the ordinary man's influence; or the frequency of such activities as organizational membership or political participation — clearly all these have important effects on the way the political system operates. It is somewhat more difficult to pin down the precise relationship between these attitudes and behaviors of ordinary citizens and the ways in which political democracies operate. The major problem is that, though we have about five thousand individual respondents, we have only five nations. Thus if we want to test statistically the relationship between two attributes of the individuals in our sample — say, the relationship between social class and political participation — we have a large number of cases with which to do this. But if we want to test the relationship between a pattern of attitudes in a nation and some characteristic of a political system — say, the relationship between frequency of political alienation and the stability of the political system — we have few cases in which to test this. This is no new problem in political analysis, and we are in fact five times as well off as most studies of this sort. What we can do is to consider our five nations as examples of types of political democracy — more or less stable democracies, more or less effective, more or less participatory. Which of these nations is highest on any dimension can be assessed either on the basis of data outside of our study (a brief glance at history will tell which of these are more stable, or an analysis of the party structures will allow a classification by type of party system), or on data within our study (one might use the frequency of various types of political activity to rank the nations by the extent to which they are characterized by high or low rates of participation). If one can then show, for instance, that in the more stable democracies there does exist a particular set of political attitudes that could theoretically further the chances of stable democracy; or that in those nations where participation is most frequent there does in fact exist a particular set of interpersonal attitudes that could theoretically further political participation, then one has come a long way toward demonstrating the probability of some connection between attitudinal patterns and systemic qualities. Furthermore, these connections between sets of attitudes and the characteristics of the political system can be made more convincing by internal analysis of the attitudes within the nations. Suppose one finds that a particular attitude toward interpersonal relations exists most frequently in a system where political participation of a particular sort is most frequent; if one also finds that it is precisely those individuals who hold that attitude who are more likely to be the political participants, one can then support the hypothesis that the particular attitude is connected with a particular kind of participatory system. By moving constantly from characteristics of the political system to frequencies of particular attitudes within the system to the pattern of attitudes within the individual members of the system, one can hope to develop plausible, testable (and perhaps, in a preliminary way, tested) hypotheses about the relationship between what we have called political culture and the workings of political systems.

We hope to have shown in the above discussion that the kind of data reported here make sense only if interpreted in terms of other types of material about the systems we study. Thus the information we have about the five political systems is not limited to areas directly under the little pinpoints of light. One must integrate into a study of this sort findings about the general shape of the system, the institutions, the history of their development, and so forth. One advantage of a cross-national study, we have suggested, is that it forces one to look at systemic characteristics. Our findings are intended not to replace, but to supplement other materials used for the analysis of political systems. It is only if material of the sort we have can be combined with other materials that we will have made progress.

CHAPTER II

Patterns of Political Cognition

IN OUR CLASSIFICATION of types of political culture, we have referred to the dimension of cognition. A participant is assumed to be aware of and informed about the political system in both its governmental and political aspects. A subject tends to be cognitively oriented primarily to the output side of government: the executive, bureaucracy, and judiciary. The parochial tends to be unaware, or only dimly aware, of the political system in all its aspects. In the five countries in our study, pure parochials and subjects are rare. Even the Mexican Indian villager has had some exposure to specialized governmental authority; and the Italian rural housewife may have some knowledge of political parties. In the five democracies we study, the parochial and subject orientations tend to rest primarily upon affective and evaluative tendencies. The Mexican villager may feel no loyalty or involvement with the Mexican nation and government. He may view it as an alien force to be avoided. His loyalty and sense of obligation go to his village, and to its norms and structures. Nevertheless, these affective and evaluative parochial and subject patterns have cognitive consequences. When affect and norms are lacking, the motivation to acquire information is weak, and thus cognition, though it may be present, tends to be vague.

In the present analysis of cognitive patterns, we do not claim to present an exhaustive description of the political "cognitive maps" of Americans, Britons, Germans, Italians, and Mexicans. What we have to offer, rather, is a limited number of measures of cognitive content and processes, which is nevertheless sufficient to bring out some of the significant differences among our countries. Four such measures are presented in this chapter.

The first of these is an attempt to discover how much importance is attributed to national and local government in each of our five countries. The second is a measure of awareness of and exposure to politics and public affairs. The third is a political information test intended to get at differences among countries in the amount of political information their adult populations possess. And the fourth is a measure of the readiness of these populations to make choices or entertain opinions about political issues and problems. Needless to say, this represents only the shallowest probing of the dimension of political cognition. But it does bring out some rather striking differences among our countries in the objects of political cognition, in the intensity and quantity of cognition, and in the sense of cognitive competence.

TABLE II.1 *Estimated degree of impact of national government on daily life; by nation*[a]

Percentage of respondents who say national government has	*U.S.*	*U.K.*	*Germany*	*Italy*	*Mexico*
Great effect	41	33	38	23	7
Some effect	44	40	32	31	23
No effect	11	23	17	19	66
Other	0	—	—	3	—
Don't know	4	4	12	24	3
Total percentage[b]	100	100	99	100	99
Total number of cases	970	963	955	995	1,007

[a] Actual text of the question: "Thinking now about the national government [in Washington, London, Bonn, Rome, Mexico City], about how much effect do you think its activities, the laws passed and so on, have on your day-to-day life? Do they have a great effect, some effect, or none?"

[b] In this and subsequent tables, variations in total percentages from one hundred percent are the result of rounding.

THE IMPACT OF GOVERNMENT

The first aspect of the cognitive dimension we shall examine is that of knowledge of governmental output. To what extent do the people in these countries perceive government as having an effect on them as individuals? To what extent do they see their lives as related to the activities of government? One of the questions asked of all respondents was designed to discover how much effect they thought the activities of their national governments had on their daily lives. The results are reported in Table II.1.

Large majorities of Americans, Britons, and Germans see their national government as having some impact on their lives. The Mexicans are at the opposite extreme, with 66 per cent attributing no effect to their national government. The Italians are in between, with just a little more than half attributing some or great importance to national government, and a little less than half attributing no importance to the national government or stating that they did not know what importance the national government had for them. Table II.2 reports the responses to a similar question regarding the effect of local government. The pattern is almost the same as that for the national government, except that a slightly

TABLE II.2 *Estimated degree of impact of local government on daily life; by nation**

Percentage who say local government has	*U.S.*	*U.K.*	*Germany*	*Italy*	*Mexico*
Great effect	35	23	33	19	6
Some effect	53	51	41	39	23
No effect	10	23	18	22	67
Other	—	—	—	2	—
Don't know	2	3	8	18	3
Total percentage	100	100	100	99	100
Total number	970	963	955	995	1,007

* Actual text of the question: "Now take the local government. About how much effect do you think its activities have on your day-to-day life? Do they have a great effect, some effect, or none?"

higher proportion of American, Italian, and German respondents attribute importance to their local governments.

What these figures suggest is that the large majority of Americans, Britons, and Germans are cognitively oriented to governmental action. That is, they perceive government as influencing their lives. Italians and Mexicans, and particularly the latter, are either less frequently aware of the impact of government or are aware of it but reject it as having no significance for them.

We are also in a position to determine whether or not the impact of government in these countries is considered favorable. A follow-up question was asked: "On the whole, do the activities of the national government tend to improve conditions in this country, or would we be better off without them?" Table II.3 shows that large majorities in the United States, Britain, Germany, and Italy who said the national government affected their daily lives also viewed this effect as beneficial. The Mexicans showed the lowest frequency of favorable responses; they, more than the others, said that they would be better off without the activities of the national government. The same pattern came out in the follow-up question on the impact of the local government.

If we combine the results of these two questions on the im-

TABLE II.3 *Character of impact of national government; by nation**

Percentage who say	*U.S.*	*U.K.*	*Germany*	*Italy*	*Mexico*
National govt. improves conditions	76	77	61	66	58
Sometimes improves conditions, sometimes does not	19	15	30	20	18
Better off without national govt.	3	3	3	5	19
National govt. makes no difference	1	1	1	1	2
Other	0	1	0	2	1
Don't know	1	2	4	5	2
Total percentage	100	99	99	99	100
Total number	821	707	676	534	301

* As described by those respondents who attribute some impact to national government.

pact of national and local government and the character of impact, the following points are suggested. The American and British respondents in the great majority perceive an impact of their national and local governments and view that impact as favorable. The German respondents resemble them, except that a larger percentage takes the skeptical position that the national and local governments sometimes improve conditions and sometimes do not. Those Italians who do attribute significance to their national and local governments (a little more than half) also attribute a favorable impact to them. On the other hand, only a minority of the Mexicans (less than one-third) attributes significance to the government, and even among this third a substantial proportion either takes a skeptical position on the benefits of government or rejects it as largely harmful in its effects.

The broad picture presented thus far suggests that in the United States, Britain, and Germany, the bulk of the population are "allegiants" in the output sense; that is, they are aware of and evaluate favorably the governmental output. In Italy and particularly in Mexico, there is a high incidence of alienated subjects and parochials. Our regular interview enabled us merely to say that around two-thirds of the Mexicans and a little less than half of the Italians either attributed no significance to government or said they didn't know if it had any significance. Our life-history interviews will help us fill in the meaning of our quantitative data.

In each of the countries we reinterviewed some 10 per cent of our respondents, repeating some of the same questions but probing more deeply and recording their responses verbatim. What we discovered in this freer, open-ended material is that those respondents in Mexico and Italy who said that government had no impact on them or that they did not know how much impact it had included both "parochials" and "alienates." Some parochial statements follow.

Asked whether government is necessary, a Mexican house servant who lives with her family in her mistress's house in Mexico City replied, "I won't answer this as I don't know what to say." She attributed no significance to government for her and her family. Asked what taxes are used for, she replied,

"What are they? I don't know." She can neither read nor write and has never voted. A Mexican housewife in San Luis Potosi replied to the question on the effect of government by saying, "Its activities have no effect on me as I have nothing to do with government." She reported that she has too many children to be able to think about anything else. She has few friends and no trust in people outside her family. The only occasion when she would consider approaching a governmental official would be if there were some possibility of getting a job for a member of her family. Insofar as the parochial is aware of government, he tends to see it in relation to family interests. Thus a poor Mexican tailor living in Oaxaca said about the government: "It has no effect. I have no family or job connections with the government."

Much more frequent among the Mexican and Italian cases were explicitly alienated respondents. Most of them were "output" alienates: government should do things for themselves and for people like them, they believed, but it was indifferent to the interests of poor people, or it was corrupt and responsive only to bribes or family connections.

Here are a few examples of the theme of governmental corruption among our Mexican respondents.

> *A Mexican Housewife, on the effect of local government on her life:* "It has an effect for them. They take all the money."
> *A Mexican Secretary, on what taxes are used for:* "Public officials say they are for improvements for the town, which seems incredible since each new governor increases taxes and does nothing for the town, only for his pockets."

Another theme of alienation is neglect.

> *A Mexican Bricklayer, on the effect of local government on him:* "There is no water in the house and my wife has to go somewhere else to get it."
> *A Mexican Female White-collar Worker, on the effect of local government:* "They have neglected the food shops and the markets where the merchandise is not of good quality and expensive. Vegetables are sometimes rotten but are sold just the same and this causes sickness among the people."

The same themes of corruption and neglect appear among the Italian alienated respondents. Thus an Italian cab-driver in Bari replied impatiently to the question on the effect of the national government on people like himself: "Of course, it has an influence, but we don't have any influence. The government officials have influence to fill up their own pockets. What effect can they have? There is nothing that one can do. My family keeps its place and is not interested." Questioned further about the local government, he replied: "All local activities are for interested parties. They make a lot of propaganda; they promise many things, but nobody does anything for the people. How can I approach the mayor, or join a party, if nobody thinks about us?"

Parochialism and alienation are not peculiar to Italy and Mexico, however. We encountered both phenomena in Germany, Britain, and the United States. Tables II.1 and II.2 suggested that these attitudes occur far less frequently in the latter three countries. But a few examples may help to make the point that the differences are relative and not absolute.

> *An English Female Garment Worker, on the effect of the national government on her:* "I don't know. I don't bother. They don't affect us at all. If we don't work, they don't give us anything."
>
> *An English Cook, on the effect of the national government:* "I should say, quite a lot . . . well, I don't know that they affect me in particular. The only thing I'm up against is that those who have been thrifty all their lives, they let them get on with it—but those who haven't, they help. That's what I don't like."
>
> *A German Laborer, on the influence of the national government:* "There is little influence. The main influence is that everyone has to pay taxes. It hardly touches my life."
>
> *A German Refugee Housewife, on the effect of government on her family life:* "When my husband brings home his pay envelope and we see the deductions — then we are in touch with the government."

Thus far we have been analyzing questions about governmental output. Those respondents who attribute significance to national and local government and who can provide examples of this significant impact are at least subjects. If they are aware of the impact of government but are dissatisfied, we can call them alienated subjects. If they are not aware at all or only dimly aware, we can call them parochials. It is of interest that many respondents, particularly among the British, answered these output questions with gratuitous input content. In other words, their "democratic" orientation spilled over into a subject context. For example, a Scottish steel worker attributed great significance to the local government, and when pressed for an example he remarked, "Well, the people are interested in things that want doing and they are not long in waiting to bring it up to the local Council or in wanting to publish it in the local paper."

Awareness of the significance of government impact varies sharply with the level of education. Thus in the United States 89 per cent of those who had had some secondary school education were aware of the significance of the national government, as compared with 73 per cent of those who had had only primary school education. In England the percentages were 76 for the university educated to 70 for the primary school educated, and in Germany the figures were 83 per cent to 66 per cent.

Although the differences are large among these three countries, the important point is that even among the minimally educated Americans, Britons, and Germans, the perception that government is significant for one's daily life is extremely widespread.

In contrast, among uneducated Italians and Mexicans, the incidence of awareness of the significance of national and local government was extremely low: 24 per cent for Italy and 25 per cent for Mexico. Italians with secondary school education had an incidence of awareness of 72 per cent, and those with university education 85 per cent. What is striking about the results for Mexico is that even the secondary- and university-educated showed a relatively low incidence of awareness of the significance of government: 35 per cent for the secondary-educated Mexicans and 57 per cent for the university-educated Mexicans.

AWARENESS OF POLITICS

Our first series of questions was intended to ascertain patterns of "output cognition." We were concerned with whether people perceived government as having an effect on them, their families, and their communities. In another series of questions we sought to determine whether or not they followed or paid attention to political and governmental affairs (including political campaigns). These questions come closer to testing the frequency of participant orientations in the five countries, for they get at the dimension of attentiveness to political input. We may assume that if people follow political and governmental affairs, they are in some sense involved in the process by which decisions are made. To be sure, it is a minimal degree of involvement. The civic culture, as we use the term, includes a sense of obligation to participate in political input activities, as well as a sense of competence to participate. Following governmental and political affairs and paying attention to politics are limited civic commitments indeed, and yet there would be no civic culture without them. They represent the cognitive component of the civic orientation.

Table II.4 tells us something about the incidence of civic cognition in the five countries. In general, the picture in Table II.4 coincides with the one reported in the discussion of subject or output cognition. The United States, Britain, and Germany are high in following political and governmental affairs, and Italy and Mexico are low. But there are two interesting qualifications to this general pattern. First, the Germans more frequently follow political affairs than do the English. And second, the Italians follow political affairs far less frequently than do the Mexicans. And a similar pattern emerges if one considers responses to a question about "paying attention to election campaigns."

The relatively high frequency with which German respondents report that they are cognitively oriented to the governmental input process — a frequency as great as or greater than that in Britain — suggests that at least in the cognitive dimension there may well be civic tendencies in Germany. If

TABLE II.4 *Following accounts of political and governmental affairs; by nation**

Percentage who report they follow accounts	*U.S.*	*U.K.*	*Germany*	*Italy*	*Mexico*
Regularly	27	23	34	11	15
From time to time	53	45	38	26	40
Never	19	32	25	62	44
Other and don't know	1	1	3	1	1
Total percentage	100	100	100	100	100
Total number	970	963	955	995	1,007

* Actual text of the question: "Do you follow the accounts of political and governmental affairs? Would you say you follow them regularly, from time to time, or never?"

democracy does not seem to have struck deep roots in German society, it is not because of lack of exposure to politics or lack of political information.

The Italian and Mexican data present an interesting contrast. On the questions about output cognition and input cognition these two nations scored lower than the other three. But in terms of their cognition of government output, the Italians much more frequently than the Mexicans expressed awareness of such activities. However, as a function of their cognition of government input — their exposure to political affairs and to political campaigns — the Italians much less frequently than the Mexicans indicated such exposure. Thus more than half of the Italian respondents said that the government had an impact on their lives; but almost two-thirds said that they never follow politics or governmental affairs, and more than half said they do not pay attention to election campaigns. In Mexico, on the other hand, a much larger proportion pays attention to campaigns and follows politics than attributes significance to the government.[1]

[1] In Chapter I we pointed out that the Mexican sample did not include that part of the Mexican population living in towns whose population was under 10,000. Since this might have affected the Mexican results, particularly in the dimension of exposure to political communication, and thus rendered invalid our Mexican-Italian comparison, we compared the Mexican sample with that part of the Italian sample living in towns of

This Mexican characteristic comes out more clearly if we compare the Mexicans who report high exposure to political communication with those who are similarly involved in the other nations. In the other four nations, less than 10 per cent of those high on exposure to communication report that neither the national nor local governments have an effect on their lives. In Mexico, on the other hand, 56 per cent of those high on exposure attribute no significance to their government.

A few comments from our life-history interviews may illustrate the difference between the Mexican and Italian patterns. A Mexican truck driver, when asked whether he was interested in political and governmental affairs, replied, "Very much, because the government can help the general conditions of life of all the Mexicans. At least this is what I wish." Asked when he first became interested in politics, he said, "About ten years ago, when I began to realize that our governors tend to benefit themselves economically without considering the needs of the other citizens." A Mexican shoemaker replied to the same question, "Yes, I like politics. I am very interested in it, because I want to see improvements and also because I want to see that everything goes well, because many political leaders, rather than help the worker, hurt him." And a Mexican stenographer commented, "I have an interest in my town that is neglected by its governor. I have compared it with other cities that were at the same level as Pueblo and now they have gone way ahead in culture and beauty." She first became interested in politics when she visited Guadalajara" . . . and saw how it had improved. I remember that last year Pueblo had the second place in the republic for its beauty and now she has lost it because her governors have neglected her."

Although there were Italian respondents who described themselves as interested in politics, the more typical reply stressed the danger and futility of interesting oneself in politics:

10,000 and over. The results differed only by a small number of percentage points and confirmed the conclusion discussed here.

An Italian Retired Worker, on his interest in politics: "Reading the paper is the most that I do, and when I read it, I read it very slowly. It takes me a whole day to read it. I don't like to take part in discussions. As I told you before, they are very lively and at times even dangerous."

An Italian Mechanic, on who is interested in politics: "The fanatics who believe in what they are doing and in their aspirations, or the ignorant people who are behind and pushed by the first."

An Italian Housewife who waits on customers in the family grocery store: "None! I have an aversion for it, because I feel nothing is just."

When we use other measures of political cognition, the same national patterns are repeated. Thus when we compare exposure to political communication in the various mass media (Table II.5), the Germans come out ahead of the British, and the Mexicans better than the Italians.

We have already seen that output cognition is closely related to level of educational attainment and socio-economic position. It also appears that education is strongly correlated with civic cognition (see Table II.6). On the university level almost all respondents in each country follow politics. On the secondary level the countries are, with the exception of Italy, uniformly high in the proportions who follow politics; and even in relation to Italy the difference between secondary-

TABLE II.5 *Following reports of public affairs in the various media; by nation**

Percentage who follow accounts	*U.S.*	*U.K.*	*Germany*	*Italy*	*Mexico*
In newspapers at least weekly	49	43	53	16	31
On radio or television at least weekly	58	36	52	20	28
In magazine (ever)	57	21	45	26	25
Total number	970	963	955	995	1,007

* Actual text of the questions: "What about newspapers (radio or television, magazines)? Do you follow (listen to, read about) public affairs in newspapers (radio or television, magazines) nearly every day, about once a week, from time to time, or never?" Only the percentages for those who report exposure are reported here.

TABLE II.6 *Following politics regularly or from time to time; by nation and education*

Nation	*Total* (%)	*Total* (*no.*)*	*Prim. or less* (%)	*Prim. or less* (*no.*)	*Some sec.* (%)	*Some sec.* (*no.*)	*Some univ.* (%)	*Some univ.* (*no.*)
United States	80	(970)	67	(339)	84	(442)	96	(188)
Great Britain	68	(963)	60	(593)	77	(322)	92	(24)
Germany	72	(955)	69	(790)	89	(124)	100	(26)
Italy	36	(995)	24	(692)	58	(245)	87	(54)
Mexico	55	(1,007)	51	(877)	76	(103)	92	(24)

* Numbers in parentheses refer to the bases upon which percentages are calculated.

school Italians and secondary-school respondents in other countries is much less than the difference between primary-school Italians and primary-school respondents in other countries. Thus on the higher levels of education one finds in all nations a uniformly high proportion who follow politics. Among those with lower educational attainment the national differences are greater. In the United States, Britain, and Germany, and to a lesser extent in Mexico, those with little education still follow politics; but in Italy few respondents on the lower level are exposed to political communication.

HAVING INFORMATION AND OPINIONS

Our measures of knowledge or cognition of the political system thus far have been subjective estimates of the significance of government and subjective estimates of exposure to political and governmental affairs. We have not yet tried to ascertain the amount of information about government and politics that the respondents actually have. Democratic competence is closely related to having valid information about political issues and processes, and to the ability to use information in the analysis of issues and the devising of influence strategies. Our survey contained two measures of information: one was based on ability to identify the national leaders of the principal parties in each country, and the second was based on ability to identify cabinet offices or departments at the national level of government.

These are simple measures of quantity of a certain kind of

information. They tap only a limited aspect of the dimension of knowledge, and they tell us nothing about the capacity to use knowledge intelligently. Furthermore, since the governmental and party structures of the five countries differ, we cannot assume that these quantitative measures of political information are strictly comparable. The ability to identify leaders of the smaller parties in Italy and Mexico may represent a higher order of cognition than the ability to identify a larger number of leaders in the American two-party system. However, when we compare the proportions at the extremes — those having either no correct information or a great deal of information — these structural differences are of less significance and our comparisons are more reliable.

The results in Table II.7 show that Germans, English, and Americans have the largest proportion of well-informed respondents by this measure of political information. The high frequency of uninformed Italian respondents is consistent with the high percentage of Italians who describe themselves as not following politics and political campaigns. On the other hand, the Mexican figures are again of great interest. Though reporting with relatively great frequency that they follow politics and political campaigns, the Mexicans show themselves to be the most poorly informed of all our national groups. Approximately half the Mexican respondents — including

TABLE II.7 *Ability to name party leaders and governmental ministries; by nation*[a]

	Percentage of total sample who could[b]			
Nation	*Name four or more party leaders*	*Name no party leader*	*Name four or more ministries*	*Name no ministry*
United States	65	16	34	28
Great Britain	42	20	34	23
Germany	69	12	40	20
Italy	36	40	23	53
Mexico	5	53	21	47

[a] Those with medium levels of information (i.e., who could name one to three in each category) have been left out of the table.

[b] Percentages in each case are of the total sample.

many who say they follow politics — could not name correctly any political leader or any government department.

If we can demonstrate this Mexican pattern, we shall have added another significant item to our characterization of the Mexican political culture. We have hypothesized that Mexican political culture combines high cognitive self-appraisal with poor cognitive performance. One way of testing this would be to determine the extent to which poorly informed respondents in our five countries are ready to express political opinions. We shall use as a measure of readiness to express political opinions a "range of political opinion" index. This index is based upon the frequency with which respondents, rather than saying they did not know, expressed opinions on a series of six general political attitude questions. These questions dealt with such matters as the content of civic obligations, judgments of interest groups and political parties, and the need for political campaigning.[2] That this combination of high cognitive self-appraisal with low information is especially characteristic of Mexico is suggested by Table II.8, which reports how frequently respondents answered these opinion questions.

It appears that the Mexicans are almost as frequently willing

[2] The six questions used to compute the "range of political opinion" index were as follows:

"1. One sometimes hears that some people or groups have so much influence on the way the government is run that the interests of the majority are ignored. Do you agree or disagree that there are such groups?

"2. We know that the ordinary person has many problems that take his time. In view of this, what part do you think the ordinary person ought to play in the community affairs of his town or district?

"3. People speak of the obligations that they owe to their country. In your opinion, what are the obligations that every man owes his country?

"4. Some people say that campaigning is needed so the public can judge candidates and issues. Others say that it causes so much bitterness and is so unreliable that we'd be better off without it. What do you think — is it needed or would we be better off without it?

"5. The ——— party now controls the government. Do you think that its policies and activities would ever seriously endanger the country's welfare? Do you think that this *probably* would happen, that it *might* happen, or that it *probably wouldn't happen?*

"6. Same as question 5, but with reference to chief opposition party."

to express opinions on all six questions as are the Germans, even though the Germans have the largest proportion of persons with high information scores and the Mexicans have the smallest. But to provide further confirmation that Mexico contains a larger proportion of "low information-high opinion" respondents than do any of the other countries, we must ascertain what percentage of respondents in each country *combines*

TABLE II.8 *Range of political opinions; by nation*

Percentage who	*U.S.*	*U.K.*	*Germany*	*Italy*	*Mexico*
Answered all six political questions	63	56	47	26	46
Said "Don't know" to one or two questions	29	37	46	37	35
Said "Don't know" to three or more questions	7	7	7	36	19
Total percentage	99	100	100	99	100
Total number	970	963	955	995	1,007

these qualities of low information and high willingness to express opinions. This analysis, expressed in Table II.9, brings out a number of points. First, it appears that in all the countries except Italy, persons who score low in information score high in the expression of opinions. Thus two out of three poorly informed Mexicans and almost all of the poorly informed Americans, British, and Germans gave some answer to four or more of the six opinion questions. On the other hand, only one out of three poorly informed Italians expressed opinions in four or more of the questions. This would seem to suggest that in all the countries but Italy, the willingness to express political opinions is widespread, affecting even the uninformed. The striking thing is that the poorly informed Mexicans are in this respect like the Americans, British, and Germans and unlike the Italians. There were almost as many poorly informed respondents in Italy as in Mexico, but most of the former refrained from offering opinions on political questions. Two inferences are suggested: first, Mexico is like the more "developed democracies," for even the cognitively incompetent feel free to express opinions, and, second, there

TABLE II.9 *Willingness to express political opinions among respondents with little political information; by nation*[a]

Nation	*Percentage of total sample low on political info.*[b]	*Percentage of total sample low on info. but answered four or more opinion questions*
United States	13	11
Great Britain	13	10
Germany	8	8
Italy	33	11
Mexico	36	23

[a] Percentages in each case apply to the total sample.

[b] Low on political information means that the respondent could name neither any party leaders nor any government ministerial post.

are many more such "aspiring citizens" in Mexico than in any of our other countries. These Mexicans (about one-fourth of the sample) are in almost all cases persons of primary or no education; persons possessing little information about the larger world of public affairs, yet quite willing to take a position on general political questions.[3] Such persons appear in all of our countries, but they appear twice as frequently in Mexico as in any of the other nations. Their existence in such large proportion in Mexico supports our interpretation that the political culture of that country contains a large aspirational component — a tendency to be willing to express opinions — along with poverty of information.

In general our findings on political cognition show the British, Americans, and Germans to be predominantly oriented toward their political systems in both the political and governmental sense. Or to use our jargon, they are cognitively oriented toward the political system in its output and input aspects. The Mexicans and Italians, on the other hand, include large numbers who are alienated or parochial. Table II.10

[3] It is important to note that we are dealing with the extent to which respondents felt *free* to express opinions, not with the extent to which they actually had opinions. Thus one reason for the infrequency of opinions among Italian respondents may be their great unease in an interview situation. This point is discussed further in Chapter III.

TABLE II.10 *Summary of patterns of political cognition; by nation*[a]

Nation	*Percentage alienated or parochial in govt. output*[b]	*Percentage alienated or parochial in govt. input*[c]	*Percentage aliented or parochial in both input and output*[d]
United States	12	20	7
Great Britain	26	33	14
Germany	26	28	13
Italy	42	63	38
Mexico	71	45	35

[a] Percentages in each case apply to the total national sample.
[b] Negative or don't know answers on local government impact.
[c] Negative or don't know answers on following politics.
[d] Negative or don't know answers on both local government impact and following politics.

provides a convenient summary of much of the argument that has been presented in this chapter. It shows that more than a third of the Italians and Mexicans are fully alienated or parochial, as compared with far smaller proportions for the other three countries. It also brings out quite clearly the imbalances in the Italian and Mexican patterns of orientation, and it summarizes evidence we have thus far presented on the predominance of aspirational tendencies among the Mexicans and of alienated tendencies among the Italians. If to the evidence summarized in Table II.10 we add our demonstration of the low political information level in Mexico, combined with an unusually frequent willingness to express political opinions, our theory of Mexican civic aspiration begins to assume a structurally elaborated form.

However, there is more to political culture than knowledge or cognition. How people *feel* about their political systems is an important component of political culture. The state of feeling or political emotion in a country is perhaps the most important test of the legitimacy of its political system. It is also the most important measure of political alienation and aspiration. This is the aspect of political culture to which we now turn.

CHAPTER III

Feelings Toward Government and Politics

ALTHOUGH WE stressed the dimension of knowledge or cognition in the preceding chapter, we included data and drew inferences about the state of feeling about government and politics in our five countries. Thus when we spoke of Italy and Mexico as having large proportions of alienates, we were implying that the citizens of these countries are cognitively oriented toward their political systems, yet they reject them either completely or in some of their aspects. In this and the following chapters we shall consider the affective dimension more directly.

In the present chapter we shall deal with generalized attitudes toward the system as a whole: toward the "nation," its virtues, accomplishments, and the like. We call this "system affect." We shall also deal with "output affect," or the kinds of expectations people have of treatment at the hands of government officials. Here we shall be describing the attitudes people have toward the executive or administrative agencies that enforce laws and toward regulations affecting them: that is, that part of the political system in relation to which they have a predominantly passive role. Finally, we shall treat "input affect," or the feelings people have both about those agencies and processes that are involved in the election of public officials, and about the enactment of general public policies. In the present chapter we shall introduce the dimension of input affect with an analysis of attitudes toward communicating about politics. In the chapter that follows we shall deal in detail with partisan attitudes and feelings in election campaigns.

We shall first treat the general dimension of "system affect," using as our measure the objects of national pride in our five countries.

SYSTEM AFFECT: NATIONAL PRIDE

Quite early in our interview we asked our respondents, "Speaking generally, what are the things about this country that you are most proud of?" In replying to this question, the respondents were not directed in any way to select political characteristics. When they gave political responses, we may assume that the expression of political pride was spontaneous. Table III.1 summarizes the results. Eighty-five per cent of the

TABLE III.1 *Aspects of nation in which respondents report pride; by nation*

Percentage who say they are proud of	*U.S.*	*U.K.*	*Germany*	*Italy*	*Mexico*
Governmental, political institutions	85	46	7	3	30
Social legislation	13	18	6	1	2
Position in international affairs	5	11	5	2	3
Economic system	23	10	33	3	24
Characteristics of people	7	18	36	11	15
Spiritual virtues and religion	3	1	3	6	8
Contributions to the arts	1	6	11	16	9
Contributions to science	3	7	12	3	1
Physical attributes of country	5	10	17	25	22
Nothing or don't know	4	10	15	27	16
Other	9	11	3	21	14
Total % of responses*	158	148	148	118	144
Total % of respondents	100	100	100	100	100
Total number of cases	970	963	955	995	1,007

* Percentages exceed one hundred because of multiple responses.

American respondents cited some feature of the American government or political tradition — the Constitution, political freedom, democracy, and the like — as compared with 46 per cent for the British, 7 per cent for the Germans, 3 per cent for the Italians, and 30 per cent for the Mexicans. In addition, the Americans and the British referred more frequently to public policy accomplishments than did the respondents in the other countries. At the other extreme, the Italian respondents, who included the smallest number of persons taking pride in their political system, had the largest number of respondents who reported that they took pride in nothing (8 per cent) or "didn't know" what they took pride in (19 per cent). The Italians had the highest proportion of "other" responses (21 per cent) and almost all of these were general statements of pride in the fact of having been born Italians.

Table III.1 also reports the nations' nonpolitical attributes in which the five peoples take pride. The German respondents, who infrequently took pride in their political system, included the largest proportion who took pride in their national economic accomplishments. They also included the largest proportion who expressed pride in the characteristics of Germans as people (frugality, cleanliness, hard work, and efficiency). Italians cited their country's contributions to the arts, the physical beauty of the country, and its cultural treasures most frequently. Mexican pride was more or less equally distributed among the political system, the economic system, the virtues of the people, and the physical beauties of the country.

On the whole, these findings in Table III.1 support the characterizations of the political culture of our five countries presented in the preceding chapter. Thus the Americans and the British with greatest frequency take pride in their political systems, social legislation, and international prestige. Italians in the overwhelming majority take no pride in their political system, nor even in their economy or society. To the extent that they have national pride at all, it is in their history, the physical beauty of their country, or in the fact of being Italian. Thus the picture of Italian alienation is deepened.

It is of great interest that Germany parts company with American and British democracy in the dimension of national pride. Germans see the significance of governmental output and they expose themselves to information about political input, but they express little pride in their political system as a whole and focus their national pride on the German economy, on the personal virtues of Germans, and on their scientific and artistic accomplishments.

The Mexican results provide a striking confirmation of the pattern presented in the preceding chapter. Though overwhelmingly alienated or parochial in relation to governmental output, the Mexicans show a relatively high frequency of interest in politics. Table III.1 also shows that, compared with the Italians and Germans, the Mexicans have a relatively high frequency of political pride. This pattern of high system affect coupled with rejection of the actual performance of the government is, we have argued, what one might expect in a nation characterized by a continuing attachment to a set of revolutionary ideals. Such a pattern of attitudes is what one might expect from people suddenly drawn into politics by a revolutionary upheaval. It is, of course, impossible to trace this set of attitudes solely to the Mexican Revolution, for it probably has many roots. But there is some evidence that the continuing impact of the Revolution as an ongoing process explains in part the type of attachment to their political system that Mexican respondents manifest. These respondents were asked if they could name some of the ideals and goals of the Mexican Revolution.[1] Thirty-five per cent could name none of the goals, while the remaining 65 per cent listed democracy, political liberty and equality, economic welfare, agrarian reform, social equality, and national freedom. What is of interest here is that, when asked what they were proud of as Mexicans, 34 per cent of those who could name some of the Revolution's goals or ideals — in contrast with

[1] The text of the question was: "Our Mexican Revolution is a very important event which is always much discussed. Could you tell me, in your opinion, what the principal ideals and goals of the Mexican Revolution are?"

only 19 per cent of those who could not name any — were proud of some political aspect of their nation.

But even more interesting are the results of a follow-up question to the one on the goals of the Mexican Revolution. Those respondents who mentioned some goal of the Revolution were then asked if these goals had been realized, or forgotten, or if people were still working to achieve them. Of the respondents who could name a goal of the Revolution (n: 614), 25 per cent thought the goals had been realized, 61 per cent thought that people were still working to attain them, and 14 per cent thought they had been forgotten. As one would expect, those respondents who thought that the goals of the Revolution had been forgotten were the least likely of the three groups to express pride in their political system. Thirty-one per cent (n: 84) of this group said they were proud of the Mexican political system. But in connection with our hypothesis about the effects of the Mexican Revolution as an ongoing process, it is interesting that, though the difference is slight, those respondents who believe that people are still working to accomplish the goals of the Revolution, rather than those who believe the goals have already been accomplished, express pride most frequently in the political system: 39 per cent of the former (n: 379) express such political pride, in comparison with 34 per cent of those who do not see the Revolution as a continuing process (n: 151). Mexican pride in nation, thus, does seem to depend to some extent on the continuing symbolic identification with the Mexican Revolution.

In the United States and Britain, where a large proportion of the respondents express pride in the political characteristics of their nation, this proportion was higher among the better-educated respondents. In the United States 92 per cent of those with some university education responded with political objects of pride, compared with 81 per cent for those who did not get beyond primary school. In Britain 75 per cent of the university educated took pride in political characteristics, compared with 41 per cent of those with only primary education. Similarly, in Mexico, 22 per cent of those with no education expressed political pride, compared with 38 per cent of the university educated. In Germany and Italy, on the other hand, level of education seems to have little relationship to the frequency with which political pride was expressed.

Similarly, persons in the more skilled and better-rewarded occupations in Britain, the United States, and Mexico were more frequently proud of their political systems, whereas occupation made relatively little difference in this respect in Germany and Italy. The main difference in objects of pride in each of the latter two countries was that the better-educated and the skilled, managerial, and professional respondents more often expressed pride in their country's achievements in the arts and sciences than did those with relatively little education or those employed in manual occupations.

The fact that education and occupational level have so little effect on national pride in Germany and Italy suggests alienation from the political system rather than parochialism or lack of awareness of the system. Higher education opens the minds of individuals to the secondary structures of their society, to the dimension of historical depth, and to the wider perspectives of the world scene. If higher-educated Germans and Italians fail to be significantly more political in their choice of objects of pride than their lower-educated compatriots, we have to conclude that the political system of each country is given a low order of preference, or is negatively appraised among those social groupings who are aware of it and follow its activities. Furthermore, we are now in a position to point out that political alienation in Germany differs from that in Italy. Alienation in Italy involves the withdrawal of attention as well as the absence of political pride. In Germany we have the interesting combination of high exposure and attentiveness to the political system, along with an absence of pride in it.

OUTPUT AFFECT: EXPECTATIONS OF TREATMENT BY GOVERNMENT AND POLICE

The feelings that people have toward governmental authorities may be inferred from their expectations of how they will be treated by them. In constructing our interview we assumed that most people preferred to be treated fairly and considerately when in contact with officials. If they expected fair and considerate treatment, we could safely assume that at least in these respects they were favorably disposed toward governmental authority. And in the opposite case, we could assume that they were unfavorably disposed. Thus our questions were intended to discover what qualities our respondents imputed to the executive side of government.

We confronted our respondents with two hypothetical situations. In the first they were asked to imagine themselves in a government office with a problem that called for official action. How did they think they would be treated? Would they be treated equally, like everyone else? We then asked them to imagine that they were explaining their point of view to the official or officials. Did they expect that they would be listened to attentively and considerately? In the second situation they were asked to imagine themselves as having some minor trouble with the police. Did they expect to be treated equally and considerately by the police? The results of the questions on equality of treatment are summarized in Table III.2.

The pattern that emerges is of great interest. The Americans and the British, who in large majorities perceived the significance of national and local government for their daily lives, who said they followed politics and political campaigns, and who most often spontaneously expressed pride in their political systems, also in large majorities expect equality of treatment at the hands of government. In theoretical terms we can say that the British and Americans are high in output and input cognition, high in system affect, and high in output affect. The Germans again conform to the British and American pattern, although the proportions expecting equal treatment are somewhat lower. Though they are low in system affect, they are high in output affect, just as they were high in output and input cognition.

The responses in Italy and Mexico confirm the high incidence of output alienation in these countries. These people are alienated in their expectations of treatment at the hands of governmental authority and police. Again, on the output side, the Mexicans show more frequent alienation than

TABLE III.2 *Expectation of treatment by governmental bureaucracy and police; by nation**

Percentage who say	*U.S.*		*U.K.*		*Germany*		*Italy*		*Mexico*	
	bureauc.	*pol.*	*bureauc.*	*pol.*	*bureauc.*	*pol.*	*bureauc.*	*pol.*	*bureauc.*	*pol.*
They expect equal treatment	83	85	83	89	65	72	53	56	42	32
They don't expect equal treatment	9	8	7	6	9	5	13	10	50	57
Depends	4	5	6	4	19	15	17	15	5	5
Other	—	—	—	—	—	—	6	6	—	—
Don't know	4	2	2	0	7	8	11	13	3	5
Total percentage	100	100	98	99	100	100	100	100	100	99
Total number	970	970	963	963	955	955	995	995	1,007	1,007

* Actual texts of the questions: "Suppose there were some question that you had to take to a government office — for example, a tax question or housing regulation. Do you think you would be given equal treatment — I mean, would you be treated as well as anyone else?" "If you had some trouble with the police — a traffic violation maybe, or were accused of a minor offense — do you think you would be given equal treatment? That is, would you be treated as well as anyone else?"

the Italians — a repetition of the pattern in the dimension of output cognition.

Table III.3 reports the frequency of expectations of considerate treatment at the hands of governmental officials and the police. Here we were concerned with whether or not our respondents imputed responsiveness to government officials, whether they felt they would be treated with dignity, on a "give and take" basis. Although there are structural differences in the bureaucratic and police organizations among our five countries, our questions were directed at those bureaucratic and police authorities with whom the respondents might come in contact in the hypothetical situations set up by the questions. (A more discriminating series of questions, which would get at differences in expectations of treatment by different levels of bureaucratic authority and different types of bureaucratic or police agencies, would no doubt have produced a more complex pattern and more reliable body of information.) Given the problem of interview length, we sought to attain comparability by specifying the type of problem (e.g., taxation, housing) or the type of offense (traffic violation, misdemeanor) that occasioned the bureaucratic or police encounter.

In all of our countries, with the exception of Mexico, the police were often viewed with as much favor as — if not more favor than — the general governmental authority. Mexican cynicism is particularly marked vis-à-vis the police, while in Britain the reported general confidence in the considerateness and responsiveness of the police is strikingly documented. It is of great interest that the Germans come out somewhat better than the Americans on expectations of considerate treatment at the hands of government and the police. Why Americans should, on the one hand, expect equality of treatment in such overwhelming proportions and then drop to only around 50 per cent for expectations of considerate treatment is an intriguing question. We would like to suggest, though it will be treated in detail below, that Americans have not as fully assimilated the role of subject in relation to administrative authorities as have the Germans and the British. Certainly these data seem to support popular impressions of

TABLE III.3 *Amount of consideration expected for point of view from bureaucracy and police; by nation**

	U.S.		*U.K.*		*Germany*		*Italy*		*Mexico*	
Percentage who expect	*bureauc.*	*pol.*	*bureauc.*	*pol.*	*bureauc.*	*pol.*	*bureauc.*	*pol.*	*bureauc.*	*pol.*
Serious consideration for point of view	48	56	59	74	53	59	35	35	14	12
A little attention	31	22	22	13	18	11	15	13	48	46
To be ignored	6	11	5	5	5	4	11	12	27	29
Depends	11	9	10	6	15	13	21	20	6	7
Other	0	—	—	—	1	2	6	6	—	1
Don't know	4	2	2	1	8	11	12	14	3	4
Total percentage	100	100	98	99	100	100	100	100	98	99
Total number	970	970	963	963	955	955	995	995	1,007	1,007

* Actual texts of the questions: "If you explained your point of view to the officials, what effect do you think it would have? Would they give your point of view serious consideration, would they pay only a little attention, or would they ignore what you had to say?" "If you explained your point of view to the police, what effect do you think it would have? Would they . . . [same choices as before]?"

TABLE III.4 *Expectation of treatment by governmental authorities and police; by education in the United States, United Kingdom, and Germany*

	U.S.			*U.K.*			*Germany*		
Percentage who expect	*Prim. or less*	*Some sec.*	*Some univ.*	*Prim. or less*	*Some sec.*	*Some univ.*	*Prim. or less*	*Some sec.*	*Some univ.*
Equal treatment in govt. office	80	84	88	81	87	88	64	73	77
Equal treatment by police	81	87	89	88	90	96	70	81	88
Consideration in govt. office	44	46	58	60	58	75	51	62	81
Consideration by police	50	59	60	75	72	71	58	65	81
Total number	338	443	188	593	321	24	788	123	26

the American as uneasy in bureaucratic situations, fuming over inefficiency and red tape.

The distinction between the United States, Britain, and Germany, on the one hand, and Italy and Mexico, on the other, still holds. Only 35 per cent of the Italians and 12 to 14 per cent of the Mexicans expect serious consideration from governmental and police authority, should they try to explain their point of view, in contrast with 48 per cent or more for the respondents in the other three countries.

Expectation of treatment by government and police also varies among educational levels. Table III.4 shows these differences for the United States, Britain, and Germany. In the United States the proportion of university-educated respondents expecting equal and considerate treatment by the government and police ranges from 8 to 12 percentage points higher than for those respondents having primary school education or less. In England the difference is similarly small, and in the case of expectations of considerateness by the police the poorly educated come out better than the well educated. This suggests that in these two countries, not only is there a general widespread expectation of equal and considerate treatment, but the less educated have these expectations almost as frequently as the more educated. Table III.4 also shows that Germany, which was high on the overall national percentage for expectations of treatment, has a sharper difference in expectation among educational levels. Furthermore, this difference is more marked in the dimension of considerate treatment than in equality of treatment. Though there is a difference of 13 to 18 percentage points in expectations of equality of treatment between Germans with primary school and those with university education, still around two-thirds of the less well-educated Germans expect to be treated equally by the government and the police. But only 51 per cent of the less well-educated Germans expect to be considerately treated by governmental authorities, as compared with 81 per cent of the university educated. The difference between these two groups with respect to considerate treatment by the police is also large — 23 per cent. The British figures present a striking contrast. Though almost three-fourths of all the British respondents expect to be considerately treated by the police, it would appear that this expectation is somewhat more widely distributed among poorly-educated Britons than among the university educated.

These findings show that in the United States and Britain both the educated and the less well educated, in large and approximately equal proportions, tend to expect "good" treatment from government. In Germany the less well educated expect to be treated equally by governmental authorities, but the expectation of considerate treatment is more frequently concentrated among the educated elements of the population.

As Table III.5 indicates, in Italy and Mexico the overall percentage of those expecting fair and considerate treatment is low, but the differences between the advantaged and disadvantaged groups is relatively large. Thus in Italy 30 per cent of those with no formal education expect to be treated equally by the police, as compared with 74 per cent for those with some university education — a difference of 44 percentage points. In Mexico only 19 per cent of those with no education expect equal treatment by government, as compared with 68 per cent for the university educated — a percentage spread of 49 points. The difference among educational groups in expectations of equal treatment by the police is similarly high in both countries. Even on the upper levels of education, the expectations of considerate treatment are low in both countries, but particularly in Mexico, where only 20 per cent of the university educated expect considerate treatment at the hands of the government and the police.

From our analysis thus far we see that the American and British respondents tend, on the whole, to have relatively favorable expectations of government; and educational differences have a relatively small effect on such expectations. In Germany overall expectations proved to be relatively high,

TABLE III.5 *Expectation of treatment by governmental authorities and police; by education in Italy and Mexico*

	Italy				*Mexico*			
Percentage who expect	*None*	*Some prim.*	*Some sec.*	*Some univ.*	*None*	*Some prim.*	*Some sec.*	*Some univ.*
Equal treatment in govt. office	30	51	65	59	19	45	58	68
Equal treatment by police	27	53	68	74	14	33	54	51
Consideration in govt. office	20	34	38	44	5	16	18	22
Consideration by police	17	34	43	48	8	13	17	22
Total number	88	604	245	54	221	656	103	24

but class differences in expectations of considerateness of treatment are also relatively large. In Mexico and Italy, and particularly in the former, overall expectations of favorable treatment are relatively low, and educational differences in expectations tend to be relatively extreme.

In our life-history interviews we pursued a similar line of questioning, but in these cases we asked our respondents whether they had ever had any direct contact with government officials. We then pressed them to describe their experiences and indicate whether they were satisfied with the treatment they received. The life-history material, consequently, can provide us with reports of personal experience at the hands of governmental authority.

The pattern in Britain is illustrated in the experience of a British house painter who approached an official of the Inland Revenue. He asked him ". . . about starting our business. He was very fair. I asked him about scales for house purchase and rates of loan." When asked whether he was satisfied or felt fairly treated, he replied, "Very satisfied. It seemed too good to be true, this about housing loans." A garage mechanic referred to an experience with the police involving a "no parking" violation. When asked whether he was satisfied with his treatment, he replied, "Well, honestly, satisfied. I didn't like it at the time." When asked if he had been treated efficiently, he replied, "Yes, too much so." There were cases of dissatisfaction among the British respondents. Perhaps the strongest case of dissatisfaction was that of a small businessman. He referred to a contact with income tax officials: "The only way was to browbeat them. Politeness didn't work at all. In the long run, I was quite satisfied, but only through my own endeavors. I find the more minor the official you deal with, the less satisfaction you get." When asked whether he had been fairly treated, he replied, "Yes, I don't think there's any distinction made between various people. Only in the case of personal friendships, which is not only done in government offices."

The American respondents similarly reported favorable contacts on the whole, but with qualifications. Thus a salesman referring to his experiences with traffic tickets said his experiences had varied. "In some ways it was ideal, in others it was disgraceful the way I was treated. One guy was looking to give a ticket and he gave it. But the police force is adequate as could be expected. Some can be very arrogant." A manufacturer's representative referred to contacts with both an alderman and the sewer department. He reported: "The alderman fixed me up fine. As to the other — yes and no. Yes, insofar as the explanation I got. No, in that I was told the City Hall had to take care of the problem — this entailed much travelling." Pressed to state whether he was fairly treated, he replied, "Yes. That's the way everyone's treated." Southern Negroes' experiences of governmental treatment are illustrated in the case of a Negro woman who reported her effort to register as a voter. "The men were so harsh and gruff, I don't know. I mean, they used that tone of voice to me I guess trying to frighten me, but I just smiled to myself and acted like I did not notice it." When asked whether she was satisfied, she replied, "No, they could have been more pleasant."

The Italian and Mexican cases bring out a general pattern of experience with corruption, discrimination, and unresponsiveness:

> *An Italian Housewife:* "I have spoken very often to governmental officials, but they take no interest in this town. My husband tried to get a pension for his father, but spent so much money that he had to stop. They don't take us into consideration. Here we advance only by recommendation."
>
> *An Italian Tree Surgeon:* ". . . my wife was sent back from the tax office. In the employment office things are not done right. . . . It is a month that I am without work, and am not on the employment list, as there is favoritism. The friends of the officials will be signed up first, and they will get the first jobs available. We are put on the list with a month and one-half delay."
>
> *An Italian Gymnastic Instructor (Communist):* "For Heaven's sake! The last time I was at a government office there was a poor man with a paper to fill out. He was asking the official how to fill it out. The official wouldn't pay attention but told him, 'Fill this paper out and that paper out and come back tomorrow.' The poor man did not know what to do. So I told the official he was there because I was paying him; everyone was paying him to be there and give explanations. He didn't open his mouth, and filled out the paper for the man."

The themes are similar among the Mexicans.

> *A Mexican Small Businessman:* "Normally the officials are not very competent. One doesn't see individuals with much education in the municipality. They are not very efficient in the way they do their business. But in the local government they will do their duty for money. . . ."

> *A Mexican Blacksmith:* ". . . the people that work in those places are not attentive. They don't do it willingly. They are despots and get angry."
>
> *A Mexican Schoolteacher:* ". . . the judges operate through money. As far as the state employees are concerned, they are generally just, although they take into account your personal appearance."

A Mexican housewife said she would go to the government authorities only if a member of her family was arrested. ". . . I would go to a judge or to a lawyer. If he [member of family] was guilty, they would let him free if I paid a big sum. If he was innocent, they would help me."

PATTERNS OF POLITICAL COMMUNICATION

We turn now to the dimension of feelings about politics, or input affect. Here and in the following chapter we present a variety of measures, including attitudes toward political communication, intensity of partisanship, feelings about voting and election campaigns. In the present chapter we deal with communication patterns in our five countries. Our treatment of political communication covers more than the dimension of input affect; we are concerned with discovering the differences in the direct (face-to-face) political communications processes among the five countries. Our questions seek to get at communications behavior as well as feelings about political communication.

If ordinary men and women are to participate in a democratic political process, they must have the feeling that it is safe to do so, that they do not assume great risks when they express political opinions, and that they can be relatively free about the person to whom they talk. To the extent that these expectations are not present, impulses to communicate politically are suppressed, and what political communication there is tends to be restricted, covert, confined to family, or "ideologically trustworthy" groups; people are not on "speaking terms" politically. Whether or not people are on "political speaking terms," whether or not there is an overt and relatively unrestricted communications process, will in turn be related to the degree of development of the media of communication and their freedom and autonomy, the relative independence of interest groups from governmental and party control, the characteristics of the party system, and the relationship between parties.

The first measure we shall use of freedom of political communication is the extent to which people in our five countries report that they discuss politics. We have already examined exposure to political communication in the press, radio, and television. The same pattern that we found there emerges in our examination of informal, face-to-face communication (see Table III.6). The chief exception is that Germany, which reported the highest frequency of following reports of public affairs in the mass media, comes out with a lower frequency of talking politics than that of either the United States or England. This is a finding of some interest. Talking politics with other people differs from exposure to political communication in the mass media in two respects. First, talking politics is an active form of political participation; mass media exposure is relatively passive. Thus German political participation, which is extraordinarily high in the dimension of passive exposure, seems to drop substantially when it comes to active political communication. Second, talking politics with other people implies some sense of safety in political communication. No one can tell what thoughts pass through the minds of newspaper readers or television viewers. Talking politics means taking a chance; in totalitarian countries, a big chance. In democratic countries the risks may not be so high, but there still are some risks. The

TABLE III.6 *Frequency of talking politics with other people; by nation**

Percentage who report they	*U.S.*	*U.K.*	*Germany*	*Italy*	*Mexico*
Never talk politics	24	29	39	66	61
Sometimes talk politics	76	70	60	32	38
Other and don't know	0	—	1	2	—
Total percentage	100	99	100	100	99
Total number	970	963	955	995	1,007

* Actual text of the question: "What about talking about public affairs to other people? Do you do that nearly every day, once a week, from time to time, or never?"

higher frequency of talking politics in the United States and Britain than in Germany suggests that there is a greater sense of safety in political communication in these countries, a greater tendency to involve family, friends, neighbors, and work-groups in the political communications process. But we shall return to this theme later.

The Mexican and Italian patterns of direct, face-to-face communication about politics and exposure to political communication in the mass media coincide. Roughly two-thirds of the respondents in each country report that they do not talk politics, and two-thirds say they do not follow political affairs through the mass media. Mexican respondents report somewhat higher percentages of inactivity.

But we are concerned here not only with the frequency of talking politics, but also with how people feel about discussing political and governmental affairs. We have a number of measures of this dimension of political feeling. One of them is the way in which people responded to our interviewers. In all of our countries we were interested in the party affiliations of our respondents. Not all of them were willing to reveal the party or parties for which they voted in recent elections (see Table III.7). The same questions were asked in all of our countries, and the interviewers were in all cases natives of the countries in which they did their interviewing. In the United States, Britain, and Mexico, practically all the respondents reported the party they had voted for in the last national election and the party they usually vote for in local

TABLE III.7 *Refusal to report voting decision to interviewer; by nation**

	National election		*Local election*	
Nation	*Refuse to report last national vote*	*"Don't know"*	*Refuse to report usual local vote*	*"Don't know"*
United States	2	2	1	1
Great Britain	2	1	1	1
Germany	16	5	14	6
Italy	32	6	31	6
Mexico	1	3	1	6

* Percentages in each case apply to the total sample.

elections. In Italy 32 per cent refused to identify their national party choice, and another 6 per cent said they didn't know what party they had voted for. Similar percentages were recorded for local party choices. In Germany about 20 per cent either refused to talk about their national and local party choices or said they didn't know. Those Italians and Germans who refused to identify the party of their choice in the last national election were relatively equally distributed among all the social strata and were not especially concentrated among the relatively poorer elements. The low percentage in Mexico is due no doubt to the fact that the overwhelming majority of Mexicans vote for the Revolutionary party, which is the dominant party in the country. In other words, Mexicans, unlike Italians of the extreme left, have nothing to conceal.

Political suspicion thus appears to be spread through all social levels in these two nations.

In all five countries our respondents were asked, "If you wanted to discuss political and governmental affairs, would there be some people you definitely wouldn't turn to — that is, people with whom you feel it would be better not to discuss such topics? About how many people would you say there are with whom you would avoid discussing politics?"

Table III.8 shows that, though almost two out of every three respondents in the United States and Britain feel relatively or completely free to discuss political and governmental affairs, only about one out of three Germans and Italians indicated this degree of freedom about political communication. The Mexican distribution falls between, with almost equal numbers reporting feelings of freedom and limitation in political communication. The fact that both Germany and Italy show equally high proportions of respondents who feel greatly limited in political communication suggests that this kind of attitude can be associated with very different kinds of political structures. In Italy there is a fragmented party system with revolutionary parties on both right and left. In this situation of sharp interparty antagonism it is understandable that many people would conceal their party preferences and would be fearful of discussing politics with most other people. In

Germany the trend has been toward the formation of a moderate two-party system and the development of autonomous interest groups and media of communication. But this and other evidence shows that these institutions have not taken root in the Germans' feelings toward politics and partisanship; earlier attitude patterns seem to persist among the people. Thus the German pattern is one of incongruity between political structures and political culture, while the Italian pattern of party fragmentation and interpenetration of parties, interest groups, and the media of cummunication is matched by a cultural pattern of intensity of partisan antagonism, withdrawal from political communication, and withholding of feeling. It is also of importance that both Germans and Italians in recent decades have lived under totalitarian systems in which political communication was rigidly controlled and heavy sanctions were imposed on even moderate criticism of the regime. It is to be expected that the habits and feelings of these earlier Nazi and Fascist periods would persist into the present, despite the formal freedoms of the contemporary German and Italian political systems.

The question reported in Table III.8 confronted respondents with the hypothetical situation: "If you wanted to discuss politics, how free or unrestricted would you feel?" We have already seen (Table III.6) that about two-thirds of the Italians and Mexicans reported that they never talked politics. In other words, in response to the question of Table III.8 a large proportion of the Italians and Mexicans who never talk politics were estimating how free they would feel to discuss political problems "if they wanted to." But if we select only those respondents who actually do talk politics with other people, we find that about half of the American and British respondents both talk politics and feel relatively free to do so with most people. Less than one-third of the Germans showed this combination of communicating about politics and feeling free about it. Only about one-fifth of the Italians and Mexicans had this combination.

These figures are of great interest, for they suggest the degree of openness of the political communications processes in these five countries. Thus in the United States and Britain

TABLE III.8 *Feeling of restriction in discussing political and governmental affairs; by nation*

Percentage who report they	*U.S.*	*U.K.*	*Germany*	*Italy*	*Mexico*
Don't feel free to discuss politics with anyone	18	12	32	34	21
Don't feel free to discuss it with many people	19	20	23	17	22
Feel free to discuss it with a few	34	35	14	15	22
Feel free to discuss it with anyone	29	29	23	22	19
Other	0	0	—	1	3
Don't know	0	4	8	11	13
Total percentage	100	100	100	100	100
Total number	970	963	955	995	1,007

around three-quarters of the respondents claimed they take part in the political communications process, and only a fifth in each country both take part and feel seriously restricted in discussing politics. In Germany, though 60 per cent claim they take part in political communication, almost half of these communications "activists" feel seriously restricted and avoid communicating about politics with many or most people. In Italy less than a third of the respondents are active in political communication, and two out of three of these activists feel free to discuss politics with most people. The Mexican pattern is similar to the Italian: only 38 per cent talk politics, and these are equally divided into those who feel relatively free and those who feel restricted. Mexico also has an historical background of violence and revolution; freedom of political organization and communications has only begun to develop in recent decades. Thus the Mexican pattern of communications freedom is similar to the Italian and German.

Both talking politics and feeling relatively unrestricted about with whom one can safely discuss politics are closely related to educational attainment. The frequency of talking politics rises sharply from the primary to the secondary to the university levels in all five countries. But the differences between the educational levels are not as sharp in the United States and Britain as in the other free countries. It is also evident that participation in political discussion is more frequent at the secondary education level in Mexico than in Italy. Thus political discussion rises from one-third among Mexican primary-educated respondents to two-thirds of the secondary-educated Mexicans. Among the Italians the increase at this level is smaller. Only four out of ten Italians with some secondary education report they talk politics, as compared with the great majorities of secondary-educated respondents in the other four countries.

We find a similar pattern of higher frequency of the sense of freedom to communicate about politics among the better-educated levels in all five countries. Though there are educational differences in the United States and Britain, about one-half of the primary-educated Americans and British report feeling relatively unrestricted in their political communication, while in the other three countries only around one-third report this feeling of freedom. But there is a sense in which the Mexican pattern is somewhat more like the British and American than like the German and Italian. The percentage spread between levels of education is smaller in Mexico than in Germany and Italy. This higher incidence of communications freedom among the poorly educated in Mexico is another indication of the strength of the revolutionary aspirational tendency in Mexican political culture.

CHAPTER IV

Patterns of Partisanship

POLITICAL theorists often discuss the kind of partisanship that is consistent with an effectively functioning, stable democracy. Common to most of these discussions is the view that the major parties accept, by and large, the rules of political competition laid down in constitution, laws, and custom; and that their goals and methods are such that either one or any of the major parties finds being in the minority or opposition an acceptable risk. This formal conception of the character of majority and opposition in effective democracies implies a particular state of popular feeling: it assumes the existence of partisan feeling. It implies taking sides, having convictions and feelings about the proper course of political action, supporting some groups and opposing others. But it also assumes a limited partisanship. A too-hostile partisanship might jeopardize the willingness to accept opposition, and could cause electoral decisions to be rejected or dispensed with altogether.

Democratic partisanship implies political feeling, and not indifference. It also implies a particular quality of feelings. They must be expressible openly. And the political atmosphere must be able to accept the expression of partisan feelings. Where either the tone of political life is so menacing that it requires, out of a concern for safety, the suppression of partisan feeling; or where partisan impulses are so negative and hostile as to require suppression (or expression only in limited and intimate circles), then the effective conditions necessary for an open and moderate partisanship are not present.

Open and moderate partisanship, then, are essential to a stable democracy. They are the "feeling correlates" of responsible majority and loyal opposition. We have already seen that there are marked differences among countries (and among groups within countries) in the respondents' feelings of freedom to communicate with others on political questions. We saw that in Britain and the United States the proportion of respondents who felt relatively unrestricted in communicating about politics was relatively high, whereas in Germany, Italy, and Mexico it was substantially lower.

Now we turn to the dimension of partisan feeling as such; to attitudes toward one's own party and other parties. We offer two measures of partisan feeling in the five democracies. The first is a comparison of "self" and "other" images: views of one's own party and of opposing parties. The second is a measure of the depth and severity of partisan cleavage, reflected in attitudes toward marriage across party lines.

IMAGES OF PARTY SUPPORTERS

All of our respondents were told, "We're interested in what sorts of people support and vote for the different parties." Then they were presented with a list of statements and asked to select those statements most appropriate to describing the supporters of the competing parties in their countries. In the tables that follow, our respondents have been divided according to their partisan affiliations. Hence we are in a position to compare people's views of their own and of opposed parties, and to measure the overlapping or polarization in these views. The list itself was a product of experimentation. In order to present the respondents with choices meaningful to them, the question was posed in open-ended form in the pretest and the list was constructed from those judgments and appraisals. The list of judgments includes favorable, unfavorable, and neutral judgments.[1]

[1] The actual interviewing instructions permitted the respondents to pick

In its actual content this question is a cognitive one. The respondents were asked to pick statements that *described* the supporters of the main political parties in their countries. At the same time, most of these statements clearly reflected the respondents' emotional disposition toward these parties. When we interpret the responses as positive, negative, and

TABLE IV.1 *Qualities attributed to Republican and Democratic supporters by Republican and Democratic voters in the United States*[a]

Percentage describing party supporters as	*Repub. views of Repub.*	*Repub. views of Dem.*	*Dem. views of Repub.*	*Dem. views of Dem.*
POSITIVE QUALITIES				
Interested in defense and independence	63	49	44	52
Intelligent people	35	25	27	31
Interested in humanity	46	41	27	49
NEGATIVE QUALITIES				
Selfish people	3	14	23	4
Betrayers of freedom and welfare	1	4	4	2
Ignorant and misguided	0	8	6	1
Fascists, imperialists, etc.	0	1	2	0
Atheists	0	1	0	0
NEUTRAL QUALITIES				
Religious people	11	6	8	13
All sorts	13	15	15	13
Other	0	0	4	2
Total percentage[b]	172	164	160	167
Total number of cases	309	309	464	464

[a] For England, Germany, Italy, and Mexico, party affiliation was determined by the respondent's statement of the party voted for in the last national election. Party affiliation in the U.S. was based on responses to a question asking respondents whether they were "members" or "supporters of" or "leaned toward" the Republican or Democratic party. This applies to all tables in this chapter.

[b] Percentages in most cases exceed 100 because of multiple responses. "Don't know" respondents omitted.

as many statements as they desired. Only the first two choices were coded and recorded for each party.

neutral, we are, of course, drawing inferences about the feelings of the respondents.

Table IV.1 provides an analysis of the American responses to this question. It is of interest that the large percentages are all to be found in the positive or favorable cells. Although Republican voters attribute patriotism, intelligence, and humanitarianism to Republicans more frequently, in large proportion they attribute these same qualities to Democrats. The same pattern is true of the Democratic appraisal of themselves and of the Republicans. The strongest negative description made by supporters of either party about the supporters of the other party was "selfish people." Twenty-three per cent of the Democrats picked this statement to describe Republicans; 14 per cent of the Republicans picked it to describe the Democrats.

In the United Kingdom the polarization between the two major parties is somewhat sharper than that reported for the United States (see Table IV.2). Thus the percentages of respondents who view their political opponents in favorable terms are a good deal smaller than those in the United States. Similarly, the negative appraisals are somewhat more frequent in Britain than in the United States. Thus 28 per cent of the British Conservative respondents say that selfish people support the Labour party, and 29 per cent of the Laborites return the compliment to the Conservatives. Almost one-fourth of the Conservative respondents view the Laborites as "ignorant and misguided," while the Laborites spread their negative characterizations, picking "militarists and imperialists" in 10 per cent of the cases and "ignorant and misguided" in 6 per cent of the cases.[2]

[2] Cf. Mark Abrams and Richard Rose, *Must Labour Lose?* London, 1960, p. 19. In this survey a similar list question with different statements was used and showed a somewhat larger overlap between the supporters of the two major British parties. Mark Abrams comments, "The survey yielded striking evidence of the tolerance of the British electorate toward their political opponents and of agreement that links the supporters of both major parties. For example, between 40 per cent and 50 per cent of Labour supporters thought that the Conservatives could do as well as their own party in standing for the nation as a whole, in giving fair treatment to all races, in respecting British traditions, and in working for peace and

TABLE IV.2 *Qualities attributed to Conservative and Labour supporters by Conservative and Labour voters in Great Britain*

Percentage describing party supporters as	*Conserv. views of Conserv.*	*Conserv. views of Laborites*	*Labour views of Conserv.*	*Labour views of Laborites*
POSITIVE QUALITIES				
Interested in defense and independence	47	8	22	27
Intelligent people	33	6	12	18
Interested in humanity	25	17	9	49
NEGATIVE QUALITIES				
Selfish people	2	28	29	3
Betrayers of freedom and welfare	1	3	3	1
Ignorant and misguided	0	23	6	1
Fascists, imperialists, etc.	1	0	10	0
Atheists	0	1	1	0
NEUTRAL QUALITIES				
Religious people	2	1	4	3
All sorts	6	13	9	8
Other	1	3	2	1
Total percentage*	118	103	107	111
Total number	358	358	376	376

* Percentages in most cases exceed 100 because of multiple responses. "Don't know" respondents omitted.

The German pattern (Table IV.3) shows just about the same degree of polarization as the British. Only one positive characteristic is attributed to the supporters of the opposition party by more than one-fifth of the voters for either party: 23 per cent of the Christian Democrats attribute humanitarianism to the SPD supporters. The negative attributions are about as frequent as in Britain and somewhat more frequent than in the United States. The striking difference between the German pattern, on the one hand, and the British and American, on the other, is the large percentage of Germans — almost identical for Christian Democrats and Socialists — who de-

against nuclear war. Of those who opposed Labour, at least 40 per cent were prepared to describe Labour as equally qualified with the Conservatives in giving fair treatment to all races, working for peace, and opposing nuclear war."

TABLE IV.3 *Qualities attributed to Christian Democratic Union and Social Democratic supporters by CDU and SPD voters in Germany*

Percentage describing party supporters as	*CDU views of CDU*	*CDU views of SPD*	*SPD views of CDU*	*SPD views of SPD*
POSITIVE QUALITIES				
Interested in defense and independence	35	16	15	40
Intelligent people	20	8	10	29
Interested in humanity	33	23	9	57
NEGATIVE QUALITIES				
Selfish people	1	19	25	2
Betrayers of freedom and welfare	0	3	1	0
Ignorant and misguided	0	10	10	0
Fascists, imperialists, etc.	0	0	4	0
Atheists	0	8	0	2
NEUTRAL QUALITIES				
Religious people	57	1	55	3
All sorts	12	20	13	14
Other	0	3	0	1
Total percentage*	158	111	142	148
Total number	333	333	235	235

* Percentages in most cases exceed 100 because of multiple responses. "Don't know" respondents omitted.

scribe the supporters of the Christian Democratic party as "religious people." This clearly indicates that supporters of both major parties agree that the CDU receives support on religious grounds, though the evaluation of that support may differ from party to party.

As we might expect, the Italian respondents show a far sharper polarization between right and left than do the Americans, British, and Germans (see Table IV.4). If we examine this table from right to left, we note that large percentages in the favorable cells and small percentages in the unfavorable cells appear in those columns that record the statements picked by the Christian Democratic (DC), Nenni-Socialist (PSI), and Communist (PCI) voters to describe themselves, as well as the statements picked by the Nenni-Socialists to describe their Communist allies and vice-versa. The two left parties' appraisals of the Christian Democrats

TABLE IV.4 *Qualities attributed Christian Democratic, Nenni-Socialist, and Communist supporters by DC, PSI, and PCI voters in Italy*

Percentage describing party supporters as	*Christian Democratic views of*			*Nenni-Socialist views of*			*Communist views of*		
	DC	*PCI*	*PSI*	*DC*	*PCI*	*PSI*	*DC*	*PCI*	*PSI*
POSITIVE QUALITIES									
Interested in defense and independence	16	2	4	4	13	5	0	14	16
Intelligent people	30	2	5	0	9	31	0	32	23
Interested in humanity	20	1	4	2	20	29	0	27	32
NEGATIVE QUALITIES									
Selfish people	0	21	17	18	4	2	25	0	0
Betrayers of freedom and welfare	0	18	11	6	2	2	9	0	0
Ignorant and misguided	1	24	20	9	7	0	18	0	0
Fascists, imperialists, etc.	1	2	1	2	0	2	2	0	0
Atheists	0	24	18	0	9	0	0	5	2
NEUTRAL QUALITIES									
Religious people	52	0	1	35	4	4	25	0	0
All sorts	11	9	18	27	26	29	7	14	20
Other	3	5	5	11	15	13	11	11	14
Total percentage*	134	108	104	114	109	117	97	103	107
Total number	353	353	353	55	55	55	44	44	44

* Percentages in most cases exceed 100 because of multiple responses. "Don't know" respondents omitted.

and the Christian Democrats' appraisals of the two left parties (the second, third, fourth, and seventh columns) are extremely low in the favorable cells and high in the unfavorable ones. Again, as in Germany, all parties agree in associating religious characteristics with the Christian Democrats, though again the evaluative connotation may differ from party to party.

The Nenni-Socialists are intermediate in this pattern of polarization. Thus the Christian Democratic appraisal of the Communists is more negative and less neutral than is their appraisal of the PSI. The Nenni-Socialist appraisal of the

Democristiani is less negative and more neutral than is the Communists'. Finally, the appraisal by the two left parties is of some interest. If we compare the fifth column with the ninth, we find that the Nenni-Socialist respondents more often pick negative and neutral statements to describe the Communists than do the Communists to describe the Socialists. Also, the two left parties differ from each other in the frequency of unfavorable responses vis-à-vis the Christian Democrats (columns 4 and 7). Thus the Communist responses are more heavily weighted on the negative side, whereas the Nenni-Socialist statements are far more heavily concentrated in the neutral categories. Further, the Nenni-Socialists more frequently say that all sorts of people can be found supporting the various parties. Over one-fourth of the supporters of this party say that one cannot generalize about the supporters of either their own party or of the other two parties. This ambiguity of position is what one would expect from a party of the middle (not that the Nenni-Socialists are a middle-of-the-road party, but they are at least between the two other parties cited in the table).

These findings suggest that at the mass voting level there are significant differences between the left-Socialists and the Communists; that the PSI tends to be more open to right and left, and that the really sharp polarization is between the *Democristiani* and the Communists.

The Mexican pattern is of particular interest. It is more balanced between positive and negative than is the Italian, and if we exclude the ambiguous "religious people" category, it is less neutral (see Table IV.5). Positive views of the right are expressed more often by the Mexican left than by the Italian left; this may be due in part to the fact that the PRI (Mexican Revolutionary party) is in power in Mexico and consequently can afford to be more generous in appraising the right than can the Communists and left-Socialists in Italy. But it is probably largely due to the fact that the Mexican Revolutionary party is not very revolutionary. It includes the overwhelming majority of the voters and is consequently more heterogeneous in its social and ideological composition. Similarly, the fact that the Mexican right is more antagonistic to the

TABLE IV.5 *Qualities attributed to supporters of the Mexican Revolutionary party and the Party of National Action by PRI and PAN voters in Mexico*

Percentage describing party supporters as	*PRI views of PRI*	*PRI views of PAN*	*PAN views of PRI*	*PAN views of PAN*
POSITIVE QUALITIES				
Interested in defense and independence	44	14	24	23
Intelligent people	38	14	16	26
Interest in humanity	31	19	15	50
NEGATIVE QUALITIES				
Selfish people	17	20	52	3
Betrayers of freedom and welfare	4	9	17	2
Ignorant and misguided	7	17	24	12
Fascists, imperialists, etc.	4	3	7	4
Atheists	1	5	8	1
NEUTRAL QUALITIES				
Religious people	17	36	7	52
All sorts	8	8	2	3
Other	2	2	5	0
Total percentage*	173	147	177	176
Total number	514	514	75	75

* Percentages in most cases exceed 100 because of multiple responses. "Don't know" respondents omitted.

left than the left is to the right may be because the PAN[3] has relatively small support, and this support is heavily upper class and clerical in character.

The images of the opponents in the five-nation study may be summarized as follows: The American responses show the least antagonism or polarization between major parties. The Republicans appear to be somewhat more favorably disposed toward the Democrats than vice-versa. The antagonism between the British parties is greater than between the German. In view of other findings about the German pattern (see Chap. VIII), this may not mean that the German political system is more consensual than the British, but, rather, that there is a general withholding of affect from the political system in

[3] This is the *Partido de Acción Nacional,* the second largest party in Mexico.

Germany: a withholding that influences partisan attitudes as well as more general attitudes toward the political system and the nation. It is also noteworthy that in Britain the right is more antagonistic to left than left is to right, which reverses the American pattern.

Italy clearly presents the most polarized pattern. In view of the extremely small proportions of positive statements, the Italian figures would suggest something approximating a "psychological clean break" between right and left. Mexico's pattern shows somewhat less antagonism than the Italian, but more than the American, British, and German. It is also of interest that the left in Mexico is less antagonistic to the right than the other way around. This appears to result from the fact that the PAN combines a conservative social policy with a proclerical position, while the PRI voters are a more mixed group, including some middle-class people as well as workers and farmers, and believing Catholics as well as anticlericals.

In all five countries interparty antagonism appears to be significantly reduced by education. Thus in the United States around 14 per cent more of the secondary educated than of the primary educated picked favorable statements to describe the opposing party. In Britain the increase was smaller (6 per cent), but the direction was the same for both parties. In Germany the average increase from primary to secondary educated was 7 per cent, and in Mexico the average increase was 13 per cent. The same pattern was manifested in Italy, except that here the increase was relatively small in the positive category. There was a decline in the proportion of negative statements and an increase in the neutral and "religious people" categories.

PSYCHOLOGICAL DISTANCE BETWEEN PARTIES: MARRIAGE WITHIN AND ACROSS PARTY LINES

Citizens of the great national societies are affiliated with many groups and associations. In addition to their national citizenship, they may have party affiliations, interest group memberships, religious affiliations, regional identifications, occupational and professional memberships, recreational and convivial associations, as well as family ties. It has been argued by Schattschneider that the fragmenting impact of interest groups in the political system is mitigated by the fact that individuals are members of many groups; these memberships are not politically cumulative but are often conflicting, thus individuals tend to moderate and combine interests in their own minds in order to reduce conflict.[4] Lane, summarizing the literature on "multiple group membership" and "cross-pressures," concludes that it is conflict on salient issues among primary and more intimate group memberships, rather than among categoric memberships (such as class, ethnic origins, and the like), that tends to make people withdraw from political choices. He also points out that political withdrawal is only one of the means available to persons confronted by this situation. Other solutions that he lists include identification with one of the conflicting groups, moderating one's viewpoint by synthesizing or diffusing, minimizing the issue, and the like.[5] Truman, drawing insights from Bentley,[6] Herring,[7] and a number of American sociologists and anthropologists, points out that multiple memberships and conflicts affect the political choices, not only of individuals, but also of groups; that is, groups tend to moderate sharp choices based upon interest, avoid or postpone them when there is an expectation that memberships might be confronted with conflicts.[8] Truman's analysis is important, for he combines political–structural with psychological considerations, whereas purely psychological treatments tend to assume a static structure producing a "cross-pressured" individual psychology. In actual fact, where there are overlapping and competing structures, the structures themselves are responsive to the multiple-membership phenomenon and tend to avoid pressing for extreme positions and exclusive loyalties.

The theory of group membership and cross-pressures is largely based upon American experience. Truman is an ex-

[4] E. E. Schattschneider, *Party Government,* New York, 1942, pp. 33ff.

[5] Robert E. Lane, *Political Life,* Glencoe, Ill., 1959, pp. 197ff.

[6] A. F. Bentley, *The Process of Government,* Chicago, 1908.

[7] Pendleton Herring, *Group Representation Before Congress,* Baltimore, 1929.

[8] David B. Truman, *The Governmental Process,* New York, 1951, chap. VI.

ception in that he sought to include non-American experience, but he found little data to work with. In actual fact, membership patterns differ from one country to the next. In the European Catholic countries, for example, the pattern tends to be ideologically cumulative. Family, church, interest group, and party membership tend to coincide in their ideological and policy characteristics and to reinforce one another in their effects on opinion. In the United States and Britain, however, the overlapping pattern appears to be more common. As Schattschneider points out, where memberships tend to be politically cumulative, the impact of group membership tends to be fragmenting; where it is overlapping, there tends to be less political polarization.

In Chaper X we shall treat in detail the patterns of voluntary association membership. Here we are concerned with the capacity of the family to tolerate partisan differences. One of our questions confronted the respondents with the hypothetical situation of the marriage of a son or daughter. The respondent was then asked: "How would you feel if he or she married a supporter of the ______ party? [The question was repeated for each of the larger parties.] Would you be pleased, would you be displeased, or would it make no difference?"

Because of its hypothetical character, the question does not measure behavior; that is, the actual extent to which interparty marriage has occurred among our respondents or their children. Rather, it measures the respondents' estimates of the effects on family ties of marriage across political party lines. Since we can safely assume that parents prefer to maintain close relationships with their children, their response to our question will be an estimate of the degree to which family ties would be either impaired by marriage outside the party or safeguarded by marriage within the party. This, in turn, reflects the intensity of partisan antagonism. It also reflects the characteristics of the family as a part of the political system. If the family can bear political heterogeneity, we may entertain the hypothesis that the family tends intermittently to be drawn into the interest articulation and aggregation processes of the polity; that is, becomes part of the interest group and party systems. (In Chapter XI we shall show that the American and British families tend to be drawn into the political communications process.)

Another way of saying this is to point out that where political feelings are relatively cool, the large, impersonal structures of the polity can mesh with the personal and intimate ones without damaging them. If that can be done, then the family can provide a relatively smooth and continuous political socialization of children into a political system characterized by competitive political parties. It can inculcate, not only pride in nation, but also a form of partisanship that is tolerant of opposition, ambiguity, and contingency. Where the edge of partisanship is too sharp, however, the family either remains out of the political system or simply increases the impact of this form of partisanship. Furthermore, given a moderate atmosphere of partisanship, we may assume that it becomes possible to bring the family and the other intimate relationships of friendship and community into the political system as informal groups in situations of special need or stress. This point is dealt with in detail in Chapter VI. Here we need only point out that the ability to cooperate politically with one's fellow citizens is associated with a kind of partisanship that does not threaten intimate ties.

TABLE IV.6 *How supporters of major parties would view marriage of son or daughter within or across party lines in the United States*

Percentage who would feel	*Repub. toward Repub. marriage*	*Repub. toward Dem. marriage*	*Dem. toward Dem. marriage*	*Dem. toward Repub. marriage*
Pleased	16	3	11	3
Displeased	0	4	0	4
Indifferent	84	93	89	92
Other and don't know	0	0	0	1
Total percentage	100	100	100	100
Total number	309	309	464	464

Table IV.6 shows us how Republican and Democratic party supporters in the United States view the possible marriage of their children across party lines. Overwhelming majorities of the respondents of both parties expressed indifference regarding the partisan affiliations of the future mates of their children. Small percentages of the respondents of both parties expressed pleasure at the thought that a son or daughter would marry within the party they support, and very few respondents expressed displeasure over marriage outside the party.

The percentage among the British respondents who said that the party affiliations of marriage partners for their children made some difference was higher than among the Americans (see Table IV.7). But it was more a Conservative than a Labour party concern. Twenty-three per cent of the Conservative respondents stated they would be pleased by a marriage with a Conservative. The Labour respondents overwhelmingly expressed indifference.

The German respondents expressed more concern than the British and far more concern than the Americans about marriage across party lines (see Table IV.8). Thus 42 per cent of the CDU respondents expressed pleasure at the thought of a

TABLE IV.7 *How supporters of major parties would view marriage of son or daughter within or across party lines in Great Britain*

Percentage who would feel	*Conserv. toward Conserv. marriage*	*Conserv. toward Labour marriage*	*Labour toward Labour marirage*	*Labour toward Conserv. marriage*
Pleased	23	0	7	0
Displeased	0	12	0	3
Indifferent	77	87	92	97
Other and don't know	0	1	1	0
Total percentage	100	100	100	100
Total number	358	358	376	376

Christian Democratic marriage, and 19 per cent expressed displeasure regarding a Social Democratic marriage. Similarly, the percentage of Socialist respondents favoring a Socialist marriage was relatively high as compared with the British and American left-wing attitudes. What we are encountering

TABLE IV.8 *How supporters of major parties would view marriage of son or daughter within or across party lines in Germany*

Percentage who would feel	*CDU toward CDU marriage*	*CDU toward SPD marriage*	*SPD toward SPD marirage*	*SPD toward CDU marriage*
Pleased	42	1	25	3
Displeased	0	19	0	8
Indifferent	48	61	62	74
Other and don't know	10	19	13	15
Total percentage	100	100	100	100
Total number	333	333	235	235

here is the cumulative impact of group affiliations. The relation between religion and party affiliation is closer in Germany than in either Britain or the United States. Hence marriage out of the CDU and into the SPD may be viewed as a double strain — that of religion and party — on family ties. Still, in Germany this reaction is more frequently expressed positively as pleasure over marriage *within* the party rather than displeasure over marriage *out of* the party.

Table IV.9 shows that among Italian Christian Democratic

TABLE IV.9 *How supporters of major parties would view marriage of son or daughter within or across party lines in Italy*

Percentage who would feel	*DC toward DC marr.*	*DC toward PCI marr.*	*DC toward PSI marr.*	*PCI toward PCI marr.*	*PCI toward DC marr.*	*PCI toward PSI marr.*	*PSI toward PSI marr.*	*PSI toward DC marr.*	*PSI toward PCI marr.*
Pleased	59	1	1	27	2	23	16	6	4
Displeased	1	58	46	0	14	2	0	6	7
Indifferent	29	28	39	59	73	64	67	71	71
Other and don't know	11	13	14	14	11	12	16	17	18
Total percentage	100	100	100	100	100	100	100	100	100
Total number	353	353	353	44	44	44	55	55	55

voters the reaction is both strongly positive toward in-party marriage and strongly negative toward marriage with Communists; it is not quite as strongly negative toward marriage with left-Socialists. The reasons for this pattern in Italy are the revolutionary and anticlerical character of the left and the closeness of the Christian Democratic party to the Catholic Church. Since the Vatican and the Italian hierarchy have declared voting for the Communist and left-Socialist parties a mortal sin and have threatened to deny the sacraments to persons voting for these parties, it is not surprising that family ties would be threatened by the marriage of a member of a Christian Democratic family with a Communist. Not all Christian Democrats are hostile, however: almost one-third of the DC respondents expressed indifference regarding such a marriage. But again, these are the less devoted Catholic Christian Democrats, as measured by frequency of church attendance (see Table IV.11). Communist respondents, on the other hand, express greater indifference toward intermarriage with *Democristiani* (see Table IV.9).

In Mexico about one-fifth to one-fourth of the supporters of the major parties express hostility toward interparty marriage — a figure larger than in the United States, Britain, or Germany, but not as large as the proportion of Italian Christian Democrats who oppose cross-party marriage. Nevertheless, indifference is the most frequent response, which may reflect the recent moderation of church–state tension. Something approximating a modus vivendi has been reached between the regime and the church hierarchy.[9] This seems to be reflected in the high rate of indifference regarding interparty marriage among both PRI and PAN voters.

In general, this series of tables tends to support the points made above. Partisanship in the United States and Britain appears to be sufficiently moderate to be combined with intimate family ties without seriously threatening them. This is less true in Germany, Mexico, and Italy. A more detailed analysis suggests that in all the countries, save the United States, these attitudes are affected by the interplay of three types of membership: political, religious, and family. Thus if we control for frequency of church attendance (Table IV.11), it is evident that conservative voters who attend church every week or more frequently in Britain, Germany, Italy, and Mexico are more opposed to interparty marriage than are

[9] Robert E. Scott, *Mexican Government in Transition,* p. 174.

TABLE IV.10 *How supporters of major parties would view marriage of son or daughter within or across party lines in Mexico*

Percentage who would feel	*PAN toward PAN marriage*	*PAN toward PRI marriage*	*PRI toward PRI marriage*	*PRI toward PAN marriage*
Pleased	23	2	22	8
Displeased	7	22	11	24
Indifferent	65	70	61	63
Other and don't know	5	6	6	5
Total percentage	100	100	100	100
Total number	75	75	514	514

those who attend church less frequently or not at all. It is of interest that this relationship between frequency of church attendance and opposition to interparty marriage is almost as strong in Britain as in Germany. However, the data also show that conservative voters in Germany, Italy, and Mexico include a far larger proportion of frequent church attenders than in Britain, so the incidence of marital parochialism is far higher in these countries than in Britain.

It is also of interest that in all five countries the left appears to be more open to marriage with the right than the other way around, even in the United States, although the difference between the parties in this respect is small. This imbalance in party attitudes toward intermarriage increases in Britain, is even larger in Germany and Mexico, and becomes quite extreme in Italy. This general pattern of greater left openness to marriage with the right may be explained as ideological and social mobility. Generally speaking, conservative movements are more traditionally oriented than are left-wing movements. Traditionality implies religious or status exclusiveness. Hence we might expect supporters of conservative parties, more frequently than supporters of left parties, to have an in-group feeling about marriage across party lines. But this attitude on the part of conservative supporters may also be due to status differences. Since the supporters of the left parties tend more frequently to be lower class, socially and economically, they may view marriage of a son or daughter with

TABLE IV.11 *Frequency of church attendance*[a] *and displeasure toward political party intermarriage (right v. left), by nation*

	Percentage of right displeased at marriage into left party			
	Attend church weekly or more often		*Attend church less than weekly or never*	
Nation	(%)	(*No.*)[b]	(%)	(*No.*)
United States (Republicans displeased at Democratic marriage)	3	(143)	4	(156)
Great Britain (Conservatives displeased at Labour marriage)	23	(74)	10	(246)
Germany (CDU displeased at SPD marriage)	25	(166)	13	(162)
Italy (DC displeased at PCI-PSI marriage)	60	(296)	44	(55)
Mexico (PAN displeased at PRI marriage)	24	(48)	[18	(13)]

[a] Data only for respondents who reported some religious affiliation.

[b] Numbers in parentheses refer to bases upon which percentages were calculated.

a son or daughter of the conservative party as upward social mobility. The contrary attitude on the part of the right may also be a status reaction; that is, they may view such an inter-party marriage as a social step down.

National differences in feelings about parties may be illustrated by our life-history material. Our respondents were asked, not about party intermarriage, but about how they would feel if a son or daughter joined their own party or one of the other principal political parties. The British and American responses about the opposition party reflected tolerance of freedom of party choice for their children:

An American Housewife (Democrat): "Well, I'd feel that was up to her. She has to make her own choice. Just because I'm a Democrat doesn't mean she has to be one too."

An American Employee in a Trucking Firm (Democrat): [If his children should become Republicans] "It may have its merits which I don't know about. I would like to discuss it with them to see what part they are taking in it. That would probably be my incentive to get interested in politics."

An English Housewife (Conservative): [If her children joined the Labour party] "If they're responsible, that's their choice. If they were irresponsible, I would have to give them a guiding hand."

An English Draughtsman (Conservative): "I would be pleased to think they were taking an interest in politics—no matter which party."

More of the English respondents than the American expressed concern, but it was a moderate concern:

An English Truck Driver (Conservative): [If his children became Conservative] "I'd advise them for this, but apart from this I'd not worry." [If his children became Labourites] "They would have their choice at this age. I wouldn't mind one way or other."

An English Skilled Worker (Labour): [If his son became a Conservative] "I should say I had done a darn good job of bringing him up, if he could mix with them, but I would be disappointed."

A common German response reflected opposition to joining any party, or recommended the purest kind of expediential behavior.

A German Postal Employee: "I should warn them of any party ties, but the CDU would still be the most bearable."

A German Housewife: "It's better for him to stay away. Under Hitler we went through that mess. I hardly think that it would be any better today."

A German Clothing Store Owner: "My son is opposed to all parties. He leaves them strictly alone. As a businessman, you can't get involved with that sort of thing."

A German Businessman: "According to my experience I should say: If you are wise, join wherever they have the most power—but not out of idealism. I don't believe that anymore."

More extreme comments were encountered among the Italian respondents, especially regarding the Communist party:

An Italian Petty Government Official (Christian Democrat): "If I knew about it, I would tell them to choose a party of the right, never of the left. If they became Communists, I would beat them like dogs and hate them."

An Italian Baker (Christian Democrat): [If his children joined the DC] "I would try to bring them up the right way. If he signed up with the DC, I would be pleased." [If they became Communists] "If they wanted to sign up, I would disown them."

An Italian Carpenter (Christian Democrat): [If his son became a Communist] "Well, I would try to prevent him, as they say so many things, and one can see that they never go to Mass."

Italian left-wing respondents were less extreme in their statements:

An Italian Housewife with left sympathies: [If her son joined the DC] "I would say: Poor son! I don't sympathize very much with the DC. I consider them hypocrites."

An Italian Farmer (Communist): [If his children joined the DC] "As long as things are done in the right way, it doesn't matter whether they are Communists, Socialists, or Christian Democrats."

The Mexican respondents, like the Germans, included a substantial proportion who opposed party affiliations in principle.

A Mexican Worker: [On any kind of party affiliation] "Not good. I think that to have tranquillity, it is necessary to keep away from this, since in politics one has to be very skillful and lucky enough to fall on one's feet."

A Mexican Housewife: "I wouldn't like it if they entered politics because it always brings problems. If one is honest, the rest don't agree with you; if one is a rascal, the people realize it and don't like you."

A Mexican Blacksmith: "I wouldn't like my children to get into politics. I would like one of my children to study law. If they were in politics, they should be very honest about it, and take no personal advantage."

THE FLOW OF FEELING FROM COMMUNITY TO POLITY

What we have demonstrated so far is that people in the United States and Britain more frequently feel free to express their political opinions openly, and that the edge of partisanship in these countries is less sharp than it is in Germany,

Italy, and Mexico. At the same time, our data show that these national differences are differences in degree, with the United States and Britain at one extreme, the Italians at the other, and Germany and Mexico in the middle.

What we are in the process of uncovering is the "capillary" structure of democracy and the affective culture that is associated with it. The analogy is a useful one if we do not press it too far. The great secondary components of the democratic infrastructure — political parties, interest groups, and the media of communication — are analogous to the veins and arteries of a circulatory system. Unless they are connected effectively with the primary structure of community — family, friendship, neighborhood, religious groups, work groups, and the like — there can be no effective flow of individual impulses, needs, demands, and preferences from the individual and his primary groups into the political system. The overwhelming majority of the members of all political systems live out their lives, discover, develop, and express their feelings and aspirations in the intimate groups of the community. It is the rare individual who is fully recruited into the political system and becomes a political man. In those societies in which the secondary political structures effectively mesh with the intimate primary structures, there is a gradation from "public" to "private"; from the full-time professional politician to the intermittently active citizen. Where the primary structures remain outside the polity or are passive objects of the polity rather than active participants within it, then the individual has only three choices: to fully involve himself in politics, withdraw from it, or become a passive object of it.

In other words, it is implied that in an effectively functioning democracy a substantial proportion of its members are involved in the political system through the meshing of the more diffuse structures of the community with the more differentiated ones of the polity. Only through this engagement of family and community by the polity can the impulses, needs, complaints, and aspirations of the average man flow into the polity and affect the form and content of political controversy and policy making. The flow of demands and claims is sustained in a flow of feeling — pleasure in attaining one's ends or in the excitement of a political contest, anger over political defeat, frustration at the chicanery of politicians, contempt over demagogy, dishonesty, or corruption. The tissue of a democracy in which the primary structures are well articulated with the secondary ones has the flush of health, the "tone" of a good circulation.

Where for one reason or another the political system fails to integrate with the intimate community structures, then the demands and feelings do not flow readily into the political system and the polity may lose touch with the intimate moods and needs of its members. People may withdraw emotionally from the political system or relate themselves to it by passively accepting the displacements, projections, and other irrationalities of extremist movements. The success of Communist movements in such countries may be attributed to the Communist technique of creating its own infrastructure, particularly its own primary infrastructure (the cell), which taps into these negative feelings and channels them *against* the legitimate structures of the polity rather than *into* them.

Lest there be any ambiguity on this score, it should be recognized that a political system such as the Italian which contains large extremist movements of the left and the right can hardly be described as lacking in political feelings. The critical point made here has to do with the *flow* of affect from the individual and the community into the legitimate political institutions. Undoubtedly, the activists and some of the supporters of the Communist, Left Socialist, and MSI parties have, and express, strong negative feelings about governmental and social institutions, and positive ones about alternative forms of political and social organization. The press, parliamentary debates, party meetings, and demonstrations document the high incidence of negative affect and evaluation at the level of elite communications. Our data will suggest that this elite pattern of partisan antagonism is associated with a withdrawn and perhaps mutinous mood among large numbers of ordinary people, a tendency to withhold loyalty from the political system (which we have already discussed), and to avoid emotional involvement in electoral contests.

Several questions in our survey sought to get at the flow of affect into and out of the polity. The great act of mass participation in a democracy is the election. Consequently, our questions dealt with feelings in election campaigns. The first of the series of four questions sought to get at feelings about voting. The respondents were asked: "Which one of these statements comes closest to describing your feelings when you go to the polls to cast your ballot?" Then they were presented with a list of statements, which included the following: "I get a feeling of satisfaction out of it; I do it only because it is my duty; I feel annoyed, it is a waste of time; I don't feel anything in particular."

The respondents were later asked the following three questions about the kind of feelings they had during election campaigns: "Do you ever get angry at some of the things that go on in election campaigns? Do you ever find election campaigns pleasant and enjoyable? Do you ever find election campaigns silly or ridiculous?" On each question the respondent could indicate whether he experienced the particular feelings often, sometimes, or never. Table IV.12 shows the percentages in each of the five countries of those reporting they felt satisfaction while voting, and occasionally or frequently felt anger, pleasure, or contempt.

A number of important country differences appear in the table. The United States is high in the expression of all feelings. Almost three-quarters of the American respondents reported feelings of satisfaction when going to the polls. Two-thirds of the Americans reported enjoying election campaigns, and more than half reported sometimes feeling angry or feeling that what went on was silly or ridiculous. Only 12 per cent of the American respondents reported having none of these feelings during election campaigns. England was second highest in expressing satisfaction about voting and about election campaigns. Germany was third highest, but there was an interesting reversal. Whereas in the United States and United Kingdom a higher percentage enjoyed election campaigns than felt anger and contempt, in Germany the percentages reporting negative affect were greater than those reporting pleasure. Italy was low in all these emotions, and 54 per cent of the respondents reported never having any of these feelings about election campaigns. Mexico was also low in reported feelings about voting and elections, but not quite as low as Italy.

The Italian pattern of low affect in election campaigns is of

TABLE IV.12 *Attitudes and feelings about voting and election campaigns in five nations*

Percentage who report they	*U.S.*	*U.K.*	*Germany*	*Italy*	*Mexico*
Feel satisfaction when going to polls*	71	43	35	30	34
Sometimes find election campaigns pleasant and enjoyable	66	52	28	18	34
Sometimes get angry during campaigns	57	41	46	20	26
Sometimes find campaigns silly or ridiculous	58	37	46	15	32
Never enjoy, *never* get angry, and *never* feel contempt during campaigns	12	26	35	54	41
Total number of respondents for each question	970	963	955	995	1,007

* This question was asked only of those who had voted in one or more of the last three national elections or in recent local elections. Number of cases for this question: *U.S.*, 693; *U.K.*, 959; *Germany*, 869; *Italy*, 923, and *Mexico*, 652.

interest when we compare it with our earlier measures of partisanship. In the extent of cleavage between the right and left parties — as measured by the reciprocal party images and the incidence of negative attitudes toward marriage across party lines — the Italians came out very high. How can we reconcile the low frequency of expressions of emotional involvement in election campaigns with the high frequency of antagonistic partisanship? The explanation would appear to lie in the fact that Italians, by and large, are not oriented toward election campaigns as contests. They do not view election campaigns as necessary; and the proportion of those who report paying no attention to election campaigns is far larger than that of any other country (see Table IV.13).

In other words, the Italians tend to be withdrawn from the

electoral process, just as they tend to be withdrawn from government and nation. One might even view the intensity of their commitment to their own party as a rejection of the *system* of parties, a rejection of the other parties as members of a system of interaction; also, they regard their own party, not as an electoral contestant, but as a church or a "way of life." Partisanship is a full and intense commitment — intensively

TABLE IV.13 *Need for election campaigning and attentiveness to elections, by nation*[a]

Nation	*Percentage who say election campaigning necessary*[b]	*Percentage who pay no attention to election campaigning*[c]
United States	74	12
Great Britain	63	29
Germany	42	27
Italy	29	54
Mexico	61	45

[a] Percentages in each case apply to the total sample.

[b] Actual text of the question: "Some people feel that campaigning is needed so the public can judge candidates and issues. Others say it causes so much bitterness and is so unreliable that we'd be better off without it. What do you think? Is it needed, or would we be better off without it?"

[c] Actual text of the question: "What about the campaigning that goes on at the time of a national election? Do you pay much attention to what goes on, just a little, or none at all?"

negative because the opposing movements are in another, and threatening, moral dimension; intensively positive because one's own party is really the church, or its secular equivalent on the left.

In our life-history interviews we asked our respondents when they had last voted and what thoughts had gone through their minds while they were casting their ballots. The Italian respondents rarely reported positive reactions. More common were expressions of anxiety or of indifference:

An Italian Housewife (Christian Democrat): "I thought I had to vote, but I thought that perhaps I didn't want to vote, as often for one vote we might ruin a family. A government might get into power that will have war and the husband will be called in the army."

> *An Italian Accountant (Christian Democrat):* "I thought, what if I didn't vote for the DC? I was not sure how to vote. I was afraid I wasn't doing the right thing."
> *An Italian Housewife (Christian Democrat):* "I am afraid. I always worry about voting and that I might do the wrong thing."
> *An Italian School Official (nonparty):* "The last time I went to the polls with a feeling almost of disgrace, of indifference."
> *An Italian Workman (Communist):* "I felt I was doing my duty even if it was useless."

Among German and Mexican respondents one also encountered feelings of distrust or futility, though somewhat less frequently. In the United States and Britain these feelings were expressed at times, but the predominant comments were expressions of pleasure or satisfaction.

In the United States and Britain the proportion of respondents reporting that they have feelings about voting and election increases with education (see Table IV.14). It is of some interest that the expression of political anger is most sharply affected by education, not only in the United States and Britain, but in Germany, Italy, and Mexico as well (see Table IV.15). The important point to be noted in Table 16, however, is that in the United States and Britain all of the "affects" rise substantially with increased education. In Germany it is of great significance that only anger increases substantially with higher education: from 43 per cent for those with some primary education to 73 per cent for those with some university education. The frequency of respondents expressing satisfaction over casting the ballot, finding elections enjoyable, or sometimes silly or ridiculous, rises somewhat with secondary education and drops with university education. It would appear, therefore, that the German pattern of high negative affect is most marked among the better-educated, "upper-class" Germans. That political anger is a characteristic of class as well as of education is indicated when we control for occupation. Thus the frequency of anger doubles from 34 per cent among German unskilled laborers to 68 per cent among professional and managerial personnel. The increases in the frequency of the other affects among German professional groups are of a far smaller order.

TABLE IV.14 *Attitudes and feelings about voting and election campaigns in the United States, Great Britain, and Germany, by education*

	U.S.			*U.K.*			*Germany*		
Percentage who report they	*Some prim.*	*Some sec.*	*Some univ.*	*Some prim.*	*Some sec.*	*Some univ.*	*Some prim.*	*Some sec.*	*Some univ.*
Feel satisfaction when going to polls*	58	75	82	41	47	57	35	37	26
Sometimes find campaigns pleasant and enjoyable	60	67	77	52	54	62	37	47	27
Sometimes get angry during campaigns	43	62	71	37	47	62	43	63	73
Sometimes find campaigns silly or ridiculous	53	56	73	37	37	54	44	51	42
Total number of respondents	338	443	188	593	322	24	790	124	26

* Shown in order of columns above, the number of cases for this question (asked only of voters): *U.S.*, 226, 309, and 151; *Great Britain*, 552, 264, and 23, and *Germany*, 729, 102, and 23.

We can now add another feature to the German political-cultural profile. We have already seen that German national pride is in economic and character attributes rather than political ones. At the same time, we have seen that Germans appreciate the impact of government on their lives and expect equal and responsive treatment from their bureaucracy and police. Now we discover that German feelings about the specifically political aspects of their governmental system tend to be negative, and that this negativism tends to be most marked among the educated middle and upper middle classes. In other words, it is precisely among these elements, which in most democratic countries tend to support democratic processes, that contemporary German democracy appears to have least support.

The political-cultural characteristics of educated Germans reflect ambivalence. On the one hand, political cognition rises with education. Thus educated Germans have higher political information scores, more frequently follow discussions of public affairs in the media of communication, and

TABLE IV.15 *Attitudes and feelings about voting and election campaigns in Italy and Mexico; by education*

	Italy					*Mexico*			
Percentage who report they	*No educ.*	*Some prim.*	*Low sec.*	*High sec.*	*Some univ.*	*No educ.*	*Some prim.*	*Some sec.*	*Some univ.*
Feel satisfaction when going to polls*	10	28	29	26	25	12	24	28	49
Sometimes find campaigns pleasant and enjoyable	9	16	24	31	35	26	36	37	46
Sometimes get angry during campaigns	12	19	23	26	39	18	25	40	65
Sometimes find campaigns silly or ridiculous	9	17	29	23	39	24	31	50	55
Total number of respondents	88	604	148	97	54	221	656	103	24

* Shown in order of columns above, the number of cases for this question (asked only of voters): *Italy,* 85, 583, 129, 93, and 50; *Mexico,* 103, 456, 75, and 18.

more frequently talk politics with other people. They also accept democratic values more frequently than the less well educated; but wherever political feelings are concerned, the educated Germans show greater alienation and negativism than the less well educated. Thus pride in the political aspects of nation and feelings of satisfaction while voting decrease with education. And now we discover that only the emotion of anger in election campaigns increases sharply with education.

Two possible explanations may be made for this German phenomenon. First, the educated middle class in Germany never developed a fully democratic culture. What we may be observing in our data is the persistence of this authoritarian subject culture, which involves imparting legitimacy to authority and bureaucracy, but not to political parties and competitive elections.

But there is another explanation for these tendencies. The German educated middle classes were deeply compromised by National Socialism and in many cases penalized (if only briefly) during the early phases of the Occupation. Their withholding of feeling toward the German nation and toward the political process may be an expression of anxiety about being involved once again in a risky business. Perhaps both factors are present: a sense of discomfort over the disorderliness and lack of dignity of democratic politics, and anxiety about any kind of political involvement, based on the Nazi trauma.

Table IV.15, showing the relationship between education and electoral feeling in Italy and Mexico, reveals the same trends that were manifested in the United States and Britain, though the percentages are substantially smaller. Thus the frequencies of all the affects in Italy at the university level are below 40 per cent, compared with the "no education" group, in which they are below 15 per cent. Mexico shows the same trend, with the range in general being substantially higher than in Italy, but lower than in the other countries. At the university level the Mexican respondents range from 46 per cent for enjoying elections to 65 per cent who report sometimes getting angry at events during election campaigns.

Our analysis of national differences in feelings about politics and partisanship has brought out the following patterns. In the United States and Britain there is a widespread sense of freedom and safety in political communication; partisan feelings are relatively cool, and feelings of all kinds flow relatively freely into the political system. In Germany people seem to feel more restricted in these communications, partisanship appears to be more intense, and anger and contempt seem to be the emotions most frequently expressed in election campaigns. In Italy the proportion of the population that feels free to communicate about politics and admits to having feelings about elections is extremely small. At the same time, the intensity of partisanship is extremely high. In Mexico political communication is restricted, but not to the same extent as in Italy. The expression of feelings about elections is also low, but not as low as in Italy, and the level of partisanship is high, but again not so high as in Italy.

TYPES OF PARTISANS

At the beginning of this chapter we suggested that an effectively functioning democracy required a form of partisanship that avoided intense antagonism at one extreme and political indifference at the other. In the preceding pages we have described the incidence of extreme partisan cleavage in our five countries, as measured by attitudes toward interparty marriage and the kinds of feelings that partisans have toward electoral contests.

We are now in a position to present a typology of partisanship based on a score that combines these two measures of attitudes. If we dichotomize the responses to both sets of questions, we have a fourfold typology, as follows:

1. *The Open Partisan.* This is the respondent who expresses indifference toward interparty marriage yet describes himself as emotionally involved in election campaigns. This "open partisan" is emotionally involved in electoral contests but not so intensely partisan as to cut himself off from relations with members of the opposing party. Table IV.16 shows that 82 per cent of the Americans, 61 per cent of the British, 44 per cent of the Germans, and 42 per cent of the Mexicans manifest this kind of partisanship, while only 14 per cent of the Italians fall into this category.

2. *The Apathetic Partisan.* It may seem a contradiction to speak of an "apathetic partisan," but this is the respondent who voted for one of the major parties, who expressed indifference about interparty marriage, and who denied having any of the three feelings about elections covered in our interview (anger, pleasure, contempt). He is the indifferent voter, found in any polity, who casts his ballot but feels little involvement in the electoral contest. We see that Italy has the highest proportion of apathetic partisans and the United States the lowest, with the other countries in between.

3. *The Intense Partisan.* This is the respondent who is concerned about marriage across party lines and who also is emotionally involved in elections. He is both sharply divided from his party opponents and emotionally involved in electoral contests. We see in Table IV.16 that this type is most frequently encountered in Germany and Mexico, with Italy, Britain, and the United States following in that order.

4. *The Parochial Partisan.* This is the respondent who, though concerned about interparty marriage, is indifferent about election campaigns. This class of partisans is relatively

TABLE IV.16 *Types of partisanship by nation*

Percentage who are	*U.S.*	*U.K.*	*Germany*	*Italy*	*Mexico*
Open partisans	82	61	44	14	42
Apathetic partisans	8	22	18	30	24
Intense partisans	10	14	25	20	25
Parochial partisans	0	3	13	36	9
Total percentage	100	100	100	100	100
Total number (all admitted major party adherents or voters, omitting those who had no opinion on interparty marriage or on the emotions they felt at campaign time)	736	719	485	300	489

uninvolved in politics; we speak of them as "parochial partisans." As will be shown below, they are predominantly religious women. Their partisanship is not a political phenomenon, but a cultural–religious one. We encounter this type in large numbers only in Italy, where 36 per cent fall into this category.

What strikes the eye in Table IV.16 is the sharp difference between Italy and all the other countries. This extreme deviation in the Italian pattern may be due in part to the very high incidence of refusals among Italian left-wing party voters to disclose their party. We know from election results that approximately four out of ten Italian voters support the Christian Democratic party, while approximately one-third support the left parties (the Communists and Nenni-Socialists). In our sample 35 per cent of the respondents identified themselves as Christian Democratic voters and 10 per cent as left party voters. Hence the Italian pattern presented in Table IV.16 is heavily biased in the Christian Democratic direction.

Indeed, if we look at the social composition of the various groups of partisans, we find that in Italy the parochial partisans tend to be women, church attenders, and supporters of the Christian Democrats. Supporters of the left parties are more likely to be open partisans. Italy thus presents us with the curious anomaly of a political system in which the formal democratic constitution is supported in large part by traditional–clerical elements who are not democratic at all, and not even political in a specialized sense. Opposed to the constitution is a left wing, which, at least in part and at the rank-and-file voter level rather than among the party elite, manifests a form of open partisanship that is consistent with a democratic system.

CHAPTER V

The Obligation to Participate

THE CITIZEN, unlike the subject, is an active participant in the political input process — the process by which political decisions are made. But the citizen role, as we have suggested, does not replace the subject role or the parochial role: it is added to them. Only the rare individual considers his role as citizen more important and salient than his role as subject or parochial, for whom politics is a matter of first priority. This has been corroborated in many surveys of political opinion. When asked general questions about what worries them, or what they consider important, people usually mention family problems, job problems, economic problems, but rarely political problems.[1] Furthermore, if the ordinary man is interested in political matters, he is more likely to be interested in the output than in the input process. He is concerned about who wins the election, not about how it is carried on; he cares about who is benefited by legislation, not about how legislation is passed. Even in relation to his vote — an act that is designed to make him an active participant in the decision-making processes of his nation — he may behave routinely,

[1] In our survey, when respondents were asked what they spent their free time on, no more than 3 per cent in any of the five nations mentioned something to do with politics; and in most cases the percentage was smaller. Other survey results show almost universally that politics is not uppermost in the minds of people.

voting for a party because of traditional allegiance or for other reasons not connected with a desire to guide the course of policy.

That most men orient themselves more as subjects than as citizens is a familiar theme. Much has been written describing this fact, sometimes deploring it. Interest in and criticism of the role of the ordinary man in his political system is especially characteristic of those writers and thinkers concerned with the problems of democracy — from the ancient Greeks to current writers on American civic affairs; for it is in a democracy that the role of the ordinary man as a participant in the political affairs of his country is significant. The man whose relation to his government is that of a subject — a passive beneficiary or victim of routine governmental actions — would not be found wanting in a traditional, nondemocratic society. Moreover, this relationship would exhaust what is expected of him. What the government does affects him, but why or how the government decides to do what it does is outside his sphere of competence. He has obligations, but the obligations are passive — he should be loyal and respectful of authority. "All that is necessary for salvation is contained in two virtues, *faith* in Christ and *obedience* to law." [2] As a subject he may be more or less competent, but his competence will be "subject competence." He will not attempt to influence the decisions of his government, but will try to see that he is treated properly once the decision is made. It is not in his sphere of competence to say what taxes should be levied, but once these are decided the competent subject will see that he is treated fairly within the boundaries of that decision. The law is something he obeys, not something he helps shape. If he is competent, he knows the law, knows what he must do, and what is due him.

In democratic societies, on the other hand, his role as subject does not exhaust what is expected of him. He is expected to have the virtues of the subject — to obey the law, to be loyal — but he is also expected to take some part in the formation of decisions. The common thread running through the many definitions of democracy is that a democracy is a so-

[2] Thomas Hobbes, *Leviathan,* London, 1945, Book III, p. 385.

ciety in which ". . . ordinary citizens exert a relatively high degree of control over leaders." [3] Democracy is thus characterized by the fact that power over significant authoritative decisions in a society is distributed among the population. The ordinary man is expected to take an active part in governmental affairs, to be aware of how decisions are made, and to make his views known.

The fact that the ordinary man does not live up to the ideal set by the normative theory of democracy has led to much criticism of his passivity and indifference. Our goal is to describe and analyze, however, and not to assign praise or blame. In any case, normative questions about the role of the individual in his political system are by no means unrelated to more descriptive and analytic questions. Certainly the political moralist in describing what an individual *should* do will probably not be unaffected by what individuals actually *do,* and certainly he will consider what he believes they *can* do. The three types of questions are not identical, but they affect one another, especially if we switch our perspective to that of the ordinary man himself. So far we have talked about the gap between what scholars, philosophers, and teachers have said the ordinary man ought to do in a democracy and what in fact he does. But what about the ordinary man himself? What does *he* think he *should* do? And how does this compare with what he thinks he *can* do and with what he does?

This chapter will deal with the first question: What does the ordinary man think he should do? Philosophers and democratic ideologists have written at length about the obligations of the citizen, but what is the ordinary man's conception of his role in politics? If the model democratic citizen is active, participating, and influential, is this what the ordinary man aspires to be? And, what may be more important, does he think of himself as capable of influencing and participating in the decisions of his government? In this chapter we shall look at the ordinary man's conception of the role he ought to play, and in the next at the conception of the role he thinks he can play.

[3] Robert A. Dahl, *A Preface to Democratic Theory,* Chicago, 1956, p. 3.

WHAT IS THE GOOD CITIZEN?

The good citizen does not equal the good man. No zealous advocate of good citizenship would argue that political participation ought to be pursued to the neglect of all other obligations. The active influential citizen described in normative political theory is not excused from the obligations of the subject. If he participates in the making of the law, he is also expected to obey the law. It has, in fact, been argued that he has greater obligation to obey because of his participation. Nor would one want his civic activity to be at the expense of his private obligations. Surely the lady described by Riesman who left her screaming children locked in their room while she attended a meeting of a neighborhood improvement association does not represent the ideal toward which the advocates of good citizenship are striving.[4] There will, of course, always be conflicts between the demands of different roles, but the obligations of one role do not replace those of another.

This point is stressed here because it introduces a complexity into our attempt to measure the extent to which the ideal of the participating citizen exists in the minds of men; for the man who believes that he should be upright in his personal life — work for the good of his family or, to quote one of our respondents, "If he is a carpenter, he should be a good carpenter" — may also believe that he should be a participating and active citizen. Similarly, the man who believes that he should pay taxes and obey the laws is a "good subject." The same man may also be a "good citizen." It is only when the individual thinks of his family's advantage as the only goal to pursue, or conceives of his role in the political system in familistic terms, that he is a parochial and not also a citizen. And it is only when an individual thinks of his relationship to his state as being exhausted by his role as subject that he is subject and not also citizen.

Attempting to see how much the role of participant has been added to those of parochial and subject in our five countries, we examined our respondents' relationships with their

[4] David Riesman, *Faces in the Crowd,* New Haven, 1952, pp. 82-83.

local community. We were interested in the extent to which respondents considered themselves to have some sort of responsibility to be active in their community — either in a formal or an informal way; either in relation to local government or in relation to fellow citizens. The local community seemed to be a good place to begin, since political and governmental problems tend to be more understandable, the organs of government less distant, the chances of effective participation for the individual citizen greater on the local level than on the level of national government. In fact, it has often been argued that effective democracy rests on the ability of the individual to participate locally, for it is only here that he can develop some sense of mastery over political affairs. As Bryce put it (and as defenders of local autonomy have constantly argued), "An essential ingredient of a satisfactory democracy is that a considerable proportion should have experience of active participation in the work of small self-governing groups, whether in connection with local government, trade unions, cooperatives or other forms of activity." [5]

NATIONAL DIFFERENCES IN THE CHARACTERISTICS OF LOCAL GOVERNMENT

In this chapter and in a good part of the next, we shall deal with attitudes toward the local government. In interpreting the responses to questions about the local government, we are faced with the problem that the structures of local government differ from nation to nation and within the nations as well. And these differences in structure partially explain differences in attitudes found among the nations. It is important that these differences be kept in mind. Though it would be impossible to describe fully the patterns of local government within the five nations — there are numerous levels of local government in all five nations and substantial variations among regions — one can specify certain similarities and differences among them.

In the first place, all five nations have some form of local government. (It is important to note here that we are dealing

[5] James Bryce, *Modern Democracies*, New York, 1921, I, p. 132. (See below, chap. 6.)

with the most local governmental units: units below the level of state, or *Land,* or province.) And the local unit, whether it be a commune, *municipio, Gemeinde,* township, or non-county borough, almost invariably has some sort of locally elected council or set of officials. Thus in each country there is a set of locally elected units on which we can focus.

But despite this similarity, local government differs sharply among the five nations. From the point of view of respondents' attitudes toward participation within the local community, there are two types of structural differences that are particularly significant: the degree of local autonomy and the degree to which local structures foster citizen participation. It is difficult to measure precisely the extent of autonomy of local governmental units within nations; there are variations within nations, the criteria of autonomy are not clear, and the data are often lacking. Nevertheless, the five nations do differ so substantially in this respect — and the variations among the nations are generally larger than the variations within each nation — that one can rank the nations with some confidence according to local autonomy. It is clear that at one extreme the pattern of local government in the United States represents the greatest amount of local autonomy. The range of subject matter over which the local communities have control — the police and schools are two important examples, and the communities not only handle administration of the schools, but in many cases they actually formulate educational policy — as well as the extent of the local governments' freedom from external control appear to be much greater in the United States than elsewhere.

It would appear that Great Britain ranks next to the United States in degree of local autonomy. The range of issues over which the local government has control is smaller — educational policy, for instance, is controlled by central government agencies to a much larger degree — and within the unitary British system of government, local autonomy is not provided for formally by home rule provisions, as it is in the constitutions of a number of American states. Nevertheless, the British have a long tradition of local self-government. And local councils are active in administrative work as well as in some limited areas of legislation where permission is given by the central government.[6]

It is difficult to rank the other three nations precisely. As to the formal structure of local government, however, it is relatively easy to specify which ranks lowest. The existence of the prefect system in Italy limits substantially any opportunity for local self-government. The communes in Italy have locally elected councils, but they have little freedom of action. All acts must be submitted to the centrally appointed prefect of the province, who passes on their legality; and certain significant matters, such as the municipal budget and the levying of taxes, must be approved by the provincial administrative committee (*Giunta Provinciale Amministrativa*), which passes on both the legality and the merit of the act. It is quite unlikely that a local government structure of this sort, in which there is a centrally appointed official with powers to oversee the activities of the locality, would foster a high level of autonomous local activity. Though there is some evidence of more local autonomy than one would expect, given the formal structure, the degree of autonomy is probably least of all the five nations.[7]

As in most cases when one is trying to array a series of units along a scale, it is the units near the middle of the scale that present the more difficult problems in categorization. In terms of the degree of local governmental autonomy, it is probably accurate to place Germany and Mexico between the United States and Britain on the one hand and Italy on the other.

[6] See, for instance, W. Eric Jackson, *Local Government in England and Wales,* London, 1960. This is not to argue that in the United States and Britain there is no external control over local government. There is obviously a large amount of external control and this control is steadily growing — a point whose implications will be discussed below. But relatively speaking, local government in these two nations has a vigor missing in the other three.

[7] See Samuel Humes and Eileen M. Martin, *The Structure of Local Governments Throughout the World,* The Hague, 1961, pp. 319-24; Harold Zink et al., *Rural Local Government in Sweden, Italy and India,* London, 1957, and Edward Banfield, *The Moral Basis of a Backward Society,* Glencoe, Ill., 1958. See, also, Robert C. Fried, *The Italian Prefects,* unpublished Ph.D. dissertation, Yale University, 1961.

But one must approach the characterization of these two nations with somewhat more caution. One reason is the wide range of variation possible within a federal system, a situation heightened in Germany by differing regional traditions and by the somewhat different heritages from the three occupying powers. There is in many areas of Germany a strong tradition of local autonomy, as well as a tendency for local communities to engage in a wide range of activities, especially among many of the older northern German cities, which have long histories of local self-government.[8] It is, however, difficult to estimate in any precise way the extent to which local self-government is firmly entrenched in other areas in Germany.

Mexico, unlike Italy but like the other three nations, has legal provision for relatively autonomous local governments on the level of the *municipio*. In actual practice, however, these local governments have been relatively uninfluential and relatively nonautonomous, largely because of central control over local finances and the pervasive influence of the PRI, the single important Mexican political party. Local government in Mexico has rarely been of great significance.[9]

The nations also differ in the extent to which the local decision-making apparatus is accessible to participation by local residents. In some communities — and again this varies within nations, but perhaps more sharply among nations — there will be greater opportunity for the individual to participate in decisions. It is somewhat more difficult to compare the nations in this respect than it was to compare them in respect to local autonomy. There are fewer studies of the degree

[8] See, for instance, Lorenz Fischer and Peter Van Hauten, "Cologne," in William A. Robson (ed.), *Great Cities of the World,* London, 1957, pp. 645-82.

[9] For a consideration of the influence of the PRI in the politics of one Mexican city, see Scott, *Mexican Government in Transition,* pp. 44-55; and William H. Form and William V. d'Antonio, "Integration and Cleavage Among Community Influentials in Two Border Cities," *American Sociological Review,* XXIV (1959), pp. 804-14. If our knowledge of and ability to measure this dimension were more precise it is possible that we might rank Mexico close to, or even below, Italy. However, more precise descriptions will depend on more precise research.

to which individuals actually participate in local affairs, for such participation depends largely upon informal as well as formal channels of participation. Some data from our own study, to be presented in the next chapter, will be useful for such categorization. In general, one would expect that the extent to which the local government is open to citizen participation in decisions would be closely related to the extent of local autonomy; and impressions of community life in these five nations, as well as the data to be presented in the next chapter, support this proposition.[10]

Consequently, in interpreting the data in this and the next chapter, we shall have to keep in mind that one reason why individuals differ in the frequency with which they adhere to participatory norms is that the structure of government and community organization changes from one nation to another. This does not make the attitudinal data any less significant. As we have suggested earlier, even if the attitudes we describe are in part determined by the structure of government and social system in each nation, this does not remove the fact that these attitudes in turn affect these same structures. The norms to which an individual adheres are largely determined by the role that the system allows him to play (though the fit between norms and structure will rarely be perfect); but these norms in turn have a feedback effect on the structure, reinforcing the structure if the fit between norms and structure is a good one; introducing strain into the system if norms and structure fit less well. And lastly, as we shall attempt to demonstrate below, attitudes toward the local government cannot be explained solely by the relationship between the individual and the local governmental structure (and the same point can and will be made about the national government as well). We shall attempt to show, for instance, that the extent

[10] But the degree of local self-government and the degree to which individuals can participate within that government may be independent of each other. It would be possible, for instance, to draw the conclusion from John Gimbel's study of *A German Community Under American Occupation: Marburg, 1945-1952,* Stanford, 1961, that the American Occupation's attempt to introduce local democracy failed for the simple reason that, though they gave power to local elites, these elites were not committed to furthering citizen participation.

to which individuals believe they can influence the government, and in particular the ways in which they would attempt to exert that influence, depend, not only on the governmental system, but upon certain social and attitudinal characteristics of the individuals.

NATIONAL DIFFERENCES IN SENSE OF CIVIC OBLIGATION

Our question to the respondents dealt with participation in local affairs. We were interested not only in political participation, but also in any sort of outgoing activity the individual might mention. We wanted to know the extent to which individuals believe they have any sort of obligation to the community — to care about more than the personal problems of the family life and job.[11]

Table V.1 summarizes the responses we received as to the role individuals should play within their local community. We have classified our respondents into those who believe that the ordinary man should take some active part in his community (this includes those who say the ordinary man should attend meetings, join organizations involved in community affairs, and the like); those who believe that one ought to participate more passively in community activities (for example: one ought to be interested in local affairs, try to understand them and keep informed, vote); those who feel that the ordinary man ought to participate only in church and religious activities; and those who do not think the ordinary man has any responsibility that involves him in the affairs of his community (here we include the respondents who feel that the ordinary man ought to maintain an upright personal life; who say that he ought to take no part in the affairs of his community; and who do not know what role the individual ought to play in his community).

Clearly, from this table the image of the citizen-as-participant is more widespread in some countries than in others. In

[11] The question read: "We know that the ordinary person has many problems that take his time. In view of this, what part do you think the ordinary person ought to play in the local affairs of his town or district?" The interviewer attempted to find out as closely as possible what the respondent specifically felt one ought to do in his community.

TABLE V.1 *How active should the ordinary man be in his local community; by nation*

Percentage who say the ordinary man should	*U.S.*	*U.K.*	*Germany*	*Italy*	*Mexico*
Be active in his community	51	39	22	10	26
Only participate passively*	27	31	38	22	33
Only participate in church affairs*	5	2	1	*	—
Total who mention some outgoing activity	83	72	61	32	59
Only be upright in personal life*	1	1	11	15	2
Do nothing in local community	3	6	7	11	2
Don't know	11	17	21	35	30
Other	2	5	1	7	7
Total percentage	100	100	100	100	100
Total number of cases	970	963	955	995	1,007

* Multiple answers were possible, but we have eliminated them from this table by listing respondents' *most active* response only (i.e., the response that would fall highest on the table). Thus an individual who mentioned active as well as passive participation would be listed under active participation only; one who mentioned church activities as well as an upright private life would be listed under the former and not the latter.

the United States and Britain a large number of respondents believe that the individual should be an active participant in the affairs of his community. Half of the Americans interviewed and 39 per cent of the British mention some active role that the individual ought to play. In Italy, at the other extreme, there are few who conceive of the citizen as active participant. Only one in ten Italians believes that the ordinary man has an obligation to take an active role in his community. The proportions of German and Mexican respondents who have some image of the active citizen lie between the American and British proportions on the one hand and the Italian on the other. One out of five of our German respondents and one out of four of our Mexicans conceive of the ordinary man as having some obligation to participate.[12]

[12] The Mexican pattern is interesting here, and we shall return to it later. Mexican respondents mention an obligation to participate more frequently than do German respondents and much more frequently than

"One ought at least to take an interest in what goes on in the community"; or, "One ought to be active in church and religious affairs": if we consider these statements an indicator (albeit a weaker one) of the existence of some norm of participation, then the contrasts among the nations are still striking. In the United States 83 per cent of the respondents talk of the ordinary man as having some commitment to his community that takes him out of involvement in purely personal affairs — even if the responsibility is minimal. The proportion in Britain is somewhat smaller at 72 per cent; in Mexico and Germany about 60 per cent talk of some outgoing role for the individual, whereas in Italy only 32 per cent do.

What sorts of community activities do our respondents have in mind when they say the ordinary man ought to play some part in his local community? As Table V.2 shows, only a small number of respondents in each country mention partisan activity as the responsibility of the individual to his community. In the United States and Britain respondents frequently mention taking part in local government bodies, attending meetings, and the like. In Germany and Mexico this is less frequently mentioned, but is mentioned more frequently than in Italy. Active community participation in a nongovernmental sense — participation in civic groups and organizations, or informal activity to help the community — is quite frequently mentioned in the United States. Such nongovernmental activity is again least mentioned in Italy, with Germany and Mexico trailing Britain. In active participation, then, the five countries can be roughly grouped: the United States and Britain are the countries in which the image of the active participating citizen is most often the normative ideal; in Germany and Mexico the ideal receives mention, but less often; and in Italy this ideal is least widespread.

Some illustrations may be useful in making explicit the specific areas of activity respondents had in mind:

---

do Italian respondents. This relatively high sense of obligation, coupled, as we shall discuss, with lower activity and information, is an aspect of the civic aspirational tendency among the Mexicans.

TABLE V.2 *What role should the ordinary man play in his local community; by nation*

Percentage who choose	*U.S.*	*U.K.*	*Germany*	*Italy*	*Mexico*
ACTIVE PARTICIPATION IN LOCAL COMMUNITY[a]					
Take part in activities of local government	21	22	13	5	11
Take part in activities of political parties	6	4	4	1	5
Take part in nongovernmental activity and in organizations interested in local affairs	32	17	9	5	10
MORE PASSIVE COMMUNITY ACTIVITIES[a]					
Try to understand and keep informed	21	11	24	6	29
Vote	40	18	15	2	1
Take an interest in what is going on	3	13	6	15	4
PARTICIPATION IN CHURCH AND RELIGIOUS ACTIVITIES[a]	12	2	2	—	—
Total percentage of respondents who mention some outgoing activity[b]	83	72	61	32	59
Total number of respondents	970	963	955	995	1,007

[a] The percentages in these categories are somewhat larger than in Table V.1, since this table contains all the responses of individuals, rather than their most active responses.

[b] Total percentages are less than the total of the individual cells, since the latter involve multiple responses.

A British Housewife: "He should take some part in public life and have a say in town-planning, education, and religion."
An American Housewife: "Everyone should take part in church and community affairs. . . . We should take an active part in making our schools better."
A Mexican Housewife: "People should have diversion, but have enough free time to occupy themselves with political and social things."
A German Worker: "Organizations should be formed that would enable [people] to discuss their problems together — for instance, parents' advisory councils [*Elternbeiräte*] at schools."

An Italian Teacher: "Each individual should be interested in an active way and should criticize justly and severely when it is necessary."

An American Postmaster: "A citizen should play an active part. . . . He might hold a local office. Other civic work such as drives, such as Red Cross. Here we have a volunteer fire company; he could help out with that."

The last quotation, from an American postmaster, suggests how the existence of structures in which one can participate affects the norms of participation that individuals hold. One would certainly not expect an individual to feel to feel an obligation to participate in such activities as "drives," the Red Cross, and volunteer fire companies in communities where such activities were nonexistent.

One theme running through many of the answers that stress active participation in the local community — a theme found largely among activists in the United States and Britain — is that the individual ought to be active as a participant in decisions; that he ought, in a rather independent way, to take part in the running of the community:

An English Female Worker: "Everyone should take a part. . . . They should get together and give opinions as to why and how this and that should be worked."

An American Housewife: "I think a person should vote. If there are any town meetings he should attend them. . . . If everyone does things in his own small way, it would add up to something big. Many people sit back and let others do things for them, then complain."

A German Farmer: "He should discuss politics, but shouldn't just accept everything, but [should] speak up too."

On the other hand, local activity means for some respondents more informal social participation, perhaps to help out one's neighbors:

A German Chauffeur: "He should not just talk, but should act too. For instance, during hay harvesting time, one should not just stick his hands in his pockets and watch the farmers exerting themselves, but should pitch in. After all, it's a matter of community welfare."

An English Businessman: "He should help in local organizations

— children's clubs, boy scouts. He should help his neighbors and be a good living person."

A number of respondents, as shown in Table V.2, thought of the individual as having a more passive sort of obligation to participate in his community; this usually involved some obligation to be informed of what is going on or to be interested in it:

A Mexican Housewife: "[He should] be interested in how the government is formed, and be active by studying books and newspapers."
An English Housewife: "He ought to know what is going on. Go to the occasional meeting to find out."
An Italian Worker: "Simply be interested."

Though the degree of autonomy of local government differs from nation to nation, in all five nations there are elections for some sort of local or communal council. For many respondents, as Table V.2 indicates, voting in these elections was considered a responsibility of the individual to his community. But insofar as the individual considered his local responsibility to be exhausted by the act of voting, we have listed this as a relatively passive form of participation in community life — though a form of participation it certainly is. In some cases, particularly among those German respondents who mention voting as an obligation, this interpretation is made explicit. The responsibility to vote is explicitly stated as exhausting the individual's responsibility and, in fact, is invoked as an act that absolves one of all other community responsibilities:

An American Disabled Worker: "I think they should do their part. Outside of voting there isn't too much the average fellow can do. . . . You ought to vote and then support any worthwhile thing your community is trying to do."
An Italian Veterinarian: "What should an individual do? Elect his representatives. That's all."
A German Retired Worker: "Choose a mayor at election time. That's all one need to do. The mayor takes care of everything."
A German House Painter: "He should vote — that's the most important thing. But he should not be politically active himself."

> *A German Housewife:* "I don't understand that. We have to work. The people in the council are cleverer after all. They'll do a good job. You just have to vote for the right ones."

As was pointed out earlier, not all respondents think of the individual as having any outgoing responsibility within his local community. As Table V.1 indicated, there were a substantial number of respondents in Germany and Mexico, and particularly in Italy, who admitted to no sense of local civic obligation. In this sense, the norms that they accept in relation to their community are certainly not those of the participating citizen. They are quite probably oriented to their communities as subjects or parochials. These can be found in all five nations, but they are most frequent in Italy (where 15 per cent of the respondents invoke these parochial values — a larger group than those who think the individual ought to be an active participant) and in Germany (where 11 per cent of the respondents talk of such parochial values). The following are some examples of the ways in which one's responsibility to the community is interpreted as an essentially parochial or subject responsibility to one's personal life:

> *An English Housewife:* "It's as much as my husband can do to go to work, never mind taking part in local affairs. We appoint councillors and leave everything to them."
> *A German Mechanic:* "Take care of one's family by working. Make one's children into decent people."
> *A German Farmer:* "I pay my taxes, go to my church, and do my work as a farmer."
> *A German Mechanic:* "Work and support one's family decently. If everyone did that, the state would have less trouble and expense."
> *A German Housewife:* "Everyone should do his work."
> *An Italian Worker:* "[He] should attend to his work . . . be a good citizen, and take care of [his] family."
> *An Italian Artisan:* "[He should be] honest and concerned about his work."

One important point about the relationship among civic, subject, and parochial norms is suggested by the data in Table V.2. If the values of active participation are widespread in a country, this does not mean that the valuation of more passive participation is missing, or that subject and parochial values are missing. In the United States, for instance, where active participation is most frequently mentioned, the more passive political participation of voting is also frequently mentioned, as is participation in church and religious activities. And many respondents who mention active participation also mention the more parochial norms. This accords with our notion that the citizen role is built on but does not replace the roles of subject and parochial.

Our data clearly suggest sharp differences among the nations in the roles that respondents think individuals ought to play in their local communities. However, our data do not suggest that all those who think the individual ought to take an active part do in fact take such active roles. The gap between civic norms and civic behavior is, as we all know, large. As one American businessman who stressed the obligation to participate actively put it, "I'm saying what he ought to do, not what I do." We are not saying that one out of two Americans is an active participant in the affairs of his local community or that four out of ten Britons are. Rather, we suggest that in these countries the norm of active citizenship is widespread. And

TABLE V.3 *Percentage who say the ordinary man should be active in his local community; by nation and education*

	Total		*Prim. or less*		*Some sec.*		*Some univ.*	
Nation	*(%)*	*(No.)**	*(%)*	*(No.)*	*(%)*	*(No.)*	*(%)*	*(No.)*
United States	51	(970)	35	(339)	56	(443)	66	(188)
Great Britain	39	(963)	37	(593)	42	(322)	42	(24)
Germany	22	(955)	21	(792)	32	(123)	38	(26)
Italy	10	(995)	7	(692)	17	(245)	22	(54)
Mexico	26	(1,007)	24	(877)	37	(103)	38	(24)

* Numbers in parentheses refer to the bases upon which percentages are calculated.

this is congruent with the structure of government. The actual opportunities to participate and the norms that one ought to participate mutually reinforce each other to foster a high level of citizen participation. In Italy, on the other hand, the relative lack of opportunity to participate in an autonomous local community is accompanied by the absence of a set of norms favoring such participation.

DEMOGRAPHIC PATTERNS

Who within each country hold to the ideal of the citizen as participant? The middle class? or those with higher education? As Table V.3 indicates, in each of the five nations it is those with some higher education who are most likely to express adherence to the norms of participation; and the least likely to report that the individual has some responsibility to participate actively in his local community are those with primary school education or less. Nevertheless, despite the fact that the distribution of adherence to participatory norms is similar in the five nations, the differences in absolute levels of such expressed adherence are still great even within similar educational groups. And within each educational group the relationship among the nations is roughly the same — American respondents tend most frequently to express adherence to such norms, followed by British, Mexican, German, and Italian respondents in that order. Furthermore, unlike some other variables, where the differences among nations tend to disappear when the all-important characteristic of education is controlled, differences still remain in the frequency of adherence to the norms of participation. In fact, a university-educated person in Germany or Mexico is no more likely to express adherence to these norms than is a primary-educated person in the United States or Britain; and the Italian university-educated respondent is less likely to do so.

If a democratic political system is one in which the ordinary citizen participates in political decisions, a democratic political culture should consist of a set of beliefs, attitudes, norms, perceptions, and the like, which support participation. Of course, the frequency of adherence to this norm will be affected by the structures of the local community. But if the norm of participation is not widespread, institutional change in the direction of fostering participation will not in itself create a participatory democracy.

It is impossible to say what is the requisite level of participatory norms and of participation in political affairs for an effective democracy. Americans more often accept norms of participation than do individuals in the other four countries, yet they have often been accused of not being civic enough. But while our findings cannot tell us whether the level of participation in the United States or Britain is "good enough," they do tell us that it is certainly higher than in Germany, Mexico, and Italy. And as this and other data on participation will suggest, where norms of participation, perceived ability to participate, and actual participation are high, effective democracy is more likely to flourish.

That an individual believes he ought to participate in the political life of his community or nation does not mean that he will in fact do so. Before the norm that one ought to participate can be translated into the act itself, the individual will probably have to perceive that he is able to act. And though the two are related, they are by no means identical. One can believe he ought to participate, but perceive himself as unable to do so. Or one can perceive himself as able to participate but not feel any obligation to do so. Certainly a great source of political discontent is the acceptance of the norms of participation coupled with the belief that one can not in fact participate. This, it has been suggested, is the danger of overselling the norms of political democracy in the schools. When the myth of democracy comes into serious conflict with the realities of politics, the results are cynicism. The society in which individuals do in fact participate in decisions — that is, the democratic society — is likely to be the society in which individuals believe they ought to participate. It is also likely to be the society in which they think they can participate and know how to go about it. It is to these questions of subjective civic competence that we now turn.

CHAPTER VI

The Sense of Civic Competence

DEMOCRACY is a political system in which ordinary citizens exercise control over elites; and such control is legitimate; that is, it is supported by norms that are accepted by elites and nonelites. In all societies, of course, the making of specific decisions is concentrated in the hands of very few people. Neither the ordinary citizen nor "public opinion" can make policy. If this is the case, the problem of assessing the degree of democracy in a nation becomes one of measuring the degree to which ordinary citizens control those who make the significant decisions for a society — in most cases, governmental elites.

Recent work on the theory of influence suggests that there are numerous means by which interpersonal influence can be exerted, and that it makes a difference which means are used. In this chapter we shall be concerned with a particular type of influence that nonelites may exert on elites: a type that we label *political* influence. We shall roughly define the political influence of a group or individual over a governmental decision as equal to the degree to which governmental officials act to benefit that group or individual because the officials believe that they will risk some deprivation (they will risk their jobs, be criticized, lose votes) if they do not so act. Thus we define political influence as both the outcome of the decision and the motives of the decision makers. The outcome will benefit the influential groups or individuals more than it would if the influence were not exercised. And the decision makers act to benefit the groups or individuals because they believe they will suffer some deprivation or, what amounts to the same thing, fail to gain a reward. The latter criterion is important. Officials may act to benefit a particular group for a variety of reasons: out of a feeling of paternalism, for instance. But it is only when officials act because they fear the consequences of not acting that a group may be considered to be politically influential and a participant in the decision.[1] If the individual can exert such influence, we shall consider him to be *politically competent;* or if he *believes* he can exert such influence, we shall view him as subjectively competent.

So far we have defined political influence as the way in which governmental elites make decisions. Our study, however, concentrates upon the perceptions and behaviors, not of governmental elites, but of the ordinary citizen. We are concerned with the ordinary man's perception of his own influence. Thinking that one can influence the government or even attempting to influence government is not the same as actually influencing it. A citizen may think he has influence over decisions, or he may attempt to exert influence over decisions, and the government official may be unmoved. Conversely, a citizen may believe that all government decisions are made without any consideration of his needs and desires or of the needs and desires of his fellow citizens, when, in fact, government officials constantly try to calculate the way in which groups will react to their acts.

If the degree to which citizens believe they can influence the course of governmental decisions is not necessarily related to

[1] This model represents, of course, a great oversimplification. If one were studying the "real" influence situation, rather than the ordinary man's perception of that situation, one would have to complicate things quite a bit. Government officials respond to many different groups for many different reasons. Furthermore, even where democratic political influence by the populace exists, the government official will have reciprocal influence, and this leads to a complex bargaining situation. Since we are not studying the "real" influence situation, however, such complications are not necessary; nor are we forced to ask which citizens exert influence over which officials in relation to which issues.

their actual level of influence, why study their subjective views of their competence? In the first place, we are interested in the state of attitudes in a country. If democracy involves high levels of actual participation in decisions, then the attitudes of a democratic citizenry should include the perception that they in fact can participate. A democratic citizen speaks the language of demands. Government officials accede to his demands because they fear some loss otherwise — the loss of his vote perhaps — or because they consider it legitimate that he make such demands. The subject, too, may want and expect beneficial outputs from the government. But he does not expect these to be accorded him because he demands them. The government official who acts to benefit him responds, not to the subject's demands, but to some other force. In a traditional society with a highly developed set of norms as to what is due each member, the government official may be responding to these traditional rules when he acts in favor of an individual. Or in an authoritarian–legalistic political system in which the behavior of government officials is circumscribed by explicit rules, he may act as he does because the individual falls within a particular category, which, according to the rules, is to receive a certain type of treatment. In these situations the official is not acting capriciously. His decision to aid the individual is determined by a set of social or legal rules. And these rules may, of course, be enforced by an administrative hierarchy to which the subject may appeal. This kind of subject influence, or administrative competence, is more circumscribed, more passive than that of the citizen. It may set in motion an action that will affect the way in which a rule is interpreted or enforced against an individual. It is not a creative act of influence that can affect the content of the decisions themselves, except in an indirect way.

Second, the perception of the ability to exert political influence is significant even if individuals rarely try to use that influence, or are frequently unsuccessful when they do try. Much of the influence that our respondents believe they have over government probably represents a somewhat unrealistic belief in their opportunities to participate. It is likely that many who say they could influence the government would never attempt to exert such influence; and it is likely as well that if they tried they would not succeed. Yet such a belief in the ordinary man's ability to participate may have significant consequences for a political system. Though individuals' perceptions of their own political ability may not mirror the objective situation, it cannot be unrelated to that situation. If an individual believes he has influence, he is more likely to attempt to use it.[2] A subjectively competent citizen, therefore, is more likely to be an active citizen. And if government officials do not necessarily respond to active influence attempts, they are more likely to respond to them than to a passive citizenry that makes no demands. If the ordinary citizen, on the other hand, perceives that government policy is far outside his sphere of influence, he is unlikely to attempt to influence that policy, and government officials are unlikely to worry about the potential pressure that can be brought to bear on them. Thus the extent to which citizens in a nation perceive themselves as competent to influence the government affects their political behavior.

Furthermore, the existence of a belief in the influence potential of citizens may affect the political system even if it does not affect the political activity of the ordinary man. If decision makers believe that the ordinary man *could* participate — and they certainly are not entirely cut off from the dominant social beliefs — they are likely to behave quite differently than if such a belief did not exist. Even if individuals do not act according to this belief, decision makers may act on the assumption that they can, and in this way be more responsive to the citizenry than they would be if the myth of participation did not exist. But whether myth or reality (and the statements we shall be talking about are probably a combination of both), the extent to which individuals think they can influence the government and the ways in which they believe they can do so are, as we shall discuss further in Chapter XIV, important elements of the civic culture.

[2] Evidence that those who believe they can influence are more likely to have actual experience in attempting to do so will be presented below, in Table VI.2.

In this chapter we are concerned with the perceptions that individuals have about the amount of influence they can exercise over governmental decisions. Several questions may be asked about their attempts to influence the government:

1. Under what circumstances will an individual make some conscious effort to influence the government? Direct political influence attempts are rare. For the ordinary citizen the activities of government — even local government — may seem quite distant. At the time that a decision is being made, the citizen is not aware that it is being made or of what its consequences for him are likely to be. It is probable, then, that only in situations of some stress, where a government activity is perceived to have a direct and serious impact upon the individual, will a direct influence attempt be stimulated.

2. What method will be used in the influence attempt? Some major dimensions in this respect include: the kinds of channels of influence that are used; whether the attempt is violent or non-violent; and whether the individual attempts to influence the government alone or attempts to enlist the support of others.

3. What is the effect of the influence attempt? The extent to which the government official changes his behavior in response to some influence attempt by a citizen is a problem beyond the scope of our study. However, since we are concentrating on the perspective of the citizen, we shall consider his view of the likelihood that an attempt made by him to influence the government will have any effect.

THE DISTRIBUTION OF SUBJECTIVE COMPETENCE

In developing our survey instrument, we took into account the fact that direct attempts to influence the government are more likely to arise in some stress situations, in which an individual perceives that an activity of the government is threatening injury to him. Our questions attempted to place the individual in such a hypothetical stress situation, so that we could ascertain how he thought he would react. We asked him to suppose that his local government or his national legislature was considering a law that he thought was very unjust and harmful. What did he think he could do about it? If the respondent thought he could do something, we probed to find out what it was. We then asked him how much effect he thought any action he took would have, and how likely it was that he actually would do something. A similar set of questions was asked about an unjust and harmful regulation being considered by the most local governmental unit.[3] These questions were about the political branches of the government, the elected governments on the national and local levels. Through these questions we hoped to get some notion of the respondent's views on the extent of his political competence and, more important, on the strategy of influence open to him.

The results for these questions on local and national subjective competence are reported in Table VI.1. Two points call for comment. First, in all five countries the sense of subjective competence occurs more frequently vis-à-vis the local government than the national government. This confirms widely held views of the closer relatedness of citizens to their local governments because of their greater immediacy, accessibility, and familiarity. American and British respondents most frequently say that there is something they can do about an unjust local regulation. More than three-quarters of those we interviewed in each of the two countries expressed the opinion

[3] The exact wording of these questions was:

On the national government —

Suppose a law were being considered by [appropriate national legislature specified for each nation] that you considered to be unjust or harmful. What do you think you could do?

If you made an effort to change this law, how likely is it that you would succeed?

If such a case arose, how likely is it you *would actually* try to do something about it?

On the local government —

Suppose a regulation were being considered by [most local governmental unit: town? village? etc. specified] that you considered very unjust or harmful. What do you think you could do?

If you made an effort to change this regulation, how likely is it that you would succeed?

If such a case arose, how likely is it that you *would actually* do something about it?

that they have some recourse if they believe the local government is considering a law they think unjust; only 17 per cent say that there is nothing they can do. In the other three coun-

TABLE VI.1 *Percentage who say they can do something about an unjust local or national regulation; by nation**

Nation	*Can do something about local regulation*	*Can do something about national regulation*
United States	77	75
Great Britain	78	62
Germany	62	38
Italy	51	28
Mexico	52	38

* Percentages in each case apply to the total sample.

tries over 30 per cent of those interviewed report that there is nothing they can do in such a situation.[4]

The second point brought out in Table VI.1 is that, although in all five countries the proportion that says it can influence the local government is higher than the proportion expressing national competence, this difference is relatively small in the American, British, and Mexican samples, and relatively large in Germany and Italy. Put briefly, three-fourths

[4] Many respondents make it quite clear that they believe there is nothing they can do, either because they consider themselves too powerless or because they consider government activities outside their sphere of competence. The following are some examples of these responses:

A German Housewife: "Nothing at all. The local council makes its decision, and there is nothing one can do about it."

A German Housewife: "I'd say nothing because I don't understand it, and I wouldn't do it right, anyway."

An American Semiretired: "Nothing. That's all because we put our trust in our elected people and we must feel they know more about these things than we do even though we don't always agree."

An American Housewife: "Not anything. No 'mam' not nothing . . . Nothing at all."

A British Retired Office Worker: "I wouldn't have much chance to do anything, being just one insignificant person."

An Italian Housewife: "What do you want me to do? I don't count for anything."

A Mexican Housewife: "Nothing. I have no one with whom to talk. I wouldn't know what to do in such a case."

of the American respondents express local and national competence; more than three-fourths and a little less than two-thirds of the British respondents express local and national competence, respectively. In Germany almost two-thirds of the respondents express local competence, whereas only a little more than one-third express national competence. In Italy the proportion drops from one-half to less than one-third. And in Mexico the proportion declines from a little more than one-half to a little more than one-third. The generalization about the greater sense of competence vis-à-vis the local government holds up in our findings, but it is most apparent in Italy and Germany.

That an individual is subjectively competent does not mean that he will in fact try to change what he considers an unfair law. Ours was a hypothetical situation, and we do not really know what our respondents would do if they ever were actually faced with such a challenging situation. But we did ask them for their opinions on whether or not they thought they would act. In all countries many who say they can do something about an unjust regulation report that in fact they probably would do nothing. But the number who report that there is at least some likelihood that they would make an effort reflects the same national pattern reported above. If we consider the responses about the local government (the responses about the national government form the same pattern), we find that 58 per cent of the American respondents and 50 per cent of those in Britain say there is some likelihood that they would actually make an effort to influence an unjust regulation. In Germany 44 per cent and in Italy 41 per cent make some such affirmation. (The question was, unfortunately, not asked in a comparable form in Mexico.)

Lastly, there is some evidence that the subjective estimate of one's propensity to act in this challenging political situation is closely related to actual attempts to influence the government. In all five nations a substantially larger proportion of those respondents who say there is something they can do about an unjust local regulation (let us, for convenience, call them "local competents") report some experience in attempting to influence the local government. (We find the same pattern in the national data.) These data are reported in Table VI.2. In all nations those who say they could influence the local government, in comparison with those who say they could not, are at least three times as likely to have attempted such influence.

Thus the sense of local and national civic competence is widely distributed among the American and British populations. In Germany and Italy local competence is widely distributed, national competence is much less widely distributed. In Mexico, though the general level of civic competence is lower than in the United States and Britain, the discrepancy between the local and national level (as reported in Table VI.1) is less great than in Germany and Italy. It also appears that there is a relation between subjective competence and political action.

Local competence and national competence are, as one would expect, fairly closely related. The man who believes he

TABLE VI.2 *Percentage who say they have attempted to influence the local government, by local competents and local noncompetents*

	Local competents		*Local noncompetents*	
Nation	(%)	(*No.*)*	(%)	(*No.*)
United States	33	(745)	10	(225)
Great Britain	18	(748)	3	(215)
Germany	21	(590)	2	(365)
Italy	13	(508)	4	(487)
Mexico	9	(531)	2	(476)

* Numbers in parentheses refer to the bases upon which percentages are calculated.

can influence the national government is more likely to think he can influence the local government than is the man who does not feel competent on the national level. Conversely, the man who feels competent locally is also more likely to believe he can influence the national government than is the man who does not have a sense of local competence. Earlier it was pointed out that local competence is more widespread than national competence. Furthermore, local competence is most widely distributed in nations in which local government autonomy and the accessibility of local government officials to ordinary citizens is most firmly institutionalized (see Chapter V). Adding these three facts together — local and national competence are related, local competence is more widespread than national, and local competence is related to the institutional availability of opportunities to participate on the local level — one has an argument in favor of the classic position that political participation on the local level plays a major role in the development of a competent citizenry. As many writers have argued, local government may act as a training ground for political competence. Where local government allows participation, it may foster a sense of competence that then spreads to the national level — a sense of competence that would have had a harder time developing had the individual's only involvement with government been with the more distant and inaccessible structures of the national government. To argue this point is to speculate beyond our data on national and local competence. But in a later chapter we shall present data to the effect that the individual's belief in his ability to affect the government derives, at least in part, from opportunities to be influential within smaller authority structures such as the family, the school, and the place of work.[5]

THE STRATEGY OF INFLUENCE

Another aspect of political competence is the strategy an individual would use in attempting to influence the government. The *way* in which those who report that they could influence the government say they could exert this influence is, of course, important. It makes a difference whether someone has only the vaguest notion of what he can do, or a clear view of the channels open to him for expressing his point of view. It also makes a difference what resources he believes he has available to use. Furthermore, the strategy that an individual would use will naturally affect the extent to which his subjective view of his ability to influence represents real influence potential — that is, it represents the sort of activity that

[5] See below, Chap. XI.

has some chance of changing the behavior of the government officials. We shall deal primarily with those who think they have influence, the "competents," and ask how they would exert that influence.

The strategies of influence that individuals report they would use in connection with the local government are summarized in Table VI.3. (Comparable data on the national government will be presented below.) Let us look first at the question of what social resources the individual feels he has available to him. This is highly significant for understanding the nature of his perceived relationship to his government. Government organizations are large and powerful, especially when compared to the individual. This is especially true of the national government, but even local government represents an institution whose resources are much greater than those of the ordinary man. Looking at the individual and his government, one is tempted to see him as lonely, powerless, and somewhat frightened by the immensity of the powers he faces. This is in fact one of the most frequent descriptions of the average man in modern political societies. In the theory of the "mass society" the individual is described as related directly as individual to the state. He has no other social resources to support him in this relationship and naturally feels ineffective and anxious.[6] However valid this theory may be concerning the actual amount of power the average man has and the social resources available to him, our data suggest that a large number of our respondents do not view themselves as the model of mass society describes them. In their relationship to their government they think of themselves as neither powerless nor, what is more important, alone.

This fact is reflected in the data reported in Table VI.3. A number of our respondents believe that they can enlist the support of others in their attempts to influence the government. What is most striking is the variation from country to country in the numbers who feel they can call on others to aid them. In the United States 59 per cent of our respondents indicated that they could attempt to enlist the support of others

[6] On this general topic see William Kornhauser, *The Politics of Mass Society,* Glencoe, Ill., 1959.

if they wished to change a regulation they considered unjust. At the other extreme, only 9 per cent of the Italians mentioned the use of this social resource. In the other countries the proportions reporting that they would try to enlist the support of others varied from 36 per cent in Britain, to 28 per cent in Mexico, to 21 per cent in Germany.[7]

Whom would citizens enlist to support them? Individuals as we know are members of a large number of social groups. They are not merely citizens of their nations; they are members of families, communities, churches, voluntary associations, trade unions, and a great variety of other groups and organizations. Basically these associations can be divided into two classes: formal organizations and informal face-to-face groups.

Much has been written about the important role of formal organizations in the political process — especially the role of political parties and associational interest groups. Both play major intervening roles between the individual and his government. They aggregate the demands of citizens and communicate these to government officials. Recently there has been growing interest in the informal face-to-face network of social groups to which an individual belongs — family, friends, work group, and neighbors. Here the main emphasis has been upon the impact of these groups on the political attitudes of their members, and on the process of communication downward; that is, to the individuals from such formal institutions as government, political parties, and the mass media.[8] Little has been said about the role of such informal assocations in what we might call the "influence-upward" process: the process by which citizens in a democracy influence the attitudes and behavior of government officials. But our findings show

[7] Since question wording can seriously affect the response received, it is important to note here that the notion that one could enlist the support of others was in no way suggested by the question or by the interviewer's probing of the question. Interviewers were carefully instructed not to ask such questions as: "Is there anyone you could get to help you?" or "Would you attempt to do this alone or with other people?"

[8] On the subject of the political functions of informal groups, see Sidney Verba, *Small Groups and Political Behavior*, Princeton, N.J., 1961. chap. 2.

TABLE VI.3 *What citizens would do to try to influence their local government; by nation*

What citizens would do	*U.S.*	*U.K.*	*Germany*	*Italy*	*Mexico*
TRY TO ENLIST AID OF OTHERS					
Organize an informal group; arouse friends and neighbors, get them to write letters of protest or to sign a petition	56	34	13	7	26
Work through a political party	1	1	3	1	—
Work through a formal group (union, church, professional) to which they belong	4	3	5	1	2
Total percentage who would enlist others' aid[a]	59	36	21	9	28
ACT ALONE					
Directly contact political leaders (elected officials) or the press; write a letter to or visit a local political leader	20	45	15	12	15
Directly contact administrative (nonelected) officials	1	3	31	12	18
Consult a lawyer; appeal through courts	2	1	3	2	2
Vote against offending officials at next election	14	4	1	1	—
Take some violent action	1	1	1	1	1
Just protest	—	—	—	12	—
Other	1	2	—	3	5
Total percentage who would act alone[b]	18	41	41	43	24
Total percentage who would act with others or alone	77	78	62	51	53
Total number of respondents	970	963	955	995	1,007

[a] Total percentages are less than the total of the individual cells, since some respondents gave more than one answer.

[b] This row includes only the respondents who replied that they could do something but did not mention working with others. Hence the total is less than the sum of the individual cells, which contain respondents who may have mentioned both group and individual activity.

most strikingly that, when it comes to the support that individuals believe they could enlist in a challenging political situation, they think much more often of enlisting support from the informal face-to-face groups of which they are members than from the formal organizations to which they belong or with which they are affiliated. In all countries except Germany, less than 1 per cent of the respondents indicate that they would work through their political party if they were attempting to counteract some unjust regulation being considered by the local government; the German figure is about 3 per cent. Clearly, no matter how important the role of political parties may be in democratic societies, relatively few citizens think of them first as the place where support may be enlisted for attempts to influence the government.[9]

In all countries more individuals report that they would attempt to work through other formal organized groups than through political parties. But when one considers the entire range of formal organizations to which people may belong, the number who report they would enlist their support is small: no more than 3 per cent of the respondents in any country. Of course, not all respondents have some formal organization at their disposal; such organizations are more frequent in some nations than in others. And the percentage who report membership differs substantially from country to country. Furthermore, not all formal organizations are equally politically relevant.

But even among those respondents who belong to a formal organization that they report is involved in politics, the number who would invoke such membership in a stress situation is much smaller than the number who are members. In the United States, where such memberships are most frequent, 228 respondents report membership in this kind of organization, but only 35 of these Americans report that they would work through that organization if they were trying to influence a local regulation. In Italy, where such memberships are

[9] To some extent the infrequent mention of a political party in this context probably understates the role of parties in this influence process. Many more respondents mentioned contacting government officials. If they explicitly mentioned that the partisan affiliation of the official was relevant in their attaining access to him, they would be coded as working through a party. But many may have considered this affiliation relevant even if they did not mention it.

least frequent, we find the same pattern. Fifty-six Italians belong to some organization they believe is involved in political affairs, but only thirteen of those members would work through it if they were trying to influence a local regulation. The aid of a formal organization would be called upon most frequently in Germany, but only half as frequently as the occurrence of membership in a politically relevant organization.

That formal organizations rarely would be invoked by individuals who were trying to influence the government does not mean, however, that these organizations are politically unimportant. They still may effect an individual's political influence, for he may have more influence over government officials merely by being a member of such a group, even if he makes no overt attempt to influence the government. And this sort of influence is of great significance — probably of greater overall significance than the overt influence attempts that ordinary citizens make from time to time. Furthermore, though an individual would not use his formal organization as the means to influence the government directly, his membership in itself enhances the prospects that he will believe himself capable of influencing the government and will actually make some such attempt. Thus he may, for a variety of reasons to be discussed below, develop greater self-confidence in his own political competence.[10]

Cooperative Political Behavior. As Table VI.3 indicates, in all nations respondents less frequently mention enlisting the support of formal groups than informal groups — arousing their neighbors, getting friends and acquaintances to support their position, circulating a petition. This in itself is striking, though it ought not, for reasons given above, to be taken to imply that these informal groups play a more significant role in the political process than do formal organizations. What is most striking is not the frequency with which informal groups are mentioned in all countries, but the sharp differences in frequency among the nations.

Thus Table VI.4 shows that 56 per cent of the American respondents, 34 per cent of the British, and 26 per cent of the

[10] See below, Chap. X, for a discussion of the impact of voluntary associations.

Mexicans reported that they would use this informal group strategy, as compared with 13 per cent of the Germans and 7 per cent of the Italians. If we consider the proportion of local competents who say they would cooperate with their fellow citizens in attempting to influence the government,[11] we find that 74 per cent of American local competents would use informal groups, whereas only 13 per cent of Italian local competents and 22 per cent of the Germans would do so. In Mexico,

TABLE VI.4 *Those who would enlist the aid of an informal group to influence an unjust local regulation*

	Percentage of total sample		*Percentage of local competents*	
Nation	(%)	(*No.*)*	(%)	(*No.*)
United States	56	(970)	74	(745)
Great Britain	34	(963)	43	(748)
Germany	13	(955)	22	(590)
Italy	7	(995)	13	(508)
Mexico	26	(1,007)	50	(531)

* Numbers in parentheses refer to the bases upon which percentages are calculated.

though the proportion of local competents is relatively low, the proportion of those local competents who would work through informal groups is quite high — 50 per cent. And in Britain the proportion of local competents who say they would seek the cooperation of others is about as great — 43 per cent.

The notions that one can cooperate with one's fellow citizens in attempting to influence the government and that such cooperation is an effective means of increasing one's own influence dominate the bulk of the responses of the local com-

[11] The percentage of respondents mentioning a particular strategy of influence can be computed either as a percentage of the entire population or as a percentage of the local competents only. Both figures are important. The first figure reflects the propensity for certain types of political behavior in a nation. But if we are interested in how nations differ in the strategies their citizens will use, we must use the second figure; for if we did not, the national differences in the percentage choosing a particular strategy might reflect merely that there are more in one country than in another who report that there is nothing they could do. In the following tables the percentages will be reported in both forms.

petents in the United States and play an important role in responses in Britain and Mexico. In all five countries, however, there are individuals who would work with others in attempting to influence the government. A few illustrations may help to convey that attitude:

An American Office Manager: "You can't do anything individually. You'd have to get a group and all get together and go to the proper authorities to complain."
An American Salesman: "Get up a petition. Get together with people who have the same objection. Taking it up with the responsible person like the mayor or police commissioner."
An American Housemaid: "I could discuss it with others and see how many others felt the same about it as I did. We could then write a letter each to some government person in charge and let him know how we felt, or we could write one letter and get a lot of people to sign it."
An English Dispatch Clerk: "Contact neighbors and friends and make a protest to the councillors. . . ."
An English Foreman Gardener: "First thing — get a petition going. Take it up to the Council offices and make yourself spokesman of a group. You could try the local M.P."
An English House Painter: "You could more or less get a petition up and show the feeling. You could discuss it with your workmates and your wife."
A Mexican Shoemaker: "Protest, join a group of citizens, and personally go to the office where it was issued and talk about it to the authorities."
A Mexican Housewife: "I would get together all the people and send a petition to the president or the governor of the state signed by all."

In a democratic political system, the belief that cooperation with one's fellow citizens is both a possible and an effective political action represents, we suggest, a highly significant orientation. The diffusion of influence over political decisions, by which we define democracy, implies some cooperative ability among the citizenry. This cooperation seems to be necessary, in terms of both the amount of influence the ordinary man can expect to have and the results of his influence on governmental decisions. By definition, the "average" man's influence over the government must be small. Compared with the forces of government — and this would apply to local as well as national government — he is a frail creature indeed. If the ordinary man is to have any political influence, it must be in concert with his fellows. Second, from the point of view of the output of a democratic government, noncooperative and completely individualistic influence attempts could lead only to dysfunctional results. Every individual demand cannot be met, or the result will be chaos. If the government is to be responsive to the demands of the ordinary man, these demands must be aggregated, and the aggregation of interests implies cooperation among men. The aggregation of interests involved in the cooperation of groups of like-minded individuals is aggregation on a rather low level, but it does suggest a propensity to work together with one's fellows, which is relevant for larger political structures as well. In any case, we may suggest that the citizen who believes he can work cooperatively with others in his environment if he wants to engage in political activity has quite a different perspective on politics from the individual who thinks of himself as a lone political actor.

Furthermore, the notion that one can affect a government decision by bringing one's peers into the dispute is a highly political notion. It represents a fairly clear attempt to use political influence in one's relations with government officials. The threat that *many* make — whether it is the threatened loss of votes or of support, or the threat of public criticism — is, other things being equal, greater than the threat that *one* can make. Thus the individual who mentions getting others to join him in his dispute with the government is more likely to see himself as a citizen able to influence his government than as a subject who lacks such influence. And the variations among the five nations in the frequency with which such groups are mentioned reflect variations in such citizen competence.

It is particularly important to note what sorts of groups are involved here. The informal groups our respondents talk of forming do not exist, at least in a politically relevant sense, before the political stress situation arises. The individual perceives himself as able to create structures for the purpose of influencing the government. These structures represent a form of influence that had not been committed to politics before the politically challenging situation arose. In this sense, the ability of the individual to create structures to aid him in his disputes with the government represents a reserve of influence on his part. He has not committed his complete support to some larger social system, as has the individual in the so-called mass society; nor is he cut off from contact with the government, as is the parochial.

That a large proportion of people in a country perceive that the informal face-to-face groups of which they are members can be rallied to their support in time of political stress represents a significant aspect of the political culture of that nation. It means that some of the most basic building blocks of the social structure have been incorporated into the political system. An individual's role as citizen, particularly as a democratic, influential citizen, fuses with his other social roles. The type of political activity sparking this fusion of informal group membership and political citizenship is also highly significant. The fusion takes place because of political demands being made by citizens upon their government. They invoke their friends and neighbors in an attempt to influence their government. Thus the fusion occurs at the heart of the democratic process — the process by which the ordinary citizen exercises some control over his government. This is profoundly different from the fusion between face-to-face groups and government that has been attempted within totalitarian states. Here the government has attempted to influence the individual: family and friendship groups are penetrated by the state to support its attempts to propagandize and control. The state attempts to control these informal groups. In the countries we studied the invocation of informal groups has a contrary meaning. It is an attempt to penetrate and control government. It represents a meshing together of polity and community, rather than an assimilation of community into the polity.

Lastly, we have stressed the importance of this propensity toward cooperation with one's fellow citizens, not merely because we believe that it has significant consequences for the political system, but because we feel it is a type of behavior that can best be understood and explained by the type of study contained in this book. In the first place, the frequency with which individuals talk of cooperating with their fellow citizens to influence the government is not as dependent upon the structure of government as is the frequency with which they say they can influence the government. Whether or not someone feels he can affect the course of government action obviously depends to a large extent upon the structure of government — the extent to which it provides citizen access. But the difference between the individual who responds that he would write a letter to the local council and the one who responds that he would write a letter to the local council *and try to induce his friends to do likewise* cannot be explained by national differences in the structure and powers of their respective local councils.[12] As we shall see shortly, these differing levels of

[12] This is not completely true. Governmental structure may be more amenable to group influence in some countries than in others. But this is more likely to occur because of the government's past experience with such groups than because of the government's formal structure. On the other hand, there is no doubt that certain structures of government foster such "banding together" protests more than do others. Structures where power is diffused among a large number of autonomous or semi-autonomous boards and councils and the like (especially elected boards and councils) are more likely to foster such protest than are structures dominated by a centrally appointed official whose domain includes a larger area (as with the Italian prefect system). But this is an example of the general proposition that interaction will occur between political orientation and political structure. In this case, however, to explain the origins of this group-forming attitude according to formal political structure alone would be unconvincing. One has to look beyond the structure of the local government.

There is, however, another way in which governmental structure may foster or inhibit the group forming propensities of a population. The legal systems of nations differ in the extent to which they ban, regulate, or in other ways make difficult the formation of non-governmental associations. Legal systems on the European continent have been more hostile to such groups than has the Anglo-American legal system. And though these regulations refer largely to formal organizations (to be discussed in Chapter X, below), they might have an effect on informal groups as well. See on this

social and economic development, while they can explain many of the political differences among the nations, cannot explain the propensity to cooperate politically. The origin of this propensity must be sought elsewhere. In a later chapter we shall try to trace it to social values and attitudes and to the degree of partisan fragmentation in society.[13]

Though the use of primary groups as a resource for influence is most common in the United States, Britain, and Mexico, there are several interesting differences between the United States and Britain on the one hand and Mexico on the other. The notion that one can mobilize an informal group as an aid in attempting to influence the government appears to be of greater significance for the actual exercise of influence in the former two countries. Earlier it was pointed out that those who report they can do something about an unjust local law (the local competents), compared with those who report the opposite, are much more likely to report some experience in attempting to influence the government. If we look only at the local competents and ask how those who would work through groups and those who would act alone differ in the extent of their experience in attempted local influence, we find that in the United States and Britain those who would work through groups are more likely to have had experience in these endeavors. In the United States 36 per cent of those who report they would work through informal groups (n: 547) also report that they have at some time actually attempted to influence the government, whereas only 25 per cent of those local competents who would use some other strategy (n: 198) report such experience. In Britain the parallel figures are 23 per cent for those who mention informal groups (n: 315) and 15 per cent for other local competents (n: 414). In Mexico, on the other hand, those who mention informal groups are a bit less likely to be the experienced re-

point, Arnold Rose, "On Individualism and Social Responsibility," *Archives Européennes de Sociologie*, II (1961), pp. 163-69.

[13] The relationship between social and economic development and the propensity to form groups will be discussed at the end of the chapter. The explanation of this group-forming propensity in terms of social values and partisan fragmentation will be attempted in Chapter IX.

spondents: 7 per cent of those who mention informal groups (n: 264) report experience, as against 10 per cent of the other local competents (n: 267).[14]

Furthermore, in the former two countries the use of informal groups as a means of influencing the government is seen, not only as a means to protest, but as the key to effective protest. In order to test the extent to which individuals felt they could influence their local government, we asked another question after asking what respondents thought they could do about an unjust local law: "If you made an effort to change this regulation, how likely is it that you would succeed?" Of interest to us here is that a large number of American and British local competents volunteered the statement that their protest would have some likelihood of success only if others joined with them. (The percentages were 30 in the United States and 20 in Britain.) In Mexico, though a good percentage felt there was some likelihood that they would succeed if they attempted to influence their local government, fewer than one per cent of the respondents suggested that this would be the case only if they had the support of others. Though the use of informal groups is perceived as a means of influence in Mexico, it is not yet perceived as the key to effective influence.[15]

One further difference deserves mention. In the United States and Britain the use of informal groups as a means of influencing a governmental decision is considered much more appropriate on the local than on the national level. In Mexico, on the other hand, the proportion who would use informal groups is about the same on the local and national levels. The fact that in Britain and the United States, more than in Mexico, the use of such groups is closely related both to

[14] In Germany those local competents who mention informal groups are somewhat less likely to have had actual influence experience. Seventeen per cent of those who mention informal groups (n. 126) report past experience, as against 23 per cent of local competents who do not mention them (n. 460). In Italy those local competents who mention groups are somewhat more likely to be experienced: 16 per cent (n. 67), as against 13 per cent (n. 438) of those who do not mention groups.

[15] In Germany the percentage of local competents who mentioned that they would succeed only if others joined them was 12; in Italy it was 5.

experience and to expectations of success, coupled with the fact that such strategy is considered more appropriate in connection with the local government in the former two countries, suggests that informal group strategy is based on a more realistic appraisal of the potentialities of such a strategy — a realistic appraisal deriving from actual experience with such groups on the local level. In Mexico this influence strategy is less well grounded in actual local experience. It appears to be another instance of the aspirational character of the Mexican political culture.

Individual Action. The respondents who spoke of themselves as acting alone in their attempt to influence the government show some variation, as Table VI.4 indicates, in the strategies they mention. In the United States and Britain respondents are more likely to say they would approach an elected government official rather than an appointed official of the bureaucracy. In Mexico and Italy respondents are as likely to say they would direct their protest toward one type of official as toward the other. In Germany, however, more respondents mention appointed officials than elected officials as the target of their protest. It is tempting to consider these results to be a reflection of a more highly developed political competence in the United States and Britain. A protest to an elected official seems to be inherently more of a political protest, in the sense of involving an implied threat of deprivation to the official if he does not comply — for the loss of the vote is the most usual deprivation with which the individual can threaten an offending official. This may partly explain the differences among the nations in the chosen targets of influence attempts; but it is more likely that these differences merely reflect national differences in the relative position and importance of elected and appointed officials within the structures of local government.

Lastly, not all of those who say they could do something about an unjust local regulation had any clear strategy in mind. As Table VI.3 indicates, 12 per cent of the Italian respondents said that they could protest if faced with a regulation they considered unjust, but when asked how or to whom they could protest, gave no more specific reply. The 12 per cent who would protest represent about one-fourth of all Italian local competents. While this answer shows a higher level of subjective competence than the answer that one could do nothing, it reflects little awareness of the political channels through which one might effectively approach the government.

NATIONAL COMPETENCE

We saw in Table VI.1 that in all nations fewer respondents say they could influence the national legislature than the local government and more say there is nothing they could do. In Table VI.5 we report the strategies respondents say they would use vis-à-vis the national government. In all nations formal organizations are somewhat more often mentioned as a resource for influencing the national government than the local government. (And if one calculated the percentage as a proportion of "national competents" rather than as a proportion of the entire sample, the difference would be sharper.) Conversely, in all nations fewer respondents mention using informal groups in connection with the national government than mentioned them in connection with the local government, though the pattern is the same; these groups are mentioned most frequently in the United States, followed by Britain and Mexico, then Germany and Italy. Generally, national influence strategies tend to rely more on the organized structures of politics, such as interest groups, political parties, and the press, or on individual approaches to elected political leaders. As we have already pointed out, this probably reflects realistic calculations. It takes a larger group and greater political skill to bring influence to bear on the national than on the local government. However, our evidence suggests that informal group competence persists significantly at the national level in the United States and Britain, even if it does not bulk as large as it does at the local level.

SOCIAL GROUPS AND SUBJECTIVE COMPETENCE

Clearly the five nations differ in the extent to which their citizens believe themselves capable of doing something should government threaten their interests; they differ, too, in the strategies the citizens would use. Why are there such differ-

TABLE VI.5 *What citizens would do to try to influence their national government; by nation*

What citizens would do	*U.S.*	*U.K.*	*Germany*	*Italy*	*Mexico*
TRY TO ENLIST AID OF OTHERS					
Organize an informal group; arouse friends and neighbors, get them to write letters of protest or to sign a petition	29	18	7	6	18
Work through a political party	1	2	6	2	—
Work through a formal group (union, church, professional) to which they belong	4	3	7	2	3
Total percentage who would enlist others' aid[a]	32	22	19	10	20
ACT ALONE					
Directly contact political leaders (elected officials) or the press; write a letter to or visit a local political leader	57	44	12	7	8
Directly contact administrative (nonelected) officials	—	1	4	4	6
Consult a lawyer; appeal through courts	—	—	1	1	4
Vote against offending officials at next election	7	3	4	1	—
Take some violent action	—	—	2	1	4
Just protest	—	—	—	3	—
Other	—	2	—	2	3
Total percentage who would act alone[b]	42	40	18	18	18
Nothing	21	32	56	50	50
Don't know	4	6	7	22	12
Total percentage[c]	123	111	106	101	108
Total number of respondents	970	963	955	995	1,007

[a] Total percentages are less than the total of the individual cells, since some respondents gave more than one answer.

[b] This row includes only the respondents who said they could do something but did not mention working with others. Hence the total is less than the sum of the individual cells, which contain respondents who may have mentioned both group and individual activity.

[c] Percentages exceed 100 because of multiple responses.

ences? The causes are many and we do not claim to deal with them all in this study. We shall concern ourselves with the more limited question of whether the differences observed are general differences among the political cultures of our five countries, or are differences that vary sharply and in the same way among subgroups themselves, whatever the country. If the former is true, one would expect most Italians to respond in the same way, no matter what their social position, and to differ from Americans of all social groups. If the latter is true, one would expect upper-status Italians to differ significantly from Italians of lower status, and to resemble Americans of similar status. There are many difficulties in making such comparisons — not the least of which is the difficulty of getting equivalent status measures across societies; but by using roughly equivalent subgroups for comparisons, we shall attempt to make them. Furthermore, by using different measures to compare these results, one can begin to distinguish those patterns that seem to depend more upon the distribution of other social characteristics within a society. If the differences among the nations disappear when one considers only social groups that are roughly matched, one has an aspect of political culture that is less specific to the particular culture. On the other hand, if the nationals in a particular social grouping of one country still differ significantly from those of a similar social group in other countries, though they resemble closely their fellow nationals of diverse social backgrounds, one is probably dealing with an aspect of political culture whose roots are in the unique experiences of that country, and not in the experiences common to all our countries.

Let us look first at the relationship between citizen competence and education. We choose education as the first variable to consider, because of its close relationship with the factors that would tend to make a man feel subjectively competent (we shall discuss this relationship more fully in Chapter XII). As Figure VI.1 clearly points out, in all countries the more education an individual has, the more likely he is to consider himself capable of influencing the local government; that is, to be what we have called a local competent. (The percentage of individuals who say they could affect a local law is measured on the vertical axis; the level of education on the horizontal.) In the United States 60 per cent of those who did not get be-

Percentage of respondents who say that they can do something about a local regulation that they consider unjust or unfair

(By nation and education)

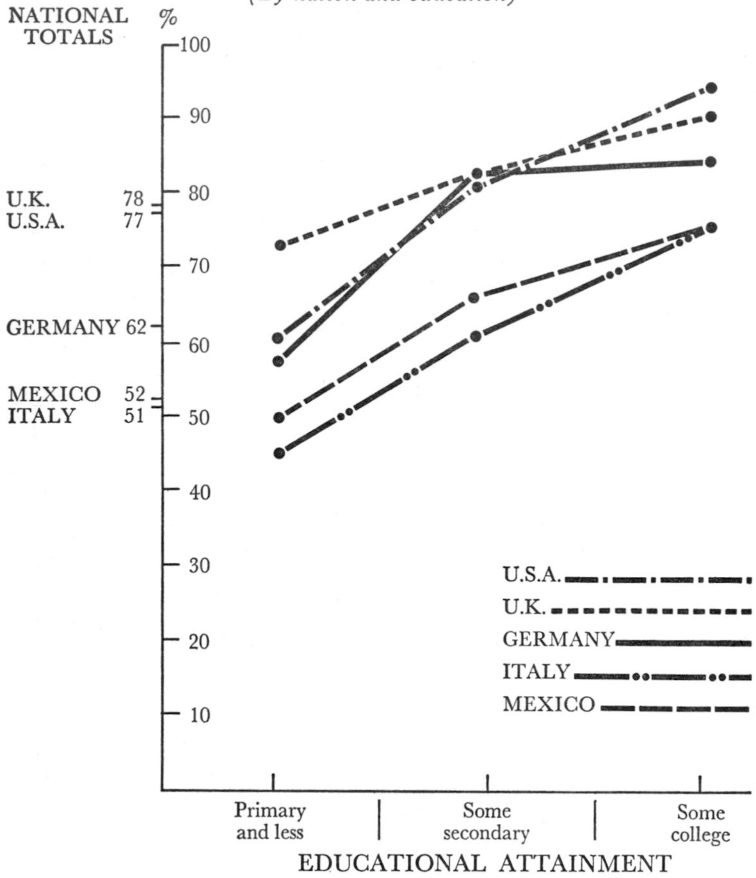

NATIONAL TOTALS

U.K. 78
U.S.A. 77
GERMANY 62
MEXICO 52
ITALY 51

%
100
90
80
70
60
50
40
30
20
10

U.S.A.
U.K.
GERMANY
ITALY
MEXICO

EDUCATIONAL ATTAINMENT

	Primary and less	Some secondary	Some college
U.S.A.	60% (339)	82% (443)	95% (188)
U.K.	74% (593)	83% (322)	88% (24)
GERMANY	58% (792)	83% (123)	85% (26)
ITALY	45% (692)	62% (245)	76% (54)
MEXICO	49% (877)	67% (103)	76% (24)

(Numbers in parentheses refer to the base upon which percentage is calculated.)

FIGURE VI.1

Percentage of local competents who would enlist the support of an informal group in order to influence a local regulation they thought was unjust

(By nation and education)

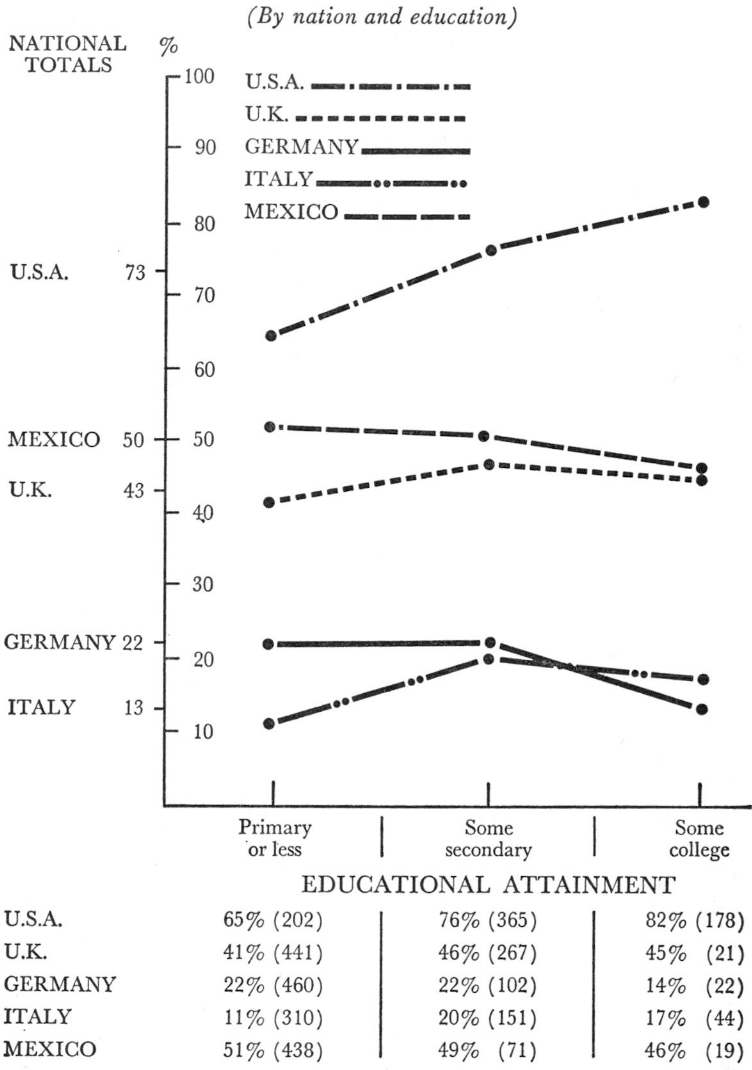

	Primary or less	Some secondary	Some college
U.S.A.	65% (202)	76% (365)	82% (178)
U.K.	41% (441)	46% (267)	45% (21)
GERMANY	22% (460)	22% (102)	14% (22)
ITALY	11% (310)	20% (151)	17% (44)
MEXICO	51% (438)	49% (71)	46% (19)

(Numbers in parentheses refer to the base upon which percentage is calculated.)

FIGURE VI.2

yond primary school and 95 per cent of those with some college education are local competents. And the pattern repeats itself in each country. This then is a clear uniformity across national lines. No matter what the frequency of local competence within a nation, the incidence of this competence is greater among those with higher education.

What about the differences among and within nations? The question is a bit harder to answer, for differences exist both among educational groups within the same country (as the slopes of the lines indicate) and within similar educational groups among nations (as the different heights of the lines indicate). Some differences among nations diminish significantly within similar educational groups. For instance, though the American and German national totals for local competents are quite different, the differences between the two countries almost disappear when similar educational groups are compared. The greatest similarity in national totals occurs between the United States and Britain, on the one hand, and Mexico and Italy, on the other; yet in each pair the members differ somewhat more from each other between similar educational groups than they do on the national level. When the primary educated of America and Britain are compared, those in Britain show a higher rate of citizen competence; and when the lower educational groups of Italy and Mexico are compared, those in Mexico show a somewhat higher competence on the lower two levels.

Thus education has a mixed effect on the differences among nations. But the following general statements can be made on the basis of Figure VI.1. On all levels of education Mexican and Italian respondents are less frequently local competents than are respondents on similar levels in the other three countries (though on the university level the difference becomes quite slight). Second, the higher the educational level, the less difference there is among nations. This fact comes out clearly if one looks at the range among the nations on each level of education. On the elementary school level the range between the nation with the greatest frequency of local competents (Britain) and the nation with the least frequency (Italy) is 29 percentage points; on the secondary school level there are 21 percentage points between the nations that have the greatest frequency (Britain and Germany) and the one with the least (Italy); and on the university level 19 percentage points separate the United States, on the one hand, from Italy and Mexico, on the other.

Which are greater, national or educational differences? The measure of these is rough, but if one compares the ranges between the highest and lowest nation within each educational group (as reported in the previous paragraph) with the ranges between the highest and lowest educational group within each nation, the results suggest that there is certainly as much — if not, on the average, more — variation among educational groups within a single nation than among individuals with similar educational attainment in different nations. In the frequency with which respondents believe themselves competent to influence the government, there is within each nation about as much, if not more, difference among the educational levels as there is cross-nationally on each educational level. The ranges between the educational group that most frequently reports itself competent to influence the government (those with some university education in each nation) and the group that least frequently reports such competence (those with only primary education or no education in each country) are: United States, 35 percentage points; Britain, 14 percentage points; Germany, 27 percentage points; Italy, 31 percentage points, and Mexico, 27 percentage points. These figures are rough, since they compare the extreme cases as to education and as to nation. But they do suggest that in overall local competence, similar educational groups compared cross-nationally resemble one another at least as much as, and perhaps more than do different educational groups within the same nation.

So far we have considered the extent to which individuals believe they can influence an unjust local regulation. But the strategy an individual would use may be more important than the simple distinction of whether or not he thinks he can do anything. In particular, the belief that one can cooperate with one's fellow citizens as a means of influencing the government appears to be important. Does this political strategy depend to as large an extent upon educational attainment as does the existence of local competence? The data in Figure VI.2 suggest that it does not.

The percentage of local competents who would work through informal groups varies sharply from country to country even within each educational group, but varies very little among educational groups within the individual countries.[16] Only in the United States does the frequency with which such activity is mentioned vary directly with educational attainment, and even here the relationship is not as strong as that between educational levels and local competence in general. Consider again the contrast between the United States and Germany. Within similar educational groups, German and American respondents hardly differ in the frequency with which they say that there is something they can do about an unjust local regulation. But if we compare the percentage of these local competents who would cooperate with their fellow citizens, we see that on each educational level German respondents are much less likely to mention such activity. Furthermore, well-educated German respondents are no more likely to talk of such activity than are less-educated ones. Unlike the situation in relation to overall local competence, where the range of difference among nations was no greater and perhaps a little less than the range of variation among one nation's educational groups, the variation among nations in the frequency with which political cooperation is mentioned is generally much greater on all educational levels than among educational groups within a nation. Here, then, may be a pattern of political culture the existence of which is independent of the educational attainment of an individual or the educational level in a nation. Education, our data suggest, may lead individuals to believe that they can influence their government, *no matter what country they live in* (providing, of course, that there is at least some institutional structure to support this attitude). Our data also suggest that as the overall educational

[16] The percentage is calculated as a percentage of local competents, not of the total population. This is to isolate the political strategy that competents would use from the fact that the frequency of competents differs from country to country.

level of nations rises, they will become more similar in this respect. But education does not necessarily increase the potentiality that individuals will create groups to support them. The ability to create political structures through cooperation with one's fellow citizens in time of stress seems to be typical of some nations and not of others. It is an element of political style, not a result of educational attainment.

Our discussion suggests that local competence varies with social grouping, while the use of informal groups as the strategy of influence is much more dependent upon national political style. Figures VI.1 and VI.2 compared respondents on differing educational levels, but the same pattern emerges if one compares respondents by occupation and by sex. But there is little variation among these groups in the frequency with which a group-oriented strategy is selected.

The data on educational, occupational, and sex differences in subjective competence suggest that whether or not one believes himself capable of influencing a local or national regulation depends a lot on who he is within his own country.[17] If he has more education, higher status, or is male, he is clearly more likely to consider himself competent. One's self-perceptions of his role as a citizen vary greatly with one's social position within a nation. But whether or not the local competent believes that his friends and neighbors are available to help him in a stress situation depends relatively little on his social position within a nation; more important is the nation he happens to live in. Political competence thus grows with higher education or occupational status, but cooperative competence seems to be rooted in specific national political cultures.

[17] The questions on "national competence" produce a similar pattern of response.

CHAPTER VII

Citizen Competence and Subject Competence

THE ROLE OF citizen represents in some sense the highest form of democratic participation. It is through such participation that the ordinary man gains influence over the course of governmental affairs. But men do not take part in political life only in their roles as citizens. As suggested in the introductory chapter, they also remain in a subject relationship to government even after they have adopted the role of citizen. Though they may take part in the making of laws, they remain the subjects of laws. In many societies the opportunity for the individual to take on the role of the citizen may be very limited, but in all societies with any form of specialized political system, individuals are subjects.

Just as the citizen role may be performed more or less competently, so may the subject be more or less competent. But the competence of the subject is different from that of the citizen. The competent citizen has a role in the formation of general policy. Furthermore, he plays an *influential* role in this decision-making process: he participates by using explicit or implicit threats of some form of deprivation if the official does not comply with his demand. The subject does not participate in making rules, nor does his participation involve the use of political influence. His participation comes at the point at which general policy has been made and is being applied. The competence of the subject is more a matter of being aware of his rights under the rules than of participating in the making of the rules.[1] And though the subject may attempt to make the government official responsive, he appeals rather than demands. His appeal may be to the set of administrative rules that are supposed to guide the action of the government official, or he may appeal to his considerateness. If the government official responds, it is because he is following these rules or because he is being considerate — not because influence has been applied to him. (Of course, administrative officials can be "influenced," as we define influence, but then one no longer has a subject relationship. We shall return to this point below.)

The civic culture, we have argued, is a political culture in which large numbers of individuals are competent as citizens: we call this competence *political* competence. But in the civic culture individuals would be competent as subjects as well (*administrative* competence). Whether or not individuals consider themselves competent in the administrative sense depends upon many factors, not the least of which are the responsiveness of the governmental bureaucracy to the individual and the existence of channels of appeal open to the ordinary man. Though we cannot measure the extent to which the governmental structure fosters a sense of administrative competence in a population, we can measure the extent of that sense of competence.

THE SENSE OF ADMINISTRATIVE COMPETENCE

Just as individuals may or may not perceive that the decision-making organs of government are amenable to political influence, so they may or may not perceive that those government officials with whom they stand in a subject relationship are responsive to their appeals. To test the extent of the sense of administrative competence, we attempted to find out what

[1] Of course, there is no hard and fast line between the making of general rules and the application of them. General rules are usually made within the legislature, but administrative agencies often have discretion to formulate fairly general policy as well.

expectations respondents had of the responsiveness of government bureaucrats. The situation presented to them was an administrative one in which attempts at political influence would be inappropriate (though in the real world it may be and often is employed). What sort of treatment, we wanted to know, did individuals expect to receive from government administrative officials? In particular, we were interested in the extent to which individuals felt they could have some voice in the proceedings if they were involved in some question in a government office. We posed two hypothetical situations. In one we asked respondents: "Suppose there were some question you had to take to a government office — for example, a tax question or a housing regulation. . . ." In the other we asked them to suppose "you had some trouble with the police — a traffic violation, maybe, or being accused of a minor offense. . . ." In both cases we asked what sort of reaction they would expect if they explained their point of view to the government officials.[2]

The relevant data were reported in Chapter III, Table III.3. As the table showed, the type of response individuals expect varies from nation to nation. It is clear that Mexican respondents rarely expect to achieve much by expressing their point of view. Only 14 per cent expect that they will receive serious consideration, and almost twice as many expect that they will be ignored; most of the rest expect to receive little attention. Italian respondents follow the Mexicans in the frequency with which they expect to be ignored and in the infrequency with which they expect to receive serious consideration. The response patterns for the other three countries are higher with the British most frequently expecting serious consideration, followed by Germans and then Americans.

As the table also revealed, the pattern is the same in relation to the police. Again the Mexicans expect very little: only 12 per cent believe they will receive serious consideration, and 29 per cent believe they will be ignored. Italian respondents again fall above the Mexicans in terms of their expectations, but below the respondents of the other three countries. American and

[2] These questions are discussed more fully in Chapter III, above.

German respondents report about as frequently that they would receive serious consideration, but Americans more frequently report that they would be ignored (11 per cent of American respondents believe they would be ignored, in comparison with only 4 per cent of the Germans). The expectation of serious consideration among British respondents is, however, well above that in any other country, with 74 per cent of British respondents expecting such treatment.

The divergences among the nations on this set of figures can hardly be overemphasized. Certainly the British live in an entirely different governmental world from that of the Mexicans or Italians. How different it is can be seen if we compare Britain and Mexico. Whereas three out of four Britons expect the police to give their point of view serious consideration and only a handful expect it to be ignored, little more than one in ten Mexicans expect such consideration and almost one in three expect their point of view to be ignored.

CITIZEN AND SUBJECT COMPETENCE

Individuals, then, may believe themselves competent as citizens or as subjects. As competent citizens, they perceive themselves as able to affect governmental decisions through political influence: by forming groups, by threatening the withdrawal of their vote or other reprisals. As competent subjects, they perceive themselves as able to appeal to a set of regular and orderly rules in their dealings with administrative officials. They will receive fair treatment from the administration, and their point of view will be considered, not because they attempt political influence, but because the administrative official is controlled by a set of rules that curbs his arbitrary power. The British, for instance, perceive themselves as able to count upon such treatment; the Mexicans clearly do not.

Citizen competence and subject competence differ but are not completely independent of each other. Nor is it likely that the existence of one type of competence will leave the other unaffected. One would expect a certain amount of spillover of political competence into administrative competence. The more politically competent a population is, the more inhibited is the bureaucracy in its ability to act arbitrarily and without consideration of the individual. But the spill-over from political into administrative competence can be of two types. On the one hand, a highly politically competent citizenry may exert pressure upon bureaucrats to follow the administrative rules. Their adherence to the rules of administrative procedure will be enforced, not merely by their own internalization of these rules or by the controls exercised upon them by administrative higher-ups, but by the threat of political reprisal: protest by citizens through political agencies if the officials do not follow these rules. In this way a high degree of citizen competence raises the level of subject competence, but it does not change the relationship of the individual to the administration — he still comes as a subject, albeit a competent one, whose appeal is to the rules of bureaucracy.

The second type of spill-over of political competence into the relations between individuals and administration is one in which political influence (and here our technical use of the term coincides with the everyday, pejorative use of the word) is brought to bear upon administrative officials, not to compel them to follow the bureaucratic rules, but to compel them to make a particular decision in favor of a particular individual or group. Political influence acts directly to enforce individual demands, not indirectly to enforce bureaucratic rules. In this way political competence does not support and increase administrative competence; rather, it tends to convert it into political competence as well. The role of citizen overwhelms the role of subject.

The relationship between the two types of competence, we suggest, represents a significant aspect of the pattern of political orientation in a nation. Let us look first at the number of respondents in each nation who consider themselves competent in the political and administrative sense. As an indicator of those who consider themselves politically competent, we shall take the responses to the questions on whether the individual believes he can do something about an unjust act contemplated by the local or national government. Political competents are those who believe there is something they can

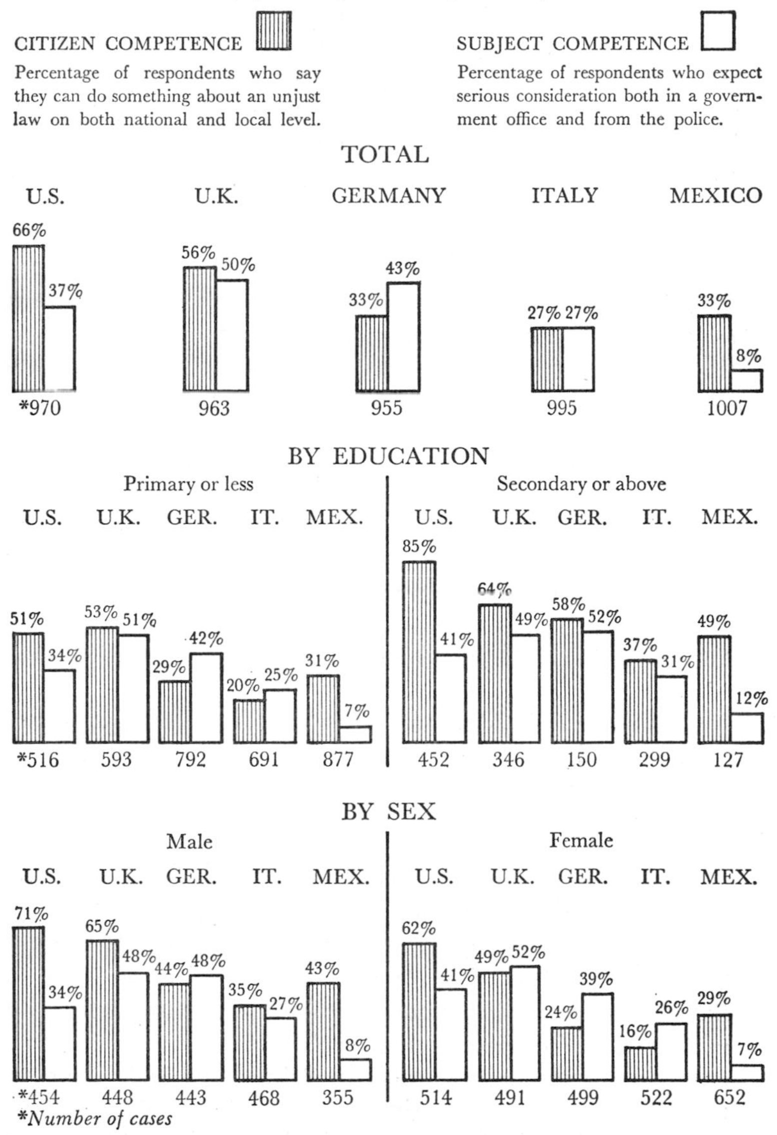
Citizen competence and subject competence
(By nation, education, and sex)
CITIZEN COMPETENCE
Percentage of respondents who say they can do something about an unjust law on both national and local level.
SUBJECT COMPETENCE
Percentage of respondents who expect serious consideration both in a government office and from the police.
TOTAL
U.S.
U.K.
GERMANY
ITALY
MEXICO
66%
37%
56%
50%
33%
43%
27%
27%
33%
8%
*970
963
955
995
1007
BY EDUCATION
Primary or less
Secondary or above
U.S.
U.K.
GER.
IT.
MEX.
U.S.
U.K.
GER.
IT.
MEX.
51%
34%
53%
51%
29%
42%
20%
25%
31%
7%
85%
41%
64%
49%
58%
52%
37%
31%
49%
12%
*516
593
792
691
877
452
346
150
299
127
BY SEX
Male
Female
U.S.
U.K.
GER.
IT.
MEX.
U.S.
U.K.
GER.
IT.
MEX.
71%
34%
65%
48%
44%
48%
35%
27%
43%
8%
62%
41%
49%
52%
24%
39%
16%
26%
29%
7%
*454
448
443
468
355
514
491
499
522
652
*Number of cases

FIGURE VII.1

do in relation to both levels of government. Administrative competents, on the other hand, expect serious consideration both from the police and in a governmental office.

Figure VII.1 reports the numbers of political and administrative competents in each nation. Some interesting differences emerge when one compares the nations in terms of the number of individuals who manifest these two types of subjective competence. In the United States the number of politically competent respondents is quite a bit greater than the number of administratively competent ones. Sixty-six per cent of the Americans believe they can exert some political influence over national and local government, whereas only 37 per cent expect serious consideration in the two administrative situations. In Britain on the other hand, there is relatively little difference between the proportions of political and administrative competents; though there are somewhat fewer administrative competents, both types are frequent. In Germany the relationship between the numbers of political and administrative competents is the reverse of that in the United States and Britain: administrative competents are more frequent than political competents. In Italy there are about as many political as administrative competents, but both types are relatively rare. And in Mexico, as in the United States, there are more political than administrative competents. However, both types of competents are less frequent in Mexico than in the United States, and the ratio of political to administrative competents is much greater: more than four times as many political competents as there are administrative competents.

This pattern of distribution of the two types of competence is generally apparent if we consider subgroups in the various nations — males and females and those with high and low education. In general, within all subgroups in the United States and Mexico the proportion of respondents who are politically competent is greater than the proportion who are administratively competent; the levels of both types of competence remain lower in Mexico. In Britain and Italy there are roughly equivalent proportions of political and administrative competents, but the frequency of both types is much lower in

Italy. And in Germany the frequency of administrative competents is greater than the frequency of political competents.

Another interesting point emerges from Figure VII.1. Among those respondents whom one would expect generally to be more competent there appears to be a heavier stress on political competence. Compare those who have secondary education or better with those respondents who have less education. As one would expect, those who have a higher level of education are more frequently competent in both the administrative and the political sense. But the increase in competence from the lower to the higher educational level is much more manifest in terms of political than administrative competence. In the United States, for instance, 35 per cent of respondents with primary education or less are administratively competent, in comparison with 41 per cent among those with secondary education or better — an increase in frequency of 7 percentage points. But 51 per cent of those with primary education or less are politically competent, in contrast with 85 per cent among those with higher educational attainment — an increase of 34 percentage points. The parallel increases between educational levels in Italy are 6 percentage points for administrative competence and 17 percentage points for political competence. And though in Germany there are generally more administrative than political competents, on the higher educational level there are somewhat more political competents.

A similar pattern emerges if one compares men and women. In every nation men are more likely than women to be politically competent, and in most cases the differences in frequency of this form of competence are quite striking. But the differences between the sexes in administrative competence are much smaller. In Mexico and Italy the differences in frequency of administrative competence are negligible, while in the United States and Britain women are somewhat more likely than men to consider themselves administratively competent.

The fact that female respondents and those respondents with lower education resemble male respondents and those with higher education much more in their administrative competence than in their political competence suggests that political competence in some way develops after administrative competence. As was suggested in Chapter I, the role of citizen develops on top of the role of subject. Those groups whose induction into full political participation has generally lagged — women and those with lower education — are more fully inducted into the role of competent subject than into that of competent citizen. Thus the distribution of the two types of competence probably reflects the historical process by which various groups have come to take part in politics. Within each of the five nations the subject role has been more generally assimilated than the citizen role. Citizen participation is a more selective and more slowly developing type of participation. It spreads from the more easily politicized to those more difficult to bring into political life.

These subgroup differences within the nations in the distribution of the two types of competence suggest an historical pattern of the spread of citizen and subject competence. A similar historical pattern is suggested if we compare the nations in these terms. Consider the United States and Britain first. Both nations stand high on our measures of political competence. British and American respondents most frequently say that they can do something about an unjust local regulation and about an unjust national law. Furthermore, as pointed out in Chapter VI, they most frequently suggest that they would form groups as a means of increasing their influence. There is one important difference between the two countries in their patterns of political strategy: informal groups are more frequently invoked as a means of influence in the United States; for though the British rank second in the frequency with which respondents mention such groups (34 per cent of them do), they mention them much less frequently than do American respondents (56 per cent of whom do). On the other hand, the British much more frequently manifest what we have called administrative competence. In the frequencies with which they expect serious consideration from government and police officials they rank first of all the five nations. The American respondents, on the other hand, are less likely to expect serious consideration from government and police officials than are British or German respondents, and more likely than either group to expect that their point of view will be ignored.

In Britain, then, a high level of political competence coexists with a high level of administrative competence. In the United States the former type of competence is more widespread than the latter. This difference between the two countries reflects the way in which the development of political institutions in each country has interacted with individuals' attitudes toward these institutions to produce a current state of competence. The development of political competence in Britain (a development that can be roughly equated with the spread of the franchise and the formation of interest groups and of political parties with roots in a mass electorate) came gradually and on top of a previously existing idea of an independent government and sovereign whose powers over individuals were limited by the rules of law. Englishmen had what we would call subject competence long before they were politically competent. They had an elaborate set of rights dating at least from the seventeenth century (their legally enforceable common law went back to the twelfth century). These legal rights were enforced, not by political means, but through the independent courts of law. For our purposes the important historical development is that the political rights acquired by Britons in the nineteenth century did not come into conflict with the idea of an independent governmental authority limited by some higher law. The notion of the independent authority of government under law has continued to exist side by side with the notion of the political power of the people. The old authoritarian institutions and symbols were not replaced by democratization, but continued to coexist with the new institutions. From the point of view of the individual, the political competence Britons received in the nineteenth century did not replace their competence as subjects under the rules of law. If anything, the growth of citizen competence raised the level of subject competence by adding a new force for the enforcement of the rules of law.[3]

[3] For a discussion of this development see Harry H. Eckstein, "The British Political System," in Samuel H. Beer and Adam B. Ulam (eds.), *Pat-*

In the United States, on the other hand, the development of political competence through the spread of the franchise, the growth of political parties, and the consequent induction of new groups into the political process has tended to conflict with Americans' subject competence. The idea of an independent governmental authority controlled by rules of law was affected by the spread of democratic participation. As popular political control over government increased, it clashed with the notion of independent government agencies that were controlled, not by popular political influence, but by a set of legal or administrative rules and norms. In the Jackson era, for instance, the franchise spread and new groups entered the political process. This increase in political democracy, however, was accompanied by a tendency for the administrative branches of the government to be subordinated to political considerations. Through the growth of the spoils system and the popular election of essentially administrative and judicial officers, popular influence over the governmental process came to mean political influence over the courts and administrative agencies. And throughout most of American political history, the spread of popular influence over the government has involved a diminution of the areas in which individuals stood in a subject relationship to the government. As new groups have been given political influence, this has meant control, not so much over legislative decisions through the right to elect representatives, as over the courts and bureaucracy through election, political pressure, and "pull." The traditional urban machine did not offer favorable social legislation to the new groups: it gave them influence over administrative decisions. The political machine offered favors in employment, "protection" by the police, aid before the courts or aid in becoming a citizen, and favors in the receipt of business. The sign that one had a voice in the affairs of government was not that the legislature was responding to one's needs through social legislation, but that one could have some trouble with the police "fixed." Thus as the American gained political

---

terns of Government, New York, 1958, pp. 57-74, and T. H. Marshall, *Citizenship and Social Class,* Cambridge, England, 1950, pp. 10-27.

competence, his role as subject declined; for political competence meant influence over just those institutions in relation to which one might expect the individual to stand as a subject.

Perhaps the major distinction between Britain and the United States in this aspect of their political histories turns on the existence of a revolutionary tradition in the United States. Whereas British political development has never involved the challenge of the existence of an independent governmental authority, the very founding of the American republic involved such a challenge. As Oscar and Mary Handlin have pointed out, the American colonists brought with them the European conception that government authority descended from the crown, but this view changed during the eighteenth century. "The marks of change were a growing habit of defiance or evasion of royal wishes, a steady loss of respect for the royal person and for the symbols of his majesty, and the disappearance of the charisma in which the throne had been enveloped. At the eve of the Revolution, the colonists could refer casually, without sense of *lèse-majesté,* to George III as a crowned ruffian. . . .

"By then Americans thought of authority, not as descending downward from the throne, but as derived from below from the choices of the people. The consent of the governed referred not to an abstract compact between ruler and governed, as in the long tradition of European political theory, but to a process by which the people delegated power to their governors." [4]

The contrast between British and American attitudes toward the police is especially relevant here. As the Handlins go on to state, Americans ". . . never acquired the respect for the cops that the English did for the Bobbies. The revolutionary experience persuaded the free citizens of the United States that a police force . . . was a threat to republican institutions." [5] Thus in the United States the revolutionary experience led to the view that there was no office that did not derive from the citizenry, hence no limit to the exercise of citizen competence. Though in Britain the competent citizen and the

[4] Oscar and Mary Handlin, *The Dimensions of Liberty,* Cambridge, Mass., 1961, p. 32.

[5] *Ibid.,* p. 39.

competent subject coexist, in the United States the competent citizen has tended to replace the competent subject.

If this is true, one would expect to find a closer relationship between political and administrative competence in the United States than in Britain. Britons' expectations of their ability to affect administrative decisions ought not to depend on the extent to which they consider themselves politically competent. In the United States, on the other hand, one would expect the individual who believes himself politically competent to generalize his political competence into administrative competence as well. That such a difference in the relationship between the two forms of competence does indeed exist is shown in Table VII.1. This table relates political to administrative competence. On all levels of political competence Britons are more administratively competent. In the United States the respondents with high subjective political competence (those who believe that both the national and local governments would be amenable to their influence) are more likely to expect serious consideration from the police and government than are respondents with intermediate political competence (those who believe that one level of government — usually the local — is amenable to their influence) and are much more likely to expect such consideration than are those low in political competence (those who believe neither level of government would be responsive). Forty-four per cent of those high in political competence express high administrative competence, in contrast with 31 per cent of the intermediates and 19 per cent of the lows. In Britain, on the other hand, the relationship between the two forms of competence is not as close. Fifty-three per cent of those high in political competence expect serious consideration in both administrative situations, in contrast with 50 per cent of those intermediate and 38 per cent of those low in political competence.

The sharpest contrast between the two nations in the relationship between the two types of competence is found among those on the higher educational level. In Britain the relative independence between the two forms of competence is most clearly seen among this group: 50 per cent of those with

TABLE VII.1 *Political and administrative competence;*[a] *by nation and education*

	Total						*Primary or less*						*Secondary or above*					
	Can influence local and national		*Can influence local or national*		*Can influence neither*		*Both*		*Either*		*Neither*		*Both*		*Either*		*Neither*	
Nation	(%)	(*No.*)[b]	(%)	(*No.*)	(%)	(*No.*)	(%)	(*No.*)	(%)	(*No.*)	(%)	(*No.*)	(%)	(*No.*)	(%)	(*No.*)	(%)	(*No.*)
United States	44	(644)	31	(179)	19	(145)	43	(262)	32	(128)	19	(126)	44	(382)	22	(51)	16	(19)
Great Britain	53	(534)	50	(245)	38	(160)	55	(312)	52	(168)	37	(108)	50	(222)	47	(77)	42	(47)
Germany	55	(314)	42	(314)	33	(314)	53	(227)	41	(270)	33	(295)	59	(87)	45	(44)	37	(19)
Italy	29	(250)	28	(277)	25	(463)	30	(133)	25	(185)	23	(368)	28	(112)	33	(92)	35	(95)
Mexico	8	(337)	9	(239)	6	(431)	7	(273)	9	(211)	5	(395)	10	(64)	12	(28)	16	(36)

[a] I.e., the proportion of respondents who expect consideration for their point of view in a government office and by the police, measured among three groups of respondents: those who believe they can influence both the national and local government; those who believe they can influence either the national or local government, and those who believe they can influence neither.

[b] Numbers in parentheses refer to the bases upon which percentages are calculated.

high political competence are high on administrative competence, in comparison with 42 per cent among those low in political competence. In the United States the close relationship between these two forms of competence is most apparent among those with higher education: 44 per cent of those with high political competence also manifest administrative competence, in contrast with 16 per cent of those low in political competence. These data suggest that there is indeed greater independence between the roles of citizen and subject in Britain than in the United States.

The pattern of political and administrative competence in Germany contrasts sharply with that of the United States. Germany seems to be a nation in which the subject orientation is relatively frequent, as against the citizen orientation. Consider the treatment Germans expect in government offices or from the police. In both cases, they (after the British) most frequently expect serious consideration for their point of view. In contrast to this is their response to unjust legislative activity. In connection with an unjust local regulation, they rank third in the frequency with which individuals feel they can do something to redress such an act; in connection with an unjust national law, they rank fourth — slightly below the Mexicans. As Figure VII.1 indicated, it is only in Germany that more respondents could be described as administrative competents rather than political competents. However, that pattern appears to apply especially to those Germans of lower educational attainment. Just as important as the number who say they can influence an unjust law are the strategies they report. Relatively few would attempt to form groups for these purposes, and German respondents frequently talk of contacting administrative officials.

This pattern of competence seems to reflect the political history of Germany. Subject competence grew, as in Britain, before citizen competence. But whereas the development of political democracy in Britain has had a long history and has added a significant degree of citizen competence to subject competence, political democracy has had a far less orderly and successful development in Germany. While in the nineteenth century the British middle class, followed by the working class, was demanding and receiving political influence over the government, the German middle class accepted the law and the order of the German *Rechtsstaat,* under which it might prosper but have no political influence. Power over governmental decisions was left in the hands of competent governmental officials; it was not distributed among the populace. But though the German was not a competent citizen, he remained a competent subject. His rights under the law were clearly defined and carefully protected by a system of courts and administration free from political influences. In contrast with Britain, then, the belief in one's political competence has not taken a firm root among the population. If in the United States the competent citizen tends to replace the competent subject, and if in Britain the two tend to coexist in harmony, in Germany the competent subject remains the dominant form of competence.[6]

If our above description is correct, then our data would seem to indicate the Italian citizens experience neither *Rechtsstaat* nor effective democracy. In subject competence the Italians rank fourth, well below the United Kingdom, the United States, and Germany. Only about one in three expects serious consideration from the government or the police. On our measures of political competence the Italians rank last in the frequency with which respondents say that they can influence an unjust local or national regulation. And among the Italian local competents the strategies suggested reveal little political competence. Very few mention the possibility of forming groups. And one out of four of those who say they can do something about a local law they feel is unjust say that they can "protest" and that is all. Citizenship competence and subject competence seem equally retarded.

[6] But if in Germany the subject role is dominant and the role of citizen has not yet been completely assimilated, there does tend to be a relationship between these two roles — a relationship somewhat stronger than that in Britain but not as strong as that in the United States. Fifty-five per cent of those Germans high on political competence are also high on our measure of administrative competence, in contrast with 42 per cent of those who are intermediate on political competence and 33 per cent who are low on this measure.

This pattern, too, is what one might expect in a nation with the political history of Italy. Before unification, Italy had experienced centuries of external tyranny by a variety of powers under whom Italians had neither political nor effective legal rights — they were competent neither as citizens nor as subjects. From such a history one would expect the development of neither citizen nor subject competence. One would expect, rather, as H. R. Spencer argues, that Italians would look upon government, not as a social institution amenable to their influence, but as a natural force — often catastrophic, like an earthquake — to be endured. "This tendency to acquiescence and submissiveness, this feeling of the individual's insignificance, this feeling that the affairs of men are governed by forces that may be endured but not swerved from their movement or organized for man's use, only taken advantage of, furtively and sporadically — is a natural conclusion for men of intelligence who are not men of political tradition." [7] The current political culture of Italy may be inappropriate for a healthy, functioning democracy. It can be understood in the light of Italian political history.

Lastly, let us consider the pattern of subject and citizen competence in Mexico. In the frequency with which they would expect serious consideration from government officials or the police the Mexicans rank clearly the lowest. The figures, when compared with those of any of the other countries, are quite striking. On political competence, however, the data are not so bleak. As to the percentage who think they can do something about an unjust regulation on the local level, the Mexicans rank slightly above the Italians; and more frequently than either the Italians or the Germans they report they can do something about an unjust national law. More important is the fact that their strategy of influence manifests some incipient political competence. The use of informal groups, for instance, is frequently mentioned.

The Mexican pattern is significant. Political competence, we have been arguing, is harder to acquire than subject competence; historically it has tended to develop later and to spread

[7] H. R. Spencer, *Government and Politics of Italy*, Yonkers, New York, 1932, p. 17.

from the more politically "advantaged" groups in a society to the less advantaged. But in Mexico we seem to have the reverse situation. The explanation probably lies, once again, in the revolutionary political culture of Mexico. The Mexican pattern of more widespread political than administrative competence is paralleled only in the United States, the other nation whose political formation has represented, as has the Mexican Revolution, a rejection of traditional authority. The Mexican Revolution meant a sudden induction of individuals into the political system. Attention was turned to the national government as the vehicle of change and to the national heroes who guided the destiny of the country. Individuals did develop a subjective sense of political competence, but it was not a competence based on experience. As we have shown, the cooperative competence found in Mexico is not based on much actual group experience, and only 9 per cent of the Mexicans who believe they can influence the local government report some experience along these lines (in contrast with 33 per cent in the United States and 18 per cent in Britain). The Mexican Revolution created political competence, but it was an aspirational or mythic sense of competence. Furthermore, the Revolution took place in a society where the institution of an independent, rational bureaucracy had not taken root; local bureaucracy was the tool of the traditional political powers. Nor did the Revolution change this fundamentally. Bureaucracy remained subordinate to political forces and today is still an arena of political struggle. Thus subject competence never developed in Mexico. In contrast to Germans, Mexicans have started to become competent citizens before they are competent subjects.

CHAPTER VIII

Competence, Participation, and Political Allegiance

IN EARLIER CHAPTERS we have shown that the frequency of various types of political attitudes and behavior differs from nation to nation. In this chapter we consider probably the most significant and certainly the most difficult question raised by the data thus far presented: how do political competence and participation affect a political system?

Though citizen competence and participation are at the heart of the definition of democracy, the problems faced by democratic governments would be much simpler if their only concern were to achieve maximum competence and participation. In fact, however, the political system that attempted to achieve that goal at the expense of all others would not long survive. Political systems, if they are to survive, must also be relatively effective and relatively legitimate; that is, what the government accomplishes must be at least satisfying enough to the citizens so that they do not turn against the government; and the system, if it is to have a long-run potential of survival, must be generally accepted by citizens as the proper form of government.

These statements about political stability are so general as to be truistic. But they focus our attention on those aspects of a political system which are most crucially affected by political competence and participation. Political competence and participation will influence a system's effectiveness as well as its legitimacy, and it is this influence that we shall attempt to explore.

Our data enable us to explore this relationship only partially. The question we ask is not what happens to the political system in which there is participation in decisions, but what happens to the individual who believes himself competent to participate in decisions. As we pointed out earlier, our respondents differ in the extent to which they believe they can participate in political decisions: in what we have called their subjective competence as citizens. What, we may ask, goes along with this subjective political competence? Aside from his sense of ability to participate, in what way does the subjectively competent individual differ from someone who does not feel that the affairs of politics and government are amenable to his influence? This is clearly not the same as asking how a participatory political system will differ from one that involves less participation, but it is closely related to it. We want to know what set of political orientations is likely to be found among a citizenry that considers itself capable of participating in governmental decisions. And those orientations — whether they involve belief in either the effectiveness or ineffectiveness of the system, whether they involve allegiance to or rejection of the system — will have implications for the stability of that system.

To facilitate this analysis of the way in which subjective political competence affects other attitudes, a scale was devised to rate respondents on the extent to which they believe themselves competent in their relations with the government. The scale is based on their responses to five questions dealing with local government. We asked whether the respondent believed he could understand local politics; whether he felt he could and would act to influence the local government; whether he had any expectations of success in influencing the local government, and whether he had ever attempted such influence.

The scale allows us to group our respondents into one of six categories, ranging from a high score of five, for those with the highest degree of subjective competence, to a low score of zero, for those who expressed the least subjective competence. The total distribution of scores on the scale for the five nations is what one would have expected from our earlier discussion of the distribution of political attitudes. The United States and Britain have the highest proportions of high scorers. Sixty-five per cent of the respondents in the former country are in the upper three categories of the scale and 62 per cent in the latter. Germany comes next with 46 per cent in the upper categories, followed by Italy with 40 per cent and Mexico with 38 per cent.

How does the self-confident citizen differ from the individual who considers himself relatively powerless? Respondents can be grouped into those with *high* subjective political competence (those who receive a score of four or five on the subjective competence scale), those with *medium* competence (scoring two or three on the scale) and those with *low* competence (scoring zero or one on the scale). Is the subjectively competent citizen more active in politics; is he more likely to think that politics benefits him; is he more likely to be in some way affectively attached to his political system? How, in short, does the man who considers himself a political participant differ in his political attitudes from the individual who does not consider himself competent?

Sense of Competence and Political Activity. The first and most obvious question that one may ask about the subjectively competent citizen is whether he is likely to be the more active citizen. This is what one would expect, and the data suggest that it is strongly the case. The more subjectively competent an individual considers himself, the more likely he is to be politically active.

Table VIII.1 shows that those high on the scale of subjective competence are more likely to expose themselves to political communications. For instance, among Mexicans with no education or only primary-school education, 34 per cent of those high in subjective competence report that they follow politics and electoral campaigns regularly, in contrast with 8 per cent of those low on subjective competence. Or, to select an educational group that follows politics quite frequently: among the Germans with secondary education or better, 77

TABLE VIII.1 *Percentage who report high exposure to political communications*[a] *among three groups of subjective competents; by nation and education*

	Total						Primary or less						Secondary or more					
	High[b]		*Med.*		*Low*		*High*		*Med.*		*Low*		*High*		*Med.*		*Low*	
Nation	(%)	(*No.*)[c]	(%)	(*No.*)	(%)	(*No.*)	(%)	(*No.*)	(%)	(*No.*)	(%)	(*No.*)	(%)	(*No.*)	(%)	(*No.*)	(%)	(*No.*)
United States	59	(506)	46	(251)	21	(212)	51	(205)	40	(146)	15	(165)	65	(301)	54	(105)	40	(47)
Great Britain	36	(366)	33	(364)	16	(230)	29	(209)	29	(219)	13	(164)	44	(147)	40	(138)	22	(59)
Germany	57	(305)	51	(279)	23	(368)	51	(230)	49	(227)	21	(334)	77	(73)	56	(50)	50	(24)
Italy	26	(243)	25	(234)	5	(514)	13	(149)	14	(138)	3	(402)	46	(93)	41	(94)	12	(111)
Mexico	39	(201)	19	(332)	9	(474)	34	(153)	16	(287)	3	(436)	54	(47)	34	(45)	15	(35)

[a] "High" exposure to politics means that respondent reports that he follows politics regularly in the mass media and that he pays attention to election campaigns.

[b] Level of Subjective Competence.

[c] Numbers in parentheses refer to the bases upon which percentages are calculated.

per cent of those of high subjective competence report that they follow politics regularly; in contrast, of those on the same educational level whose sense of subjective competence is lower, 50 per cent report following politics regularly. This pattern is noticeable in each nation.

The self-confident citizen is not only more likely to be the recipient of political communications: he is also more likely to take some part in the political communications process himself. In all five nations those respondents high on the subjective competence scale are more likely than those lower on the scale to engage in political discussion. This relationship applies to groups where such discussion is relatively rare. Italians with primary education or less are an example: 14 per cent of those low in subjective competence discuss politics, in contrast with 36 per cent high on this measure. It applies as well to groups where discussion is carried on more frequently. An example would be American respondents in the higher educational categories, among whom 64 per cent of those low in subjective competence discuss politics, as compared with 92 per cent of the highly subjectively competent citizens. Thus the self-confident citizen is more likely to be aware of what is going on in politics and to make his voice heard in political discussion.

Somewhat similar results are apparent in regard to partisan affiliation. Compared with those low in subjective competence, respondents higher on the scale are more likely to be party activists (either members of some political party or active campaign workers) and somewhat less likely to report no partisan affiliation. The relationship between partisan activity and sense of competence, however, is not as close as that between the measures of nonpartisan activity and sense of competence. Thus subjective competence has a definite effect upon the level and the kind of political activity within a society.

That the subjectively competent citizen is also likely to be the active citizen is not an unexpected finding. It is but the beginning of our inquiry into the implications of subjective competence. Of greater significance in understanding political participation is the relationship between sense of ability to participate and the individual's allegiance to the system as reflected in his evaluation of the legitimacy and effectiveness of the system. One of the advantages a democratic political system is supposed to have over other systems is that those who are able to participate in decisions will thereby be more satisfied with the decisions, and will be more attached to the system than are those who cannot participate. According to this hypothesis, a mutually beneficial exchange occurs between the individual and the political system. In response to his influential inputs, the system produces outputs that are in some way more beneficial for the individual than they would be without those inputs. The beneficial outputs, in turn, lead the individual, through his satisfaction with the system, to a higher level of attachment to that system. In this way, if all else is equal, democratic political systems will be, from the point of view of the participants, both more effective (participants will be more satisfied with the output of the system) and more legitimate (participants will generally consider the political system to be the proper one per se).

With our data we can test the psychological form of this hypothesis. We cannot test the hypothesis that the more individuals participate in decisions, the more likely they are to receive beneficial outputs from the system in which they participate. As has been pointed out, measuring this kind of participation involves a much more complicated analysis of citizen-elite interaction than is possible in our study; and the techniques available for measuring the performance of systems are quite crude. We can, however, test the hypothesis that the perception that one can participate is related to great satisfaction with the performance of the system and to a higher level of attachment to that system. And this psychological form of the participation hypothesis is significant for the democratic political system. It seems likely that the combination of high participation and high system performance will increase the chances of stable democracy only if both the high participation and the high system performance are perceived as such by the citizenry. If a citizenry does not consider the outputs of the system as beneficial, it is hard to see how participation can have any effect on system stability. Thus in testing the psychological form of the participation hypothesis — i.e., the relationship between participation and satisfaction with the political system — we are testing a crucial form of the hypothesis.

Satisfaction with the political system can take several forms. We have been dealing with three types of orientation to the political system: (1) to the structure of political influence (the input structure), (2) to the structure of governmental output (the output structure), and (3) a more general, diffuse orientation to the political system as a whole. If one wants to relate satisfaction to the sense of competence to participate, it is useful to look at these three orientations. In the first place, the perceived ability to participate in decisions ought to be associated with greater satisfaction with an individual's role within the political input structure; that is, the more he thinks he has influence over the government, the more he ought to be satisfied with his role as participant. Second, one would expect that the individual who considers himself capable of affecting decisions, compared with the one who believes he has no voice, would be more likely to consider the output of those decisions favorable to him. Thus the subjective competent ought to be more positively oriented to his input role as well as to the output of the political system. But the effect of subjective competence upon his more general orientation to the system as a whole may be the most crucial issue in the relationship between participation and the potential for stability of a system. Satisfaction with governmental output may lead an individual to support his political system, and high levels of such satisfaction are therefore likely to foster political stability. For long-run stability, on the other hand, a more diffuse sense of attachment — one that is less closely tied to performance — may be more significant. Satisfaction with political output usually varies with system performance. The more diffuse sense of attachment to the system (or what we have called system affect), though in the long run not unrelated to specific output, can be expected to be a more stable kind of satisfaction. It is the kind of "rain or shine" attachment that will enable a system to weather a crisis in its performance.

Table VIII.2 presents data on the relationship between the sense of ability to participate in politics and the satisfaction with the role of participant. To measure their satisfac-

TABLE VIII.2 *Percentage who report satisfaction with their voting participation, among three groups of subjective competents; by nation and education*

	Total						*Primary or less*						*Secondary or more*					
	High[a]		*Med.*		*Low*		*High*		*Med.*		*Low*		*High*		*Med.*		*Low*	
Nation	(%)	*(No.)*[b]	(%)	*(No.)*	(%)	*(No.)*	(%)	*(No.)*	(%)	*(No.)*	(%)	*(No.)*	(%)	*(No.)*	(%)	*(No.)*	(%)	*(No.)*
United States	78	(400)	72	(183)	44	(109)	68	(164)	67	(111)	42	(85)	84	(237)	79	(72)	50	(24)
Great Britain	51	(330)	43	(330)	30	(198)	49	(195)	43	(205)	30	(149)	54	(126)	45	(119)	30	(44)
Germany	42	(284)	38	(251)	26	(332)	42	(219)	41	(208)	25	(303)	43	(63)	24	(41)	37	(19)
Italy	40	(225)	35	(218)	21	(476)	38	(145)	33	(135)	21	(385)	45	(80)	40	(81)	21	(90)
Mexico	50	(161)	32	(233)	26	(258)	50	(123)	30	(197)	25	(236)	51	(38)	38	(36)	34	(22)

[a] Level of subjective competence.

[b] Numbers in parentheses refer to the bases upon which percentages are calculated.

tion with participation in the political process, we asked respondents how they felt when they went to the polls to vote: did they have a feeling of satisfaction? a feeling that they were voting merely as a duty? did they feel annoyed at the effort it took to vote? or did they feel nothing in particular? As Table VIII.2 indicates, those voters higher in subjective competence are more likely to report a feeling of satisfaction with their vote. For instance, 26 per cent of the Mexican voters who are low in their sense of competence report satisfaction with their vote, whereas 50 per cent of those high in subjective competence report satisfaction. And this general pattern is found in all groups. Furthermore, fewer voters on the higher levels of subjective competence report that they feel nothing in particular or that they do not know what they feel at the polls. The self-confident citizen, this table suggests, is also the citizen who is most likely to derive satisfaction from his participation. In all nations subjective competents are more likely than others to find their role in the input structure a satisfying one.

Satisfaction with one's political role, however, is not the only satisfaction that might be related to the sense of ability to participate. One would also expect that the individual who believes himself capable of participating in decisions would be more likely to be satisfied with the outcome of those decisions. Table VIII.3 indicates that this is generally the case. As an indicator of satisfaction with governmental output, we have taken a question on whether the activities of the local government tend to improve conditions in the area.[1] Thus we are comparing the individual's sense of competence vis-à-vis the local government with his evaluation of the output of the local government. In general, as Table VIII.3 indicates, the more subjectively competent an individual feels, the more likely he is to report that the output of the local government tends to improve conditions in his area. Among Italian respondents with low levels of subjective competence, 63 per cent believe

[1] For the purposes of this analysis, we consider only those respondents who on a previous question indicated that the activities of the local government had an impact on their lives. Further discussion of this question can be found in Chapter III.

TABLE VIII.3 *Percentage who report belief in the beneficial effect of local government activities, among three groups of subjective competents;*[a] *by nation and education*

	Total						*Primary or less*						*Secondary or more*					
	High[b]		*Med.*		*Low*		*High*		*Med.*		*Low*		*High*		*Med.*		*Low*	
Nation	(%)	*(No.)*[c]	(%)	*(No.)*	(%)	*(No.)*	(%)	*(No.)*	(%)	*(No.)*	(%)	*(No.)*	(%)	*(No.)*	(%)	*(No.)*	(%)	*(No.)*
United States	76	(471)	72	(223)	57	(155)	73	(177)	67	(124)	58	(119)	78	(294)	78	(99)	53	(36)
Great Britain	74	(296)	68	(282)	63	(130)	74	(166)	67	(165)	64	(95)	75	(120)	68	(110)	61	(31)
Germany	75	(244)	61	(225)	62	(233)	72	(181)	62	(181)	61	(211)	84	(62)	57	(42)	76	(17)
Italy	75	(175)	69	(155)	63	(240)	72	(99)	67	(90)	62	(173)	79	(75)	72	(64)	66	(67)
Mexico	46	(79)	52	(109)	44	(122)	38	(61)	45	(91)	41	(112)	71	(17)	79	(18)	[71	(10)]

[a] But only among those respondents who on a previous question indicated that the local government had an impact on their lives.

[b] Level of subjective competence.

[c] Numbers in parentheses refer to the bases upon which percentages are calculated.

that the local government tends to improve things in the area, in contrast with 75 per cent of those high in subjective competence. The proportions of British respondents who attribute this beneficial impact to the local government are 63 per cent among those low on local competence and 74 per cent among those high on such competence. And the same pattern is found in the United States and Germany — those low on the subjective competence scale are less likely to say that the local government improves local conditions than are those high on the scale. When the level of subjective competence is held constant, the similarity among these four nations in the frequency with which local government activities are positively evaluated is quite striking.

The results for Mexico, however, form a sharp contrast to those in the other four nations. Here the sense of ability to participate is apparently unrelated to an individual's evaluation of the output of the government. Moving up the scale of subjective competence, one does not find an increasing proportion of respondents who express the belief that the activities of the local government tend to improve conditions in the area. Whereas in all the other nations the individual who believes himself to be capable of participating in decisions is more likely to evaluate the governmental output positively, the Mexican who considers himself competent to participate does not differ from others in his evaluation of the government's output. In regard to the degree of activity of citizens and their satisfaction with their participatory roles, the subjective competence scale produced a close relationship in all five nations. In regard to the evaluation of governmental output, we now find a break in the uniform pattern. In Mexico the competent citizen is not more likely to evaluate actual government performance positively. Before discussing this deviation from the pattern, let us look at the relationship between subjective competence and system affect.

The attitude most relevant to long-term political stability may not be the individual's level of satisfaction with governmental output or with his role as participant. Rather, long-run political stability may be more dependent on a more diffuse sense of attachment or loyalty to the political system — a loyalty not based specifically on system performance. The question that can be raised is: does the ability to participate within the political system lead to this kind of attachment? In contrast with, say, the individual's evaluation of system output, the more diffuse sense of attachment to the political system is somewhat hard to measure. To measure system affect we shall use our question on what the individual is proud of about his country; in particular, we shall use the frequency with which individuals report pride in some aspect of their political or governmental system. The advantage of using this question is that references to the political system are spontaneous. (For a fuller discussion of the response to this question, see Chapter III.)

The relationship between subjective competence and pride in one's political system is reported in Table VIII.4. The most interesting point about this relationship is the difference between the United States, Britain, and Mexico, on the one hand, and Germany and Italy, on the other. In the United States, Britain, and Mexico those who consider themselves competent to participate in governmental decisions are more likely than those who do not feel this way to express pride in the political aspects of their nation. In Britain, for example, 50 per cent of those high in subjective competence indicate pride in their political system, as compared to 36 per cent of those low in subjective competence. And this generally applies to both levels of education. Furthermore, those on the high level of subjective competence are less likely than those below to say either that they are proud of nothing about their nation (a rather overt statement of alienation) or that they do not know if they are proud of anything or of what they are proud.

In Germany and Italy the pattern is quite different. There is apparently little relationship between one's sense of political competence and the likelihood that one will express pride in the political system. High scorers on the subjective competence scale are not more likely to say that they are proud of a political aspect of their nation than are low scorers on the scale. Furthermore, although the "high" competents are less likely than the "low" competents to say that they do not know what they are proud of as Italians or Germans, they are each as likely to give the rather extreme alienative response that they are proud of "nothing." In both countries the sense of political competence is related strongly to satisfaction with one's role as participant and to satisfaction with the specific output of the government. Unlike the situation in Britain, Mexico, and the United States, however, it does not appear to be related to more general system affect. Yet there is one difference between Italy and Germany in this respect. In Italy the lack of relationship between sense of competence and system affect is found on both educational levels. In Germany, on the other hand, this lack of relationship appears confined to those with no more than primary school education.

The data in Tables VIII.3, VIII.4, and VIII.5 suggest that there is much validity to the hypothesis that the degree of participation in decisions affects the degree of satisfaction with the system in which one participates. In general, satisfaction increases with participation. In the United States and Britain the relationship between satisfaction and a sense of participation is found on all three measures of satisfaction; in the other three nations the relationship is found on two of the three measures. In this respect, the democratic government that fosters a sense of ability to participate in decisions does appear to reap the benefit of this participation.

But the data do not unambiguously confirm the participation hypothesis. Rather, they suggest that the impact of an individual's sense of competence on his sense of satisfaction with and attachment to the political system may differ somewhat from nation to nation. In all five nations the citizen with a strong sense of ability to participate is more satisfied with his role as participant than is the citizen whose sense of ability is weaker. On the other hand, a positive relationship between sense of participation and satisfaction with the performance of the government is found in only four out of five nations. In Mexico the sense of competence is not related to output satisfaction. And the relationship between system affect and the sense of ability to participate is apparent in only three out

TABLE VIII.4 *Pride in nation among three groups of subjective competents; by nation and education*

TOTAL

What respondents are proud of about their country	*United States*			*Great Britain*			*Germany*			*Italy*			*Mexico*		
	High[a]	*Med.*	*Low*	*High*	*Med.*	*Low*	*High*	*Med.*	*Low*	*High*	*Med.*	*Low*	*High*	*Med.*	*Low*
Governmental and political system	92	87	67	50	49	36	9	5	6	3	8	2	38	31	26
Other aspects[b]	7	12	20	46	44	43	81	85	70	80	76	61	60	60	48
Nothing	0	0	4	2	4	8	5	3	9	8	4	11	0	2	5
Don't know	0	0	9	3	4	13	5	6	15	9	12	26	2	7	21
Total percentage	99	99	100	101	101	100	100	99	100	100	100	100	100	100	100
Total number of respondents	506	251	212	366	364	230	305	279	368	243	234	514	201	332	474

PRIMARY OR LESS

What respondents are proud of about their country	*United States*			*Great Britain*			*Germany*			*Italy*			*Mexico*		
	High[a]	*Med.*	*Low*	*High*	*Med.*	*Low*	*High*	*Med.*	*Low*	*High*	*Med.*	*Low*	*High*	*Med.*	*Low*
Governmental and political system	87	86	64	47	44	34	8	5	7	3	4	2	35	30	25
Other aspects[b]	11	12	21	47	47	44	82	85	69	77	72	56	63	60	48
Nothing	1	0	5	1	5	9	6	4	10	10	5	11	0	3	4
Don't know	1	1	10	4	5	13	5	7	15	10	19	31	2	8	23
Total percentage	100	99	100	99	101	100	101	101	101	100	100	100	100	101	100
Total number of respondents	205	146	165	209	219	164	230	227	334	149	138	402	153	287	436

SECONDARY OR MORE

What respondents are proud of about their country	*United States*			*Great Britain*			*Germany*			*Italy*			*Mexico*		
	High[a]	*Med.*	*Low*	*High*	*Med.*	*Low*	*High*	*Med.*	*Low*	*High*	*Med.*	*Low*	*High*	*Med.*	*Low*
Governmental and political system	95	90	74	52	56	42	12	8	0	3	12	2	49	38	37
Other aspects[b]	4	10	15	44	40	41	79	88	96	85	83	80	51	59	50
Nothing	0	0	4	2	2	5	3	0	0	4	2	8	0	1	5
Don't know	0	0	6	2	2	12	5	4	4	8	3	10	0	1	8
Total percentage	99	100	99	100	100	100	99	100	100	99	100	100	100	99	100
Total number of respondents	301	105	47	147	138	59	73	50	24	93	94	111	47	45	35

[a] Level of subjective competence.

[b] "Other aspects" refers to those respondents who were proud of some aspects other than the political system. Respondents who report pride in the political system as well as something else are in the top row.

of five of the nations. In Germany and Italy participation does not appear to lead to more frequent positive evaluation of the system as a whole.

These differences in the types of satisfaction associated with participation have important implications. As was reported and discussed in Chapter III, German and Italian respondents report least frequently that they are proud of the political aspects of their nations. Expressions of pride are directed at other national objects, but not at the political system, which is readily understandable in view of the recent political histories of these two nations. The present systems of government are rather new and, to some extent, have been externally imposed. In contrast with the United States and Britain — and even in contrast with Mexico, whose government has undergone a rather gradual evolution for the past forty years or so since the Mexican Revolution — politics in Germany and Italy have shown sharp discontinuities.

But the absolute *level* of expression of national pride is not in question here. Granting the differences in absolute level, we are searching for the *relationship* between sense of participation and the expression of national pride. And here the important point emerges that, whereas in the other three nations the sense of ability to participate in political decisions seems to be translated to some degree into general pride in the political system, little of this process is apparent in Germany and Italy. In these two nations even the individual who considers himself highly capable of influencing the government is no more likely to express pride in the political aspects of his nation than is the individual who feels no such sense of competence; and the self-confident citizen is as likely as the other citizen to express alienation from his nation. In the United States, Britain, and Mexico the sense of ability to participate appears to yield a general attachment to the political system. In Germany and Italy, though there is some opportunity to participate and though there are respondents who consider themselves competent to do so, this participation has not led to a greater sense of identification with the political system. Thus the positive relationship between subjective competence and system affect found among Germans with secondary education or better becomes important. It suggests that the ability to participate is beginning to be translated into attachment to the political system among those who have attained some higher educational level. In Italy, on the other hand, the gap between participation and system affect is wider.

As the data for Germany and Italy suggest, any positive attachment to the political system that derives from participation in that system tends to be rather pragmatic. The citizen who believes himself capable of participation, compared with the one who holds no such belief, does tend to be more satisfied with his political system, but it is satisfaction with the specific performance of the system. If our hypothesis about the significance of system affect for the long-run success of a political system is correct, it would appear that the sense of ability to participate within governmental decision making — an attitude that has developed in Germany and Italy since the formation of democratic governments — will foster the stability of those democratic systems as long as the performance of the system is kept at a high level. If the performance of the system lags, the fact that some Italians and Germans consider themselves capable of participating within it might add little to the chances of survival of democracy in these two nations.

The relationship between satisfaction and sense of participation in Mexico differs significantly from that found in Germany and Italy. In Mexico, as in all the other nations, subjective competence is positively related to satisfaction with one's role as participant. Furthermore, in Mexico, as in the United States and Britain (but unlike the pattern in Germany and Italy), the sense of political competence is related to general system affect. In Mexico, however, unlike the other four nations, there is no apparent relationship between sense of competence and satisfaction with the specific performance of the political system.

We cannot be sure why the pattern of Mexican responses should deviate from the participation hypothesis in this way, but the parallel between this finding and some earlier data suggests an explanation. In Mexico the sense of competence is related to general system affect, but not to a more favorable view of the actual performance of the system. This may be the pattern one would expect to find associated with a revolutionary or aspirational orientation to politics. Interest and involvement in politics, we have suggested, did not develop gradually among the Mexican people. Instead, the ordinary citizen's awareness of politics and, indeed, of his membership in a nation probably derived from the dramatic upheavals of the Mexican Revolution. Participation in politics did not spread gradually through the nation, nor was the first experience with political participation related to some specific issue.[2] Rather, the first sense of participation was in a heavily affective-laden nationalistic uprising. And the symbolic importance of the Revolution in Mexican politics has persisted to the present day. Participation, then, is not closely related to the day-to-day operations of the Mexican government; indeed, a highly active sense of participation and patriotism coexists with a low evaluation of actual government performance. Participation exists on an aspirational level. The Mexican with a strong sense of participation is positively oriented to his nation as symbol and to his political system on the more general level. He does not expect any better performance from the actual government.

The most thoroughgoing relationship between sense of ability to participate and satisfaction with the political system exists in the United States and Britain. The subjective competents are more likely to express satisfaction with their roles as participants and with the specific performance of the system; and they are also more likely to express general pride in the political system. In Britain and the United States one finds neither the gap between sense of participation and general attachment to the system apparent in Italy and Germany, nor the gap between sense of participation and satisfaction with the system performance apparent in Mexico. Participation is neither on the unreal aspirational level, as in

[2] For an example of the way in which mobilization into politics may develop gradually, through the spread of the franchise and (what may not be the same) of voting from 'central" to more "peripheral" segments of society, see Stein Rokkan, "Trends in Political Mobilization" (a paper prepared for a UNESCO Conference on Comparative Political Behavior, Bergen, Norway, June 1961, mimeographed).

Mexico, nor on the pragmatic level, as in Italy and Germany. Rather, it involves a more positive orientation to the state on the most general level, as well as more positive specific expectations of system performance.

Here then is striking evidence for the existence of a "balanced" democratic political orientation in the United States and Britain. Participation in politics in these two nations is linked with both affective orientation to the political system and specific pragmatic expectations of the system. One has neither political participation that is related only to specific system performance nor political participation related to the political system on the symbolic level but not to actual politics.

COMPETENCE AND DEMOCRATIC VALUES

If our data in the previous section are correct, democratic systems do have some of the advantages imputed to them. At least from the point of view of the individual participant, the opportunity to participate in political decisions is associated with greater satisfaction with that system and with greater general loyalty to the system. (This conclusion, though, requires all the qualifications introduced in the previous section.) Everything being equal, the sense of ability to participate in politics appears to increase the legitimacy of a system and to lead to political stability.[3]

If, in addition to being satisfied with their political system, subjective competents believe that a participatory system is the proper system to have, then the potential stability of a democratic system has been increased even more. If those who consider themselves more competent to participate also value the participation of their fellow citizens more highly — believe in electoral democracy, believe that the ordinary man ought to be a participant — then participation within politics will increase the democratic potential of a nation by increasing the citizens' commitment to democratic values.

[3] This point needs some qualification. High levels of participation may have unstabilizing effects on a system. But the *sense* of competence, especially when coupled with a somewhat lower actual fulfillment of this competence, does play an important role in political stability. See Chapter XIII below for a further discussion of this point.

Our data suggest that this is the case. Those who consider themselves competent to participate are also more likely to believe that a democratic participatory system is the proper system to have. In each nation those respondents higher on the subjective competence scale are more likely than those below to report that election compaigning is a good thing.[4] In Mexico, for instance, 71 per cent of the respondents high on the scale report that election campaigns are needed, whereas 52 per cent of those low on the scale hold this view.

That subjective competence seems to be related to adherence to formal democratic rules is shown perhaps more clearly by the relationship between sense of political competence and the frequency with which respondents report that the average man has an obligation to be an active participant in his local community. As reported in Chapter VI, there are national differences in the frequency with which respondents report that the citizen ought to participate in the affairs of his community. Despite these differences in evaluation, in all nations those who consider themselves most competent to participate are also most likely to believe that the ordinary man has an obligation to be a participating citizen. The relationship is quite close between the belief in one's own participatory capabilities and the norm that people ought to participate, and it is found both where adherence to the norm is widespread (e.g., America) and where it is less frequent (e.g., Italy). Among American respondents who most frequently report that the individual has an obligation to be a participant in his community, 61 per cent of those high on subjective competence report that the ordinary man has such an obligation, in contrast with 23 per cent of those low on the subjective competence scale. Of those Italians who are high in subjective competence, 19 per cent report that the individual has an obligation to be active in his local community, in contrast with 4

[4] The question was phrased so as to make it easy for those who were opposed to electoral campaigns to express their opposition. It read: "Some people feel that campaigning is needed so that the public can judge candidates and issues. Others say it causes so much bitterness and is so unreliable that we would be better off without it. What do you think — is it needed or would we be better off without it?"

per cent of those low in subjective competence. In general, then, the individual who feels competent to participate is also more likely to place a high value on participation by the ordinary man.

THE SELF-CONFIDENT CITIZEN: CONCLUSION

The citizen, as he has been defined in this study, is the man able to take some part in the running of his political system. He has influence over the decisions that are made in it. Throughout this study we have stressed the importance of the extent to which individuals consider themselves to be citizens in this sense. The frequency with which they rate themselves competent to participate in their political system may be taken as an index of the extent to which they consider their nations democratic. Since these individuals may be wrong about their influence potential, it would be mistaken to take the frequency of positive self-evaluations as an objective index of democracy. Nevertheless, because we are studying the political orientation associated with democracy, data on citizens' subjective competence are crucial.

Besides being an index of the extent to which citizens consider their political systems democratic, subjective competence seems to be closely related to many other attitudes vital for understanding the nature of democratic political orientations.

Compared with the citizen whose subjective competence is low, the self-confident citizen is likely to be the active citizen: to follow politics, to discuss politics, to be a more active partisan. He is also more likely to be satisfied with his role as a participant and, subject to certain exceptions discussed above, likely to be more favorably disposed toward the performance of his political system and to have a generally more positive orientation toward it.

Finally, the self-confident citizen is more likely to express adherence to the values associated with a democratic system. He is more likely to believe that election campaigns are needed and to believe that the ordinary man has an obligation to participate in the affairs of his community.

In many ways, then, the belief in one's competence is a

key political attitude. The self-confident citizen appears to be the democratic citizen. Not only does he think he can participate, he thinks that others ought to participate as well. Furthermore, he does not merely think he can take a part in politics: he is likely to *be* more active. And, perhaps most significant of all, the self-confident citizen is also likely to be the more satisfied and loyal citizen.

CHAPTER IX

Social Relations and Civic Cooperation

IN WHAT WE have presented thus far we have been concerned with specifically political qualities and attitudes, their distribution in the five countries, and their interdependence as a democratic syndrome. To separate out political qualities and attitudes from general cultural characteristics is analytically justifiable. Only in that way can we treat political culture as a separate variable, examine its component parts and their interrelationships, and establish the ways in which national political cultures differ from one another. To do so, however, is not to imply that political attitudes are autonomous and unrelated to other social attitudes. They are in fact closely related to other social attitudes, but it is only by separating them out that we can then relate them to their more general social context. In order to analyze the relationship between such social and psychological variables and political attitudes, we shall first describe some findings on the differences in general social and interpersonal attitudes among the five nations. We concentrate on the individual's nonpolitical relations with his fellow man: the extent to which he is engaged in social relations with him, his attitudes toward him. These attitudes toward his social and interpersonal environment, we believe, might help explain the individual's view of the specifically political aspects of his environment. After describing these social and interpersonal attitudes and how they are distributed among the five nations, we shall turn to their relationship with political attitudes.

LEISURE TIME AND SOCIABILITY

How can one measure the extent to which social interaction is valued in a society? Certain kinds of social relations are in a sense involuntary, and the actors' interest in them is not indicative of the value they place on social interaction. Interacting with members of one's family, for example, is unavoidable. Family members living in a household must interact with one another, though undoubtedly there are cultural differences in the extent to which family interaction or "togetherness" is valued, or in the extent to which the culture encourages individuation among the family members. Similarly, social interaction is unavoidable in many, perhaps most, work situations. Consequently, in our question designed to get at "sociability" or social interaction, we deliberately directed the respondent away from these more or less compulsory situations, and toward the leisure time of his daily life; and we sought to discover whether he preferred the leisure activities of a group or of an individual sort. The question was asked at the very beginning of the interview and was open-ended. Hence we may view the responses as spontaneous statements of preference and behavior. The actual text of the question with interviewer instructions was:

> We'd like to start out by talking about some of your more general interests. Now aside from your work and your family, what are the activities that interest you most, that you spend your free time on? [Probe] Is there anything else?" [For those who say they have no free time:] "If you had more free time and opportunity, which activities would you like to engage in?

The responses were coded under the categories listed in Table IX.1. It is of interest that in all five countries the percentages of respondents expressing interest in specifically political activities during their leisure time are extremely small. The first three rows of the table recording the frequency of

TABLE IX.1 *Preferred leisure activities; by nation*

Percentage interested in	*U.S.*	*U.K.*	*Germany*	*Italy*	*Mexico*
Civic-political activities	2	2	3	1	0
Economic interest groups	0	0	1	0	0
Other interest groups	3	0	0	0	0
Charitable and welfare activities	8	5	2	2	1
Religious activities	20	7	4	2	4
"Social" activities	18	18	8	3	6
Total percentage choosing outgoing activity**	40	30	16	7	11
Hobbies, sports, etc.	70	73	61	42	51
Cultural activities (reading, TV, radio, etc.)	33	44	52	33	58
Travel	0	3	7	8	13
Other only	0	5	15	17	4
Nothing	3	6	6	10	2
Don't know	0	0	1	3	1
Total number of respondents	970	963	955	995	1,007
Total percentage respondents	100	100	100	100	100
Total percentage responses*	157	163	160	121	140

* Percentages exceed one hundred because of multiple responses.

** Percentages in this row are less than the sum of those above since some respondents chose more than one outgoing activity.

civic-political, economic interest group, and other interest group activity contain only very small percentages. This confirms the proposition that the proportion of individuals for whom civic activity is highly salient tends to be small in all countries.

This is not the case, however, for social activity. In the United States and Britain the percentages of respondents reporting interest and participation in charitable and welfare activities, religious group activities (other than church attendance proper), and social activities are markedly higher than in Germany, Italy, and Mexico. If one considers all respondents who mention some activity that brings them into social interaction with other people, the proportions vary from 40 per cent in the United States to 7 per cent in Italy. The remainder of the activity categories are largely individual pursuits, such as hobbies of one kind or another, reading, viewing television, listening to the radio, or travelling.

These data suggest that in the stable democracies there is a higher incidence of social interaction outside of the more or less compulsory relationships of family and work group. This voluntary social interaction expresses "moral" purposes (social, welfare, and religious] as well as more recreational and social purposes. One may infer that the pattern of voluntary social interaction is relatively well established in the stable democracies, and that this in turn reflects feelings of confidence and safety in the social environment. Thus in those countries where there is a higher incidence of cooperative civic competence, there also appears to be a higher incidence of social interaction in other than political contexts. Furthermore, our analysis shows the frequency of mention of outgoing activities is relatively independent of educational attainment. There is some tendency for those with higher education to report such activities more frequently, but compared with other educational patterns the differences are slight.

VALUING OUTGOING CHARACTER QUALITIES

Some writers have suggested that the populations of stable democracies place a high value on "open" or "outgoing" character qualities. The logic of this hypothesis is as follows. If an effectively functioning democracy requires a high incidence of civic competence, and if this in turn is based on a capacity to join with others in seeking civic and political goals, then we would expect to see a high value placed on character qualities that are related to cooperating and working with others.

In one of our questions we confronted our respondents with a list of statements describing different character qualities. Respondents were asked to choose the two characteristics they admired most.[1] The most decided difference among the nations lies in the greater frequency with which American and British respondents report that they admire generosity and considerateness. When asked to name the characteristic they admire most in people, 59 per cent of the American respondents and 65 per cent of the British mention these out-

[1] Actual text of the question was: "All of us have ideas about what people should be like. Here is a list of characteristics you might find in people Could you select the quality you admire the most?"

going, interpersonal virtues; these characteristics are mentioned by 42 per cent in Germany, 25 per cent in Italy, and 36 per cent in Mexico. Furthermore, the selection of generosity and considerateness as admirable qualities rises sharply with educational and occupational status in the United States, Britain, Germany, and Italy.

In Mexico, on the other hand, higher education seems to have less effect on the frequency with which generosity and considerateness are selected. A similar national pattern emerges when we control for occupation. In the United States, Britain, and Germany we find a sharp rising curve as we move from unskilled workers to professional and managerial personnel, whereas in Italy and Mexico the differences are quite small. These findings would seem to suggest that in the United States, Britain, Germany, and, to a lesser extent, Italy, these "protocivic" or "precivic" qualities of valuing "outgoingness" exist most frequently among those whose educational and occupational advantages are greatest. But the sharpest variation in the frequency with which the "outgoing" virtues of generosity and considerateness are valued is not within, but among, the nations. In the United States and Britain these are more frequently mentioned even within matched educational and occupational groups.

FEELINGS OF SAFETY AND RESPONSIVENESS

The frequency with which people interact with one another and the kinds of character qualities they admire are in turn related to the qualities they impute to their social environments. We would expect that people who frequently engage in group activities and who place a high value on outgoing character qualities would also view the human environment as safe and responsive. To get at these feelings and expectations about social relations in our five countries, we used questions developed by Morris Rosenberg to measure "faith in people." [2] The first two are statements reflecting distrust of others; the

[2] Rosenberg, "Misanthropy and Political Ideology," *American Sociological Review,* XXI pp. 690-95; and "Misanthropy and Attitudes Toward International Affairs," *Journal of Conflict Resolution,* I (1957), pp. 340-45.

The five items in the scale were:

TABLE IX.2 *Social trust and distrust; by nation*

Percentage who agree that	*U.S.*	*U.K.*	*Germany*	*Italy*	*Mexico*
STATEMENTS OF DISTRUST					
"No one is going to care much what happens to you, when you get right down to it."	38	45	72	61	78
"If you don't watch yourself, people will take advantage of you."	68	75	81	73	94
STATEMENTS OF TRUST					
"Most people can be trusted."	55	49	19	7	30
"Most people are more inclined to help others than to think of themselves first."	31	28	15	5	15
"Human nature is fundamentally cooperative."	80	84	58	55	82
Total numbers of respondents	970	963	955	995	1,007

first of this pair reflects alienation or distrust, and the second reflects the desirability of caution in dealing with others. The first statement of alienation brings out sharp differences be-

---

"*1.* Some people say that most people can be trusted. Others say you can't be too careful in your dealings with people. How do you feel about it?

"*2.* Would you say that most people are more inclined to help others, or more inclined to look out for themselves?

"*3.* If you don't watch yourself, people will take advantage of you.

"*4.* No one is going to care much what happens to you, when you get right down to it.

"*5.* Human nature is fundamentally cooperative."

To form a "faith in people" scale, respondents were given one point for responding that "most people can be trusted," that "people are more inclined to help others"; for disagreeing with items *3* and *4,* and for agreeing with item *5.* Those who gave the opposite answers to those listed above were given a score of -1 for each of these answers. Equivocal answers, such as "it depends" or "some people can be trusted and others not," were given a score of zero. The respondents were then classified into three groups, depending on their level of "faith in people." In the high group are those whose scores ranged from $+2$ to $+5$; in the middle are those whose scores ranged from -2 to $+1$, and in the low group are those whose scores ranged from -3 to -5. This scoring differs from that which Rosenberg used for his scale.

tween the American and British respondents, on the one hand, and the Germans, Italians, and Mexicans, on the other. The second statement of distrust, which gets at the desirability of being cautious in relation to others, seems to be almost universally supported in all five countries.

The more moderate of the two positive statements about social responsiveness and trust (i.e., the statement that most people can be trusted) brings out sharp differences among the countries: the American and British respondents show the highest frequencies of trustfulness, the Italians and Germans the lowest, and the Mexicans are in between. The stronger statement on interpersonal trust (most people are more inclined to help others) produces less frequent agreement, but again the percentages are higher for the American and British respondents. The fifth question, on whether or not human nature is fundamentally cooperative, offered in effect a "free ride" toward optimism and faith. It did not direct respondents' attention toward the immediate situation and realistic expectations. The percentages in all five countries are high, but again the German and Italian percentages are substantially lower than the American, British, and Mexican.

If we look down the columns we discover three national patterns. First, the American the British responses are on the whole at the low end of the continuum on the measures of social distrust and at the high end on the measures of trust. Second, the German and Italian responses show relatively high distrust and low trust. The Mexican pattern is mixed. More Mexicans than Italians and Germans agree with the alienative statements. And, with one exception, more Mexicans than Italians and Germans agree with the last three positive statements. In other words, the Americans and British tend to be consistently most positive about the safety and responsiveness of the human environment, the Germans and Italians more negative, and the Mexicans inconsistent.

In all five countries confidence in the human environment tends to increase among the better educated and economically more privileged elements of the populations.

SOCIAL ATTITUDES AND POLITICAL COOPERATION

The data presented in the previous section suggest that the five nations differ in general social attitudes. Our next task is to see how these social attitudes relate to political attitudes. The particular political attitude whose roots we shall seek in social attitudes is what we have labeled "civic cooperation" — the propensity to work with others in attempting to influence the government. Why do some individuals believe that they can cooperate with their fellow citizens in political activity whereas others do not? Why is it, for instance, that the American who wants to get something accomplished politically thinks immediately of talking to his friends and neighbors about his problem and getting them to help him, whereas this possibility would rarely occur to an Italian?

In the following chapters we shall attempt to find some of the social sources of political activity and of the feeling of political competence. In this chapter we shall deal not with the roots of the belief in one's ability to affect the government, but, rather, with the question of why some people who think they can influence the government would attempt to do so alone, while others would cooperate with their fellow citizens. Thus we shall be looking, not only for the social roots of certain orientations toward the government, but also for the roots of certain orientations toward one's fellow political actors.

Why concentrate on the sources of the propensity to work along with others in political affairs? There are several reasons. In the first place, one would expect political cooperation to be influenced by one's view of the social environment. And, furthermore, this type of political behavior has significant implications both for the political perspectives of the individual who engages in it and for the political system in which such activity is common. The reasons why such cooperative political behavior is important were discussed at some length in Chapter VI, and they only need mention here. Briefly, these include: (1) cooperation with one's fellow citizens is a means of raising the individual's influence potential vis-à-vis the government; (2) the ability to form political groups in time of political stress represents a "reserve of influence" on the individual's part; (3) the belief that one's primary group affiliations are available to aid one politically represents an integration of some of the most basic social units with the political system — an integration that greatly affects the democratic potential of a nation, because it occurs in relation to the "input structure" of politics, the process whereby individuals attempt to influence their government; and (4) the belief that one's fellow political actors will cooperate with one represents at least an incipient tendency to aggregate one's demands on the government with the demands of one's fellows — a process that is necessary for democratic decision making.

The extent of political cooperation differs strikingly among the five nations — another reason for concentrating on this topic. As the data in Chapter VI indicated, the propensity to form political groups is almost absent in some nations and exceedingly common in others. In fact, one has the impression that this propensity, in whatever degree it exists, is one of the most important aspects of political culture. This, of course, is a finding that other observers of politics have made. Tocqueville, for one, comments at length on the number of political groups observed in America:

> No sooner do you set foot upon American ground than you are stunned by a kind of tumult; a confused clamor is heard on every side, and a thousand simultaneous voices demand the satisfaction of their social wants. Everything is in motion around you; here the people of one quarter of a town are met to decide upon the building of a church; there the election of a representative is going on; a little farther, the delegates of a district are hastening to the town in order to consult upon some local improvements; in another place, the laborers of a village quit their plows to deliberate upon the project of a road or a public school. Meetings are called for the sole purpose of declaring their disapprobation of the conduct of the government; while in other assemblies citizens salute the authorities of the day as the fathers of their country. Societies are formed which regard drunkenness as the

principal cause of the evils of the state, and solemnly bind themselves to give an example of temperance. . . .[3]

And the vast difference in the tone of politics between a political system where such activity is rife and a system where it is rare can be illustrated by quoting at some length from the first few pages of a book on an Italian village by an acute student of American local politics:

Americans are used to a buzz of activity having as its purpose, at least in part, the advancement of community welfare. For example, a single issue of the weekly newspaper published in St. George, Utah (population 4,562), reports a variety of public spirited undertakings. The Red Cross is conducting a membership drive. The Business and Professional Women's Club is raising funds to build an additional auditorium for the local junior college, by putting on a circus in which the members will be both clowns and "animals." The Future Farmers of America (whose purpose is to "develop agricultural leadership, cooperation, and citizenship through individual and group leadership") are holding a father-son banquet. . . . The Chamber of Commerce is discussing the feasibility of building an all weather road between two nearby towns. "Skywatch" volunteers are being signed up. . . . Meetings of the Parent Teachers Associations are being held in the schools. . . .

Montegrano [the small Italian community] . . . presents a striking contrast. . . . Twenty-five upper class men constitute a "circle" and maintain a clubroom where members play cards and chat. Theirs is the only association. None of the members has ever suggested that it concern itself with community affairs or that it undertake a "project." . . . There are no organized voluntary charities in Montegrano. . . .

To the peasants, many of whom are desperately anxious for their children to get ahead, the lack of educational opportunity is one of the bitterest facts of life. Upper class people are affected too; some of them would like to live in Montegrano but cannot do so because it would cost too much to send their children away to a boarding school. One might think, then, that the improvement of the local school might be an important issue — one on

[3] Alexis de Tocqueville, *Democracy in America,* ed. Phillips Bradley, New York, 1948, I, pp. 249-50.

which people would unite in political parties or otherwise. . . . However, such possibilities have not been considered. . . .[4]

The national differences in the propensity for civic cooperation take on heightened importance from the fact that cooperative political behavior appears to be of greatest significance in the two most successful democracies, the United States and Britain, and of relatively little significance in Germany and Italy. And it also appears to a significant degree in Mexico (the nation we have termed an "aspirational democracy"), though here it seems to be based on less actual experience with such groups than is the case in Britain and the United States.

Finally, the search for the sources of political cooperation is especially intriguing because the propensity to form political groups does not seem to depend on the differing levels of social and economic modernization within a country. Most other significant political attitudes and behavior — interest in politics, political discussion, voting, knowledge of politics, and general sense of competence to influence the government — were found to vary strongly with an individual's educational attainment or his socio-economic status. The relationship was often so close that one could expect that as education became more widespread, the degree of political participation and competence would increase substantially. But unlike the political attitudes and behavior that seem heavily dependent on social position within a nation, the strategy of using informal groups as a means of influencing the government seems to be relatively independent of social position. If an individual thinks he can influence his government, the probability that he will try to form a group for this purpose appears to depend on the nation in which he lives, and not on other social characteristics. If we are seeking the reason for differences in political "style" among societies, the search for the roots of this political style — a style that cannot be explained by level of economic development — should prove rewarding.

[4] Edward C. Banfield, *The Moral Basis of a Backward Society,* Glencoe, Ill., 1958, pp. 15-17, 30-31.

How can we explain why the "confused clamor" of group activity exists in some countries and not in others? [5] Though no final answer can be given to a question of this sort, our data do suggest some of the sources of the belief that one can cooperate with one's fellow citizens. We shall not, in this chapter, look for the sources of the belief that one can influence the government. Rather, we shall concentrate mostly on those who believe they have such potential influence, and seek some explanation of why they would attempt to exert it through the formation of groups.

As we suggested in Chapter VI, the informal groups that our respondents talk about forming are a social resource that they use in attempting to influence the government. If an individual attempts to use (or reports that he would attempt to use) a particular resource in relation to the government, one would expect that: (1) he believes this resource offers a valuable base for influence over the government officials, (2) the resource is available to him, and (3) there is no special reason inhibiting the *political* use of this resource. Similarly, the individual who mentions that he would seek the cooperation of his peers in an attempt to influence the government must (if he is responding reasonably) believe that: (1) government officials are responsive to a group appeal (or, at least, more responsive to such appeals than to individual appeals), (2) he has available to him such informal groups (i.e., he has a family, friends, neighbors, whom he trusts and

[5] That this sort of question *can* be raised and that one can attempt to answer it illustrates, incidentally, the advantage of "discovering" the propensity to form groups in a study of this sort rather than through the keen but unsystematic observations of a Tocqueville. Not only can we now know about this propensity in some new way (those of us who work on studies of this sort like to believe the knowledge is now more reliable, if sometimes less colorful), but our knowledge is also more precise. We can tell who it is that is likely to engage in such behavior — men or women, college graduates or those with less education. More important, we can go further in trying to find out how those who say they would work through groups differ from others who do not say this; that is, we can learn why such groups can be formed. Not only is the knowledge (hopefully) more reliable, it is also more useful, for it can lead to further knowledge.

from whom he expects help), and (3) these friends, neighbors, and other associates can be used for *political* activity. The last criterion is important. The man who is well integrated into a number of primary groups — values his membership in these groups, trusts the members of the group, believes he can depend on them for help — may still not think of those groups in time of political stress. He may consider politics a special realm, where the ordinary day-to-day relationships of trust and confidence are irrelevant. He may have a rich social life, yet may not translate it into political competence. Thus in searching for the roots of political cooperation, one has to look, not only at the extent of cooperative social activities in a nation, but also at the extent to which these are translated into political resources. The propensity to cooperate with one's fellow citizens, we suggest, is based, not only on an individual's attitudes toward politics and his position in the political system, but also on his attitudes toward his fellow citizens and his position in the social system as well.

The first requirement for the maintenance of a group-forming political style is that individuals believe such an influence strategy will work. This attitude is present in the United States and Britain to an extent not found in the other nations. As was pointed out in Chapter VI, when asked if there was any chance that an attempt to influence the government would succeed, a substantially larger proportion of American and British respondents than of any other respondents volunteered the statement that success was likely only if others joined them in making the attempt.[6] Other responses in our survey support the position that the formation of groups is considered highly effective in these two countries. In another question in the interview, subsequent to the open-response question on influence strategy, respondents were given a list of five possible strategies for influencing the government and were asked to select the most effective. The five choices were: working through personal and family connections, writing to government officials, getting people interested and forming a group, working through a political party, and organizing a protest demonstration. In the United States, 37 per cent of

[6] See Chapter VI above.

the respondents selected "getting people interested and forming a group" as the most effective strategy. In Britain, 35 per cent selected this response. In Germany the proportion was 12 per cent, in Italy 13 per cent, and in Mexico 15 per cent. Clearly, one reason why individuals in the United States and Britain are more likely to think of using groups as a means of influencing the government is that they believe this method will work.[7]

CIVIC COOPERATION AND FREEDOM TO COMMUNICATE

But even if one believes that with the help of others one can influence the government, one may still not believe that the help of others is available in time of political stress. The perceived availability of others would appear to depend on a number of social characteristics. In the first place, of course, other people must be present. But more than physical presence is needed. There must also exist no severe impediments to communication among individuals. Whereas these informal political groups we have been considering may be created on the spot for political activity, group formation can probably only take place if there are pre-existing channels of communication among the potential members of the group; if there has been some previous contact among them. Table IX.3 suggests that this pre-existing communications network helps explain the existence of group competence. Among those who think they can influence the government (the local competents) in each country, those who report that they discuss political affairs are more likely to choose a group strategy as the means they would use. In Britain, for instance, 45 per cent of the local competents who discuss politics choose the group strategy, whereas 38 per cent of those who do not discuss politics choose such a strategy. And in each of the other coun-

[7] Again, we must point out that these beliefs do not exist in a vacuum. The respondents are probably right: government officials are probably more responsive to such group activity in Britain and the United States than in the other countries. And this is one source of the beliefs. But the effect of government action on political beliefs is probably reciprocal. Probably one reason why government officials are more likely to respond to group activity is that people believe that they will respond and therefore attempt such group pressure.

tries those local competents who discuss politics are more likely to say they would work through some informal group than are those local competents who do not discuss politics. Though the differences are not great, the uniformity from nation to nation is convincing.[8]

The relationship is not as strong among those with secondary education or better. In their propensity to form groups, there is no difference between the American local competents who discuss politics and those who do not; in Italy and Mexico there is a slight opposite tendency: those who do *not* talk politics invoke informal groups a bit more often. However, for each nation as a whole, and especially on the lower educational levels, the relationship holds. The existence of a political communications network (as roughly measured by our question on political discussion) does make it more likely than not that an individual will think of using his primary group relations in an attempt to influence the government. At best, however, the relationship is a mild one.

CIVIC COOPERATION AND SOCIAL VALUES

Table IX.3 divides respondents into those who discuss politics and those who do not. Thus it deals with the relationship between a specifically political activity and civic cooperation, and not with more general social activities and attitudes. Yet we are interested in the sort of informal groups that are essentially nonpolitical but are mobilized for political activity in response to a particular challenge; thus one might expect to find that the availability of these groups derives, at least in part, from more general social and interpersonal attitudes. An individual may have a wide range of informal associations, but may believe that the individuals with whom he associates cannot be relied upon for cooperative political behavior, that they cannot be trusted, or that they are unlikely to be helpful.

[8] It must be remembered that Table IX.3 analyzes local competents only. One would expect those who discuss politics to be the more competent citizens. Table IX.3 makes a more interesting point: those local competents who discuss politics are more likely than those who do not to say they would work with others in trying to exert political influence.

TABLE IX.3 *Two types of local competents and their propensity to form groups; by nation and education*

	Total				*Primary or less*				*Secondary or more*			
	Local competents who discuss politics		*Local competents who don't discuss politics*		*Discuss politics*		*Don't discuss politics*		*Discuss politics*		*Don't discuss politics*	
Nation	(%)	(*No.*)[a]	(%)	(*No.*)	(%)	(*No.*)	(%)	(*No.*)	(%)	(*No.*)	(%)	(*No.*)
United States	75[b]	(621)	68	(123)	68	(252)	62	(84)	79	(369)	79	(39)
Great Britain	45	(571)	38	(177)	45	(312)	36	(126)	45	(243)	38	(45)
Germany	24	(421)	17	(169)	24	(309)	18	(150)	22	(111)	[7	(14)]
Italy	15	(221)	11	(275)	15	(102)	8	(202)	15	(119)	21	(73)
Mexico	50	(236)	48	(295)	53	(178)	48	(260)	47	(56)	51	(34)

[a] Numbers in parentheses refer to the bases upon which percentages are calculated.

[b] I.e., 75 per cent of local competents who discuss politics mentioned a group-forming strategy.

Just as the United States and Britain differ from the other three nations in the frequency of cooperative political behavior, as evidenced by the propensity to form groups, so do they differ in the frequency of expression of cooperative interpersonal values and perceptions. We have already seen that British and American respondents value generous and considerate behavior more than do the respondents in other nations, and they are also more likely to perceive their fellow citizens as cooperative and trustworthy. This set of social attitudes, one might expect, would open the way for the individual to turn to his fellow citizens for political help. And it is perhaps this set of interpersonal perceptions and values that explains the propensity to engage in cooperative political behavior. Whether or not an individual attempts to form a group to influence the government would depend on his perception of the probable response of the government to such an appeal and on his ability to communicate with his fellow citizens. But it would also depend on his perception of the characteristics of those who are his fellow actors in the political system.

Our questions about interpersonal values and perceptions were asked in a nonpolitical context; they were asked about people in general. We now ask how much these general and diffuse social and interpersonal attitudes are related to political attitudes. Since these interpersonal attitudes are nonpolitical in content, one must consider not only their frequency but also the extent to which they have an effect upon or are translated into political attitudes. It is possible that general interpersonal trust is unrelated to the existence of a trusting attitude in political affairs. One might trust people in general, but not in relation to politics. Thus in order to see if the belief that one's fellow citizens can be called on for political aid is rooted in social and interpersonal attitudes, one would have to find (1) that social and interpersonal attitudes fostering cooperation and trust are widespread among those who believe in the political availability of their informal groups, and (2) that the existence of the cooperative interpersonal attitudes does indeed affect the belief in one's group-forming powers.

We have seen that the nations differ markedly in the

frequency with which respondents report that they admire generosity and considerateness in people. In the two nations in which the propensity toward cooperative political behavior is most widespread (America and Britain), admiration of general cooperativeness among people is, as we pointed out at the beginning of this chapter, also most widespread. To what extent are those related? Table IX.4 relates admiration of generosity and consideration to the frequency with which informal groups are mentioned as a means of influencing the government. In the United States and Britain there is some relationship between the admiration of such outgoing characteristics and the frequency with which local competents choose a strategy that involves the formation of groups. In the United States, for instance, 76 per cent of the local competents who say they admire generosity and considerateness would work through informal groups in trying to influence the government, in contrast to 68 per cent among those who admire less outgoing virtues. The relationship, though not a very strong one, exists on all educational levels. Thus in the United States and Britain, not only are supportive interpersonal activities admired by individuals more frequently than in the other three nations, but also this admiration of generosity and consideration is related to the willingness of individuals to form political groups. Interpersonal consideration is highly valued and appears to be translated into a positive evaluation of the efficacy of cooperative activities in relation to the government.

In contrast to the pattern in the United States and Britain, the degree to which individuals of the other three nations value outgoing interpersonal activities is not related to their belief in the efficacy of cooperative political activity. In Italy those who value generosity and considerateness are no more likely than those who do not to suggest using a group strategy; and in Germany and Mexico the relationship is actually reversed: those who value cooperative, interpersonal behavior are less likely to invoke informal groups as a means of influencing the government. In the three countries in which group formation is a relatively smaller part of the dominant political style, not only are interpersonal cooperative virtues

TABLE IX.4 *Two types of local competents and their propensity to form groups; by nation and education*

Nation	*Total*				*Primary or less*				*Secondary or more*			
	Local competents who value generosity		*Local competents who don't value generosity*		*Value generosity*		*Don't value generosity*		*Value generosity*		*Don't value generosity*	
	(%)	(*No.*)[a]	(%)	(*No.*)	(%)	(*No.*)	(%)	(*No.*)	(%)	(*No.*)	(%)	(*No.*)
United States	76[b]	(483)	68	(263)	68	(165)	65	(172)	81	(318)	75	(91)
Great Britain	46	(495)	39	(253)	46	(276)	38	(165)	45	(206)	43	(82)
Germany	18	(275)	25	(315)	18	(185)	25	(276)	16	(88)	30	(37)
Italy	14	(135)	13	(370)	10	(71)	11	(239)	19	(64)	17	(131)
Mexico	45	(190)	53	(341)	43	(151)	53	(287)	51	(38)	47	(52)

[a] Numbers in parentheses refer to the bases upon which percentages are calculated.
[b] I.e., 76 per cent of local competents who value generosity in others mentioned a group-forming strategy.

less frequently admired, but also admiration for them is not translated into political behavior.

CIVIC COOPERATION AND TRUST IN PEOPLE

The tendency to engage in cooperative activity within the political influence process appears, therefore, to be rooted at least partially in a set of social values that stress cooperative behavior among individuals. In the two countries in which this fusion is most complete the dominant social values stress cooperative behavior; and the degree to which cooperative interpersonal behavior is valued is directly related to the propensity to create political structures.

High valuation of cooperative behavior can be expected to affect actual interpersonal behavior if those who value such behavior also believe that people will in fact behave cooperatively in their relations with each other. In this respect as well, Britain and the United States differ from the other three nations as was shown above in Table IX.2. The responses to several questions dealing with their expectations of the behavior of others indicate that British and American respondents are more likely to expect other people to be trustworthy, helpful, and cooperative.

The relationship between the propensity to form political groups and the belief that one's fellow men are cooperative, trustworthy, and unselfish may be demonstrated by relating an individual's general "faith in people" to his expressed belief in his ability to form political groups. In order to tap the extent of our respondents' faith in people, we employed Rosenberg's "faith in people" scale, which consists of five items (reported above in Table IX.2). Each item dealt with the respondents' general attitudes toward their fellow citizens; none referred in any way to political activity. The respondents were then scored along a "faith in people" scale, according to how frequently they chose the question-response that indicated strong faith in people.[9]

How does one's generalized belief in the cooperativeness and unselfishness of human nature affect one's strategy of influence vis-à-vis the government? Table IX.5 indicates that

[9] See note 2 for a discussion of this scale.

in the United States and Britain the more one has such faith in people, the more likely he is to believe that he can work with his fellow citizens in attempting to influence the government. In the United States among those with strong faith in people, 80 per cent report that they would attempt to form a group to influence the local government, whereas this is reported by only 58 per cent of those low on faith in people. Those local competents whose faith in people is moderate are also moderate in the frequency with which they report they would attempt to form political groups. And in Britain the same pattern is apparent: 50 per cent of those local competents high in faith in people would form such groups, in contrast with 33 per cent of those low in faith in people. And the relationship persists on both higher and lower educational levels.

In contrast with the pattern in the United States and Britain, faith in people does not increase one's propensity to form political groups in the other three nations. In Germany and Mexico there is some tendency for those with stronger faith in people to be *less* prone to think of group strategies to influence the government, and in Italy there is little regular relationship between general trust in people and the ability to form groups.

In the United States and Britain the belief that people are generally cooperative, trustworthy, and helpful is frequent, and it has political consequences. Belief in the benignity of one's fellow citizen is directly related to one's propensity to join with others in political activity. General social trust is translated into politically relevant trust.[10] In the other three nations the absence of a cooperative, group-forming political

[10] Rosenberg reports a similar relationship between general social trust and political trust in an American sample. He finds that those who score high in "faith in people" are less likely than the low scorers to be cynical about politics and politicians; see his "Misanthropy and Political Ideology," *American Sociological Review, op. cit.*

A study carried on in a small city in the western United States yields similar results. A positive correlation was found between trust in people (as measured by a low score on a "personal cynicism" scale) and trust in politics. See Robert E. Agger, Marshall N. Goldstein, and Stanley A. Pearl, "Political Cynicism: Measurement and Meaning," *Journal of Politics,* XIII (1961), pp. 477-506.

TABLE IX.5 *Three types of local competents and their propensity to form groups; by nation and education*

Nation	*Total*						*Primary or less*						*Secondary or more*					
	Faith in people						*Faith in people*						*Faith in people*					
	High		*Med.*		*Low*		*High*		*Med.*		*Low*		*High*		*Med.*		*Low*	
	(%)	(*No.*)[a]	(%)	(*No.*)	(%)	(*No.*)	(%)	(*No.*)	(%)	(*No.*)	(%)	(*No.*)	(%)	(*No.*)	(%)	(*No.*)	(%)	(*No.*)
United States	80[b]	(286)	73	(338)	58	(122)	74	(94)	70	(160)	51	(83)	83	(192)	76	(178)	74	(39)
Great Britain	50	(210)	44	(379)	33	(159)	50	(100)	44	(229)	34	(112)	49	(103)	45	(143)	29	(42)
Germany	22	(96)	20	(374)	27	(120)	22	(60)	20	(299)	27	(102)	22	(36)	18	(71)	22	(18)
Italy	19	(31)	12	(193)	14	(281)	[27	(11)]	10	(116)	10	(183)	15	(20)	14	(77)	20	(98)
Mexico	41	(24)	47	(217)	54	(290)	[48	(14)]	46	(170)	53	(254)		(c)	48	(46)	53	(36)

[a] Numbers in parentheses refer to the bases upon which percentages are calculated.
[b] I.e., 80 per cent of those "high" in "faith in people" mentioned a group-forming strategy.
[c] Too few cases.

style appears to be related, not only to the lower frequency of expression of general social trust, but also to the fact that even that trust which is expressed does not increase the probability that an individual will think of working with others in trying to influence the government. A gap remains between general social attitudes and political attitudes. Politics appears to be a separate, independent sphere of activity for which one has a set of political attitudes not particularly grounded in general social attitudes. In the United States and Britain one's view of the realm of politics appears closely related to one's view of social life. In the other three nations there is less fusion between social and political attitudes.

The above data go a long way in explaining why there is a "buzz" of group activity in Britain and especially in the United States, and why this activity is not as apparent elsewhere. The explanation of the difference is intriguing: it is not only that general social values and attitudes that would foster cooperation with one's fellow citizens are more widespread in Britain and the United States; beyond that, these general social attitudes are more closely related to political attitudes in these two nations than in the other three nations. And this explanation adds weight to an interpretation we advanced earlier of the meaning of the propensity to invoke one's primary group in time of political stress. This tendency to use one's primary associations in political influence attempts, we suggested, represented a close fusion of the basic primary group structures of society with the secondary structures of politics; a fusion that led to a more integrated political system. That the use of such primary groups does represent a fusion of this sort on the structural level is strongly supported by the discovery of a parallel fusion on the level of attitudes in the same nations where the integration of primary and political structures was most complete. The close overlap of society and polity that we have been suggesting for the United States and Britain is thus evidenced on the levels of both structure and attitude. Though the structures of government in both nations are modern, functionally specific, and formally differentiated from other social structures, they are linked to the primary units of the social structure by the use of these primary structures as a resource for political influence. And the political structures are linked with the rest of the social structure, as well, by a diffuse set of attitudes that apply both to general social relations and to political activities.[11]

This suggested explanation of the sources of cooperative political behavior is particularly interesting because of the further questions it raises. Why, for instance, do British and American respondents express relatively higher degrees of interpersonal trust? And why is there no gap between these social attitudes and political attitudes, as there is in the other three nations? We leave the first question to others who are able to probe more deeply than we have into cross-national differences in social structure and personality. We shall attempt some answer to the second question.

The answer to such a complicated question can only be partial and tentative. In searching for the reason why general social attitudes are more closely related to political attitudes in some nations than in others, and why primary group affiliations are considered available for political activity in some nations but not in others, one might begin by looking at the political characteristics of Britain and the United States, to see if there is something about the way in which politics is carried on there that might explain the absence of a gap between primary social structures and attitudes and the political system.

[11] The next question that suggests itself is how this combination of trust in people and willingness to cooperate with them in political activities is learned. One possible answer is that from childhood on, individuals in the United States and Britain are given opportunities to take part in group activities with others. McClelland reports a study of secondary-school students in Germany and the United States, in which respondents were asked to list their leisure activities. American students mention on the average five group activities (clubs, school publications, social gatherings and the like), while German students mention on the average one such activity; see David McClelland, *The Achieving Society,* Princeton, N.J., 1961, pp. 199-201. This early experience with groups — and one would assume it begins even earlier than secondary school — may be a major source of civic cooperation. See Chapter XI for a further consideration of political socialization in family and school.

INTENSITY OF PARTISANSHIP AND THE INTEGRATION OF POLITY AND SOCIETY

The state of partisanship in a nation may help us explain the way in which social relationships mesh with the political system. An individual's attitudes toward political parties and, more important, toward the supporters of political parties — his own and the opposition — are, in a sense, the political equivalent of his general attitudes toward people. If there is a disparity between general attitudes toward interpersonal relations and more specific attitudes toward relations with people when they are given a political label (identified in the mind of the individual as either politically sympathetic or hostile), this indicates a lack of integration of social structure with political system.

We have already seen that the structure of partisanship in the United States and Britain differs from that in Germany, Italy, and Mexico. The two former nations have had long and relatively stable political developments. Both systems have been able to manage problems of change and the entry of new groups into politics without resort to violence. And though there have been and still are partisan conflicts, these have rarely led to a fragmentation of society into deeply ideological, closed, and antagonistic political groups. The absence of partisan fragmentation in recent decades is reflected in our data. As was pointed out in Chapter IV, respondents in the United States and Britain are less likely than those in the other three nations to report that they consider supporters of an opposition political party ineligible for membership in the primary group. In response to a question on their reaction to the marriage of a son or daughter to a supporter of an opposition party, American and British respondents rarely said they would be opposed to such a marriage and almost invariably said that such partisan considerations do not matter in this situation. In Italy, on the contrary, a much higher level of partisan antagonism was observed; and the level of partisan antagonism in Germany and Mexico lay somewhere between the two extremes.

Can this lack of partisan fragmentation help explain both

the propensity to cooperate politically with one's fellow citizens and the use of informal groups in the political influence process? At first glance, the data on the use of informal groups in Britain and the United States and the data on interparty marriage in these countries appear somewhat inconsistent with each other. We have argued that the propensity to form political groups represents a close meshing of primary structures and the political process. Yet the responses in Britain and the United States to the question of interparty marriage suggest that political affiliation is not considered a relevant criterion for membership in the primary group. This is, after all, what respondents are saying when they reply that it would not matter if their child married a supporter of the party they opposed. And other data in our study also suggest that this combination — a belief that one's primary group is available for aid in time of political stress and a desire to keep politics from disturbing primary group relationships — exists in these two nations. For instance, in response to a question on whether or not there are any people with whom they would avoid political discussion, the most frequent reason given by American and British respondents who say there are such people is that the discussion can cause disharmony within the primary group: it can create unnecessary arguments with friends or relatives. (In the other nations the most frequent reasons given for avoiding political discussion are that it is useless, that other people are too biased, ignorant, or fanatic, or that the discussion can get one into trouble.)

The data in our study indicate that there is no contradiction between the perceived availability of one's primary group in time of political stress and the beliefs that membership in the group ought not to depend on political affiliation and that the group ought not to be disrupted by political conflict; rather, it is these two beliefs that make the primary group available in time of political stress. If the criteria for entry into the primary group were partisan in nature, the ability to form groups easily in time of stress would be inhibited. Moreover, the usefulness of the group would be limited: it would be useful only if the government officials one wanted to contact were members of the same political party; whereas if the

TABLE IX.6 *Three types of local competents and their propensity to form groups; by nation (supporters of major parties only)*[a]

Nation	*Oppose marriage to an opposition-party supporter* (%)	(*No.*)[b]	*Favor marriage within own party, but would not oppose marriage out* (%)	(*No.*)	*Think partisan criteria irrelevant for primary group admission* (%)	(*No.*)
United States	59[c]	(22)	73	(37)	74	(547)
Great Britain	26	(42)	44	(55)	44	(476)
Germany	16	(55)	24	(58)	24	(220)
Italy	8	(118)	[21	(14)]	14	(85)
Mexico	55	(84)	47	(16)	53	(206)

[a] There are too few cases to allow the usual educational control, but education has little relationship to either of the variables — social distance among political parties and the propensity to form informal groups — in this table.

[b] Numbers in parentheses refer to the bases upon which percentages are calculated.

[c] I.e., 59 per cent of local competents who oppose inter-party marriage mentioned a group-forming strategy.

primary group is essentially nonpartisan, its usefulness is more general. In a sense, the intervention of the primary group in politics is made possible by the fact that it has no partisan commitment.

Table IX.6 shows the connection between the partisan fragmentation of social relationships (as measured by the extent to which respondents feel distant from opposition-party supporters) and respondents' propensity to form political groups. Respondents are divided into three types according to the degree to which they accept partisan political affiliation as a criterion for admission to the primary group — that is, the degree to which they consider partisan affiliation a relevant criterion for the selection of a marriage partner by a son or daughter.[12] The three types of respondents are: (1) those who express opposition to marriage of a son or daughter with an adherent of the opposition party; (2) those who are not opposed to such marriage, but would be pleased if a son or daughter married a supporter of their own party; and (3)

[12] See Chapter V for a discussion of these questions.

those who consider the partisan affiliation of a prospective family member to be irrelevant. The respondents in the first group prefer a social world that is relatively closed to cross-party affiliations; they express a negative reaction to those of other partisan affiliation. Those in the second group do not express hostility to people outside their own party, but they do express some positive affect toward their own party affiliation; they would be pleased if a child married someone of like political belief but not displeased if he or she married someone of opposing views. In the last group we have those who express indifference to the partisan affiliation of a potential family member.[13]

As Table IX.6 indicates, there is a relationship between the extent to which partisan criteria are considered relevant for primary group membership and the propensity to form political groups. Compare the column on the left of the table (those who oppose marriage into the family of a supporter of the opposition party) with the column on the far right (those who say that partisan criteria are irrelevant). In general, those whose primary groups are "closed," in the partisan sense, are less likely to think of cooperating with their fellow citizens in time of political stress than are those whose primary groups are "open." And in this case the relationship beween attitudes toward one's fellow citizens and the propensity to cooperate with them politically is found, not only in the United States and Britain, but in Germany and Italy as well. In Britain, for instance, 26 per cent of those in closed primary groups report that they would try to enlist the cooperation of others in trying to influence the government, in contrast to 44 per cent of those whose primary groups are open. And in Germany the respective proportions of respondents who would work with others in trying to influence the government are 16 per cent

[13] Table IX.9 reports attitudes toward party intermarriage among the supporters of the two largest parties in each nation: in America, Republicans' attitudes toward marriage of a child with a Democrat; in Britain, Conservatives toward Labour; in Germany, CDU toward SPD; in Mexico, PRI toward PAN; and vice versa in each case. In Italy three parties are involved. Table IX.15 reports the attitudes of DC supporters toward marriage with a Communist supporter, and the attitudes of PCI and PSI supporters toward marriage with a Christian Democrat.

among those in closed primary groups and 24 per cent among those whose groups are not closed. In some cases the numbers upon which percentages are based are quite small, but the cross-national uniformity is convincing.

Our hypothesis that a close relationship between social and political attitudes exists in Britain and the United States but not in the other nations, makes it interesting to note that, whereas there was no relationship between general attitudes toward people and political cooperation in Italy and Germany, there is in these two countries a relationship between attitudes to people as political actors (i.e., people who are given a partisan label) and political cooperation. Unlike general interpersonal attitudes, political interpersonal attitudes are related to the propensity to cooperate in political action.

The deviant case in Table IX.6 is Mexico. Here those who have closed primary groups are as likely to speak of cooperation with their fellows as are those whose primary groups are open. One cannot, of course, be sure why. But the most likely reason is that Mexico is essentially a one-party nation. Where there is only one party of significance, hostility to those outside the party cannot have as great an effect on one's ability to work with others as it would if there were more than one party. If, for instance, 85 per cent of the Mexicans who express support for some party express support for the major party, the PRI (as our data indicate they do), or if 90 per cent of the votes go to that party (as voting data on the 1958 election indicate),[14] then hostility to those outside the party cuts one off from few potential collaborators. And where all government, local and national, is controlled by this one party and appears likely to remain so indefinitely, partisan informal groups do not appear to be limited in the generality of their use. Thus the impact of partisanship in a one-party nation will obviously differ from that in a nation where there are competing parties with relatively large support, where there are at least some governments on the local level controlled by

[14] Though ours is a sample of little more than one thousand Mexicans, our data on party support may be somewhat more accurate than the voting statistics. Ballots in Mexico are counted by the incumbent party in what may not be a completely nonpartisan manner.

the opposition, and where the opposition is a possible successor to office on the national level.

One other aspect of the data in Table IX.6 is interesting. Consider the frequency with which those respondents in the middle column — i.e., those who say they would be pleased if a child married a supporter of their party, but who also say they would not be opposed to marriage with a supporter of the opposition party — report that they would cooperate with their fellow citizens. In the United States, Britain, Germany, and Italy the frequency with which this group mentions using primary group affiliation as a source of political influence is much closer to (and in Britain and Germany, exactly the same as) the frequency with which such groups are mentioned by those who consider partisan affiliation irrelevant (column 3) than to the frequency with which such groups are mentioned by those whose primary groups are "closed" to political opponents (column 1). This distinction is important, for it takes us one step further in our analysis of the relationship between partisanship and political cooperation. It helps specify what *type* of partisanship inhibits informal political cooperation. Those who say they would be pleased if a child married a supporter of their own party are expressing an affective orientation toward their own political party: they are saying that partisan affiliation is not completely irrelevant to primary group membership. But as long as this positive attachment to their party is not coupled with a negative reaction to those of an opposition party, their ability to form political groups does not appear to be impaired. The Conservative party supporter who would be pleased if his child married a Conservative but not displeased if the child married a Labourite appears as free to form political groups as is the Conservative party supporter who would be neither pleased by marriage to a Conservative nor displeased by a marriage to a Labourite.

It is not the existence of an affective tie to one's own political party or a preference for those of like mind that blocks the free formation of groups; it is only when these ties involve the *rejection* of those of opposing views that group formation is inhibited. This appears significant in understanding the relationship between affective orientation to politics and the maintenance of a participatory political system that is not rent by harsh political disputes. An intense affective orientation to politics, insofar as it involves rejection on personal grounds of those of opposite affiliation, is a barrier to the type of cooperative influence activity discussed in this chapter. But if the affective orientation is a "managed" affective orientation — that is, if it involves essentially positive loyalty and attachment to one's own political views, but does not involve rejection of those with opposing views — then this orientation is not a hindrance to the free formation of political groups at times of political stress.

The hypothesis that it is not partisanship per se but negative or hostile partisanship that impedes political cooperation receives additional confirmation if respondents are divided by another measure of partisanship: not their attitude toward others of opposing views, but their affiliation with their own party. Respondents can be divided into party activists (those who take an active role in their political party), party supporters (those who express support for a party but are not active), and nonpartisans (who express support for no political party).[15] The extent to which an individual is positively associated with a political party has little effect on his group-forming propensity. Party activists are generally as likely to speak of using informal groups as a means of influencing the government as are party supporters or nonpartisans. The fact that one is a partisan — that one is active in a political party or supports a political party — does not impede his ability to cooperate with one's fellow citizens. It is only when partisanship becomes so intense as to involve rejection, on personal grounds, of those of opposing political views that the state of partisanship in a nation may be said to limit the ability of its citizens to cooperate with each other in political affairs.

[15] Party activists in Britain, Germany, Italy, and Mexico are those who report membership in a political party. Party activists in the United States are those who report having taken an active part in a political campaign for a party. Party supporters in all countries are those who say they support or lean toward a particular party but who report no activity. Nonpartisans are those who say they neither support nor lean toward a party. Respondents who refuse to answer on party affiliation are omitted from the table.

CONCLUSION

The data presented in this chapter offer some explanation for the phenomenon of group formation noticed by Tocqueville and by many others since. In searching for the reasons why political cooperation with one's fellow citizens appears easier and more frequent in some countries than in others, we have considered a number of important characteristics of basic social and political attitudes in five nations. We have paid special attention to certain general attitudes and values connected with interpersonal relations, and to attitudes connected with the state of partisanship in these nations. And in doing so we have had to consider some basic differences among the nations.

In Italy, Germany, and Mexico our data suggest that there is a gap between political attitudes and the more general attitudes toward interpersonal relations. Not only are the levels of interpersonal trust relatively low, but what interpersonal trust there is is not related to the willingness or ability to cooperate politically with one's fellow citizens. Nor are those who value such outgoing characteristics as considerateness and cooperation any more likely than those who do not value them to think of engaging in cooperative political activity as a means of influencing the government. Politics appears to be a special realm where the norms and attitudes of more general interpersonal relations do not prevail.

In Italy and Germany this lack of integration between general social attitudes and political attitudes appears explicable, at least in part, by the existence of a high degree of partisan fragmentation. Those who carry political antagonisms into their personal lives (and the proportions who do are greater in Germany, and greater still in Italy, than they are in the United States and Britain), are less likely than others to think of cooperating with their fellow citizens in political activity.

These characteristics of the other three political systems highlight the pattern of attitudes in the United States and Britain that seem to explain the propensity for citizens to cooperate with one another in politics. In these two nations the ability freely to form groups for political activity appears to be related to the general nature of the citizens' commitment to politics: it is "balanced" or "managed." Americans and Britons are involved in politics, but the involvement is held within limits. They are neither parochials, cut off from politics, nor intensely partisan in ways that might lead to political fragmentation. And this balance, as we have said, is needed for a successful democracy: there must be involvement in politics if there is to be the sort of participation necessary for democratic decision making; yet the involvement must not be so intense as to endanger stability.

The balance between commitment to politics and autonomy from politics is illustrated in our data on the relationship between primary groups and politics in America and Great Britain. On the one hand, these groups are a resource that is available to the individual in time of political stress. They are a means of increasing his influence vis-à-vis the state and of making him less dependent on "mass" political institutions. Furthermore, this balanced commitment to politics seems to be related to the existence of more basic social values — widespread social trust and a high evaluation of considerateness and generosity in people — *and* to the fact that these values permeate the political system. The latter point is the significant one. It is not just that there are many Americans and Britons who trust their fellow citizens: more important, this social trust affects political trust and the willingness to cooperate with others. The political system this suggests is penetrated by overarching social values.

These overarching social norms are reflected as well in the data on interparty marriage. One can infer that the 90 per cent or so of the respondents in the United States and Britain who say that it would make no difference if their child married a supporter of the opposition party are saying, in effect, that personal relationships ought to be governed by values other than political ones. The family ought not to be allowed to be divided by partisan considerations. It is not that partisan differences are unimportant, it is just that they are not absolute values. In certain social situations there are other, more general interpersonal attitudes that are considered binding.

In Germany and especially in Italy primary groups are also insulated from inharmonious political relationships that might strain the group. In fact, one would expect the primary groups of any society to be protected by some social mechanism — for the integration of the primary groups is of key social importance. But in Italy and Germany these groups are insulated by norms that bar from entry those of opposing political views.[16] Political conflict is probably so intense that the primary group can be protected from such conflict only by exclusion. In Britain and the United States partisanship has a more moderate character, and the challenge to primary group integration by divisive partisan attitudes can be met by less drastic means. Those of opposing views can be allowed into the primary group, but the potential fragmentation is managed by the set of norms that places integrative, primary group values above the partisan, divisive ones.

This is not to say that politics is unimportant in Britain and America. Respondents report that it plays a significant role in their lives, it is of interest to the populace, it is a topic of conversation. It is all these things frequently — more frequently, in fact, than in the other three nations. Yet politics is "kept in its place." The values associated with it are subordinate in significant respects to more general social values, and these more general social values act to temper political controversy within the two nations. In this way, again, we have a "managed" or "balanced" involvement in politics: an involvement

[16] Data on voting in the continental European countries, on the other hand, might suggest that there is quite a split within the family on partisan affiliation. Women in general vote more heavily for the Christian parties, men more heavily for the left parties. In the German Bundestag election of 1953, for instance, the CDU received 2,200,000 more votes from women than from men. However, this difference in the voting behavior of men and women does not necessarily imply that this particular split occurs in many families. It has been pointed out that in Germany the bulk of this female surplus for the Christian parties comes from women who are unmarried, widowed, or divorced. (See Gabriele Bremme, *Die Politische Rolle der Frau in Deutschland,* Göttingen, 1956, p. 98.) And Duverger makes a similar point for women and the MRP in France; see Maurice Duverger, *The Political Role of Women,* Paris, 1955, pp. 49ff. It is likely that a similar pattern exists in Italy.

In any case, as we shall discuss in Chapter XIV, the norms relating to marriage of a child to an opposition party supporter may be more important than the actual behavior.

that is kept from challenging the integration and stability of the political system.

In this close relationship between primary groups and the polity, each modifies the other. On the one hand, partisanship tends to be less intense in these two countries, and therefore constitutes less of an objective threat to the stability of primary relationships. On the other hand, it would appear that the American and British families tend to be somewhat more "modern," more participating, more secularized in their communications patterns and decision-making mechanisms.[17] Consequently, they are better able to handle partisanship without being damaged. Perhaps what we are describing in these two countries is an overall pattern of greater secularization, which implies a great capacity for affective neutrality in all relationships, more of a multiple-value orientation, more tolerance of ambiguity. Furthermore, it may be that the greater secularization of the political market in England and the United States and the presence of primary-group protective mechanisms have a feedback effect, tending to mitigate conflict at the level of party elites. It is not accidental that the ritual of shaking hands by winner and loser and the sending of the congratulatory telegram by the loser to the winner are common occurrences in the United States and Britain, whereas they are rare on the European continent. It is almost as though a bargain had been struck between the community and the polity. If the primary group is to be open to the partisanship of the polity, then the polity must assimilate some of the cohesive properties of the primary group. In Britain this is effectively symbolized in the widespread acceptance of the quasi-sacredness of the Royal Family, a sacredness that makes "Her Majesty's government" and "Her Majesty's loyal opposition" members of the same national family. In the United States this quality of quasi-sacred community is symbolized in a number of roles and institutions — the national representative role of the presidency, the supralegal symbolic qualities of the Constitution, the special status of the Supreme Court, and the like.

[17] See Chapter XI for a further discussion of family patterns in the five nations.

It is this very mixture of the values of community and polity in Britain and the United States, this set of mechanisms that mitigate partisan cleavage, that create the psychological conditions necessary for the propensity to form informal groups. The nature of partisan and interest-group commitment is such that the individual can mobilize his own personal and community network in situations of political stress or threat. In a sense it is the old "right of revolution" now institutionalized in a widespread capability to act outside the organized infrastructure of democracy; the reserve power of the democratic citizen that gives him a right of independent access to political influence.

Thus the "buzz" of group activity in the United States and Britain, this characteristic tone of their politics, appears to be rooted in some fundamental characteristics of the social system. That people can so easily cooperate with each other in political activities is based on the fact that, despite political differences, they are tied to their fellow citizens by a set of interpersonal values, and these values overarch the political and nonpolitical aspects of the system. Though the two political systems are highly "modern" — highly differentiated, with functionally specific interest groups, political parties, and governmental agencies — they are in a sense embedded in a "national community." The "modern" political system has within it the seeds of great fragmentation — among political structures, along partisan lines, between polity and society. But in Britain and the United States this fragmentation is impeded by the force of shared social values and attitudes, which permeate all aspects of society.

CHAPTER X

Organizational Membership and Civic Competence

A CIVIC CULTURE, we have argued, rests upon a set of nonpolitical attitudes and nonpolitical affiliations. Many of these attitudes that we have discussed — general attitudes toward other people, sense of social trust — have little explicit political content, and many of the affiliations we have dealt with, primary group affiliations in particular, are quite distant from the political system. Our concentration on this level of social structure has not meant to imply that larger, secondary, nonpolitical groups (voluntary associations are the main example) play an insignificant role in the democratic polity. Quite the contrary: though primary associations play an important role in the development of a citizen's sense of political competence and reflect an incipient capability to aggregate one's demands with others, they would, by themselves, represent a weak link between the individual and the polity. As Kornhauser has pointed out, primary groups are still small and powerless compared with the mass institutions of politics. Larger institutions, close enough to the individual to allow him some participation and yet close enough to the state to provide access to power, are also a necessary part of the democratic infrastructure.[1]

[1] William Kornhauser, *The Politics of Mass Society*, Glencoe, Ill., 1959.

Voluntary associations are the prime means by which the function of mediating between the individual and the state is performed. Through them the individual is able to relate himself effectively and meaningfully to the political system. These associations help him avoid the dilemma of being either a parochial, cut off from political influence, or an isolated and powerless individual, manipulated and mobilized by the mass institutions of politics and government. The availability of his primary groups as a political resource in times of threat gives him an intermittent political resource. Membership in voluntary associations gives him a more structured set of political resources, growing out of his varied interests.

If the citizen is a member of some voluntary organization, he is involved in the broader social world but is less dependent upon and less controlled by his political system. The association of which he is a member can represent his needs and demands before the government. It can make the government more chary of engaging in activities that would harm the individual. Furthermore, communications from central governmental authorities are mediated by the associational memberships of the individual because individuals tend to interpret communications according to their memberships in social groupings — that is, they are likely to reject communications unfavorable to the association to which they belong — and because they may also receive communications from their associations and are thereby provided with alternate channels of political communication. Above all, from the point of view of the individual member, affiliation with some voluntary organization appears to have significant effects on his political attitudes. We shall try to specify these effects in this chapter.

In dealing with the data on associational membership, we must consider one further point. Associational membership may involve a low level of individual participation and competence: associations may be quite large; opportunities for participation limited. Thus the existence of a high frequency of membership may tell us more about the political institutions of a society than it does about the state of citizenship in that society. For the latter we shall have to know more about the nature of the membership — how active individuals are in their organizations and what effects their memberships have upon them.

THE DISTRIBUTION OF VOLUNTARY ASSOCIATION MEMBERSHIP

Voluntary association membership is more widespread in some countries than in others. This is apparent from Table X.1. In the United States over half the respondents are members of some such organization.[2] In Britain and Germany somewhat less than half the respondents are members of some organization, whereas in Italy and Mexico the proportions are 29 per cent and 25 per cent, respectively.

To what sorts of organizations do individuals in the five countries belong? The range of specific organizations is wide. But Table X.2 suggests some of the main types. In all countries organizations representing economic interests — unions, business organizations, farm organizations, and, perhaps, professional organizations — are frequently reported. Social or-

TABLE X.1 *Membership in voluntary associations; by nation*

Nation	(%)	(*No.*)*
United States	57	(970)
Great Britain	47	(963)
Germany	44	(955)
Italy	29	(995)
Mexico	25	(1,007)

* Numbers in parentheses refer to the bases upon which percentages are calculated.

[2] These data are based on responses to this question: "Are you a member of any organizations now — trade or labor unions, business organizations, social groups, professional or farm organizations, cooperatives, fraternal or veterans' groups, athletic clubs, political, charitable, civic or religious organizations, or any other organized group? Which ones?" The amount of voluntary association membership depends heavily upon the wording of the question and on the definition given the respondent of a voluntary association. The inclusion of trade unions, for instance, results in a somewhat higher figure than has been found in other studies. However, what is relevant here is not the absolute level of membership in any one nation, but the relative position of each of the five nations. What is significant, then, is that the same question was asked in all five nations.

TABLE X.2 *Membership in various types of organizations; by nation*

Organization	*U.S.*	*U.K.*	*Germany*	*Italy*	*Mexico*
Trade unions	14	22	15	6	11
Business	4	4	2	5	2
Professional	4	3	6	3	5
Farm	3	0	4	2	0
Social	13	14	10	3	4
Charitable	3	3	2	9	6
Religious[a]	19	4	3	6	5
Civic-political	11	3	3	8	3
Cooperative	6	3	2	2	0
Veterans'	6	5	1	4	0
Fraternal [b]	13				
Other	6	3	9	6	0
Total percentage of members	57	47	44	30	24
Total number of respondents	970	963	955	995	1,007

[a] This refers to church-related organizations, not to church affiliation itself.

[b] U.S. only.

ganizations are mentioned by 10 per cent or more of our sample in the United States, Britain, and Germany; and in the United States religious, civic-political, and fraternal organizations are also mentioned by 10 per cent or more of the respondents. One point to note is that the extent of "politicization" of these organizations, that is, the extent to which they are overtly engaged in politics, probably varies greatly. Some of the economic organizations are obviously deeply politicized; some of the social ones may be completely nonpolitical. We

TABLE X.3 *Percentage of respondents who belong to some organization; by nation and sex*

Nation	*Total* (%)	*Total* (*No.*)*	*Male* (%)	*Male* (*No.*)	*Female* (%)	*Female* (*No.*)
United States	57	(970)	68	(455)	47	(515)
Great Britain	47	(963)	66	(460)	30	(503)
Germany	44	(955)	66	(449)	24	(506)
Italy	30	(995)	41	(471)	19	(524)
Mexico	24	(1,007)	43	(355)	15	(652)

* Numbers in parentheses refer to the bases upon which percentages are calculated.

shall return below to the implications of this for political attitudes.

The distribution of organizational membership is also interesting. If we look at the proportion of men and women who are members of some organizations, we see some striking results (see Table X.3). The national differences in the number of individuals participating in associations can be largely explained by differences in the proportion of women who report such membership. Thus the high level of associational membership in the United States depends to a large extent on the high level of female participation. If only males are considered, associational participation in the United States is no more frequent than it is in Britain or Germany. It is, in fact, striking how similar the frequency of membership is among the three nations: about two-thirds of the male respondents in each of the three nations report such membership. Among females, on the other hand, participation in the United States is substantially more frequent than in Britain and about twice as frequent as in Germany. In Mexico and Italy the level of participation by both males and females is lower than in the other three countries. However, a similar relationship between frequency of male participation and frequency of female participation is found in all nations except the United States; that is, men participate in voluntary organizations about two to three times as frequently as do women. In the participatory role of women, then, the United States differs substantially from the other four countries, for American women, though they participate less frequently than American men in voluntary associations, do not differ from men in this respect as much as do women in other countries.

Just as men participate more frequently in voluntary associations, so do individuals with higher education. This is seen in Table X.4. In all countries there is a sharp increase in organizational membership as one moves up the educational ladder. Among those with primary school education, memberships are much less frequent than among those with higher education, suggesting one of the reasons for the close relationship between education and political competence. Education has compound effects upon political competence. Not

TABLE X.4 *Percentage of respondents who belong to some organization; by nation and education*

Nation	Total (%)	Total (No.)*	Prim. or less (%)	Prim. or less (No.)	Some sec. (%)	Some sec. (No.)	Some univ. (%)	Some univ. (No.)
United States	57	(970)	46	(339)	55	(443)	80	(188)
Great Britain	47	(963)	41	(593)	55	(322)	92	(24)
Germany	44	(955)	41	(792)	63	(124)	62	(26)
Italy	30	(995)	25	(692)	37	(245)	46	(54)
Mexico	24	(1,007)	21	(877)	39	(103)	68	(24)

* Numbers in parentheses refer to the bases upon which percentages are calculated.

only does the more highly educated individual learn politically relevant skills within the school, but he is also more likely to enter into other nonpolitical relationships that have the effect of further heightening his political competence. Associational membership is one form of such nonpolitical participation. The individual with less education, and therefore less political competence, is also less likely to enter into relationships that would develop political competence in later years. The data, then, do suggest that the various functions performed by voluntary associations are performed more frequently for those with higher education.[3]

We are interested in the way in which voluntary association membership affects political attitudes. But the types of associations we are dealing with are many and varied, and one would expect different effects from membership in different types of organizations. One way in which the organizations vary is in the extent to which they are concerned with public affairs. Some of the associations are purely social, others are directly and overtly politically oriented. One can argue — and, indeed, this is one of the major hypotheses about voluntary association membership — that membership in even a nonpolitical organization will affect political attitudes. The experience with social interaction within the organization, the opportunity to partici-

[3] Similar data could be presented for the distribution of organizational membership among the occupational strata. Higher occupational status generally involves more frequent voluntary association membership, though the relationship is not as close as that between education and affiliation.

pate in the decisions of the organization (if there is such participation), and the general broadening of perspectives that occurs in any sort of social activity — all would be expected to increase an individual's potential for political involvement and activity. Nevertheless, one would also expect to find that those organizations more directly involved in politics would have greater effects on the political perspectives of their members.[4]

Unfortunately, our data do not allow us objectively to divide the voluntary organizations into different types, based on the degree to which they take an active political role. We do, however, know whether or not the individual member perceives of his organization as taking some part in politics. Respondents were asked if any organization they belonged to was "in any way concerned with governmental, political, or public affairs; for instance, do they take stands on or discuss public issues or try to influence governmental decisions?" It must be remembered that this question probes the perceptions of the respondents: it asks for their own definition of political affairs. Furthermore, many members may not be aware of the activities of their organizations. A member of a veterans' group that is actively lobbying for veterans' benefits or for certain foreign policies may perceive his group in essentially social terms. Thus these data do not necessarily reflect the actual state of political activity by voluntary associations. But we are interested in the impact of membership in political and nonpolitical organizations on political attitudes, and so these data on the individual's perception of the political role of his organization may be sufficient.

Table X.5 reports the frequency with which respondents in our five countries perceive that their organizations take some part in politics. In the United States about one in four respondents belongs to an organization that he perceives to be

[4] Similarly, such organizations would probably also have greater effects on the operation of the political system. Even those that take no active role in politics — do not press for legislation, are politically unconcerned — may have a significant role in political decisions. Their very existence as *potential* political organizations may affect the decisions of government officials in ways that would not happen if these particular groups were not organized. Yet all else being equal, one would expect an overtly political group to have more of an impact on political decisions.

TABLE X.5 *Respondents who believe an organization of theirs is involved in political affairs; by nation*

Nation	*% of Total population* (%)	(*No.*)*	*% of Organizational members* (%)	(*No.*)
United States	24	(970)	41	(551)
Great Britain	19	(963)	40	(453)
Germany	18	(955)	40	(419)
Italy	6	(995)	20	(291)
Mexico	11	(1,007)	46	(242)

* Numbers in parentheses refer to the bases upon which percentages are calculated.

involved in politics.[5] This proportion falls off to 6 per cent in Italy. Though the nations differ in the percentage of the *total population* who perceive that an organization of theirs is involved in political affairs (column 1), the proportion of *organizational members* who hold this perception is strikingly uniform among the nations (column 2). With the exception of Italy, approximately the same proportion of organizational members in each country — 40 to 45 per cent — perceives itself to be part of a politically active organization. For about one-fifth of the Italian members and about two-fifths of the members in each of the other nations, being part of an organization does involve (in terms of the individual's awareness) recruitment into the political system.

[5] That the frequency with which an individual reports affiliation with a political organization varies with his definition of politics is suggested by a finding made by Woodward and Roper: 31 per cent of their sample responded positively to the question, "Do you happen to belong to any organizations that sometimes take a stand on housing, better government, school problems, or other public issues?" In contrast, 24 per cent in our sample answered our question positively. The difference may be due to the fact that many of our respondents would not consider "school problems" a political question. See Julian L. Woodward and Elmo Roper, "Political Activity of American Citizens," *American Political Science Review,* XLIV (1950), pp. 872-85.

ORGANIZATIONAL MEMBERSHIP AND POLITICAL COMPETENCE

Political and Nonpolitical Organizations. What effect, if any, does organizational membership have on political attitudes? Do those individuals who are members of some organization differ in their political perspectives from those who are not members? And does membership in any sort of organization, political as well as non-political, affect one's political views? Or is it only membership in a politically relevant organization that influences one's perspectives on politics? The political attitudes we are interested in are those associated with democratic citizenship, as we have defined it. If organizational membership fosters the development of a democratic citizenry, one would expect the members, in comparison with those who are not members, to feel more confident of their ability to influence the government, to be more active in politics, more "open" in their political opinions, and, in general, more committed to democratic values.

Let us look first at the relationship between organizational membership and the individual's sense of ability to influence the government. This sense of competence, we have suggested earlier, is a major attitudinal variable in understanding the political perspectives of the individual, and it has significant implications for a wide range of other important political attitudes. Table X.6 reports the proportion of respondents receiving high scores on the subjective competence scale among (1) those respondents who are members of organizations they consider to be involved in politics, (2) those who are members of nonpolitical organizations, and (3) those who are members of no organization. The results are striking, and quite uniform from nation to nation. In all nations those respondents who are members of no organization are generally lower in the scale than our organizational members. And among organizational members, those respondents who consider their organization to be involved in politics are most likely to receive high scores on the scale. In Great Britain, for instance, 80 per cent of the members of a politically oriented organization are to be found in the highest three scores of the subjective compe-

TABLE X.6 *Percentage of respondents who scored highest in subjective competence*[a] *among members of political and nonpolitical organizations; by nation and education*

	Total						Primary or less						Secondary or more					
	Member political organiz.		Member nonpolitical organiz.		Non-member		Member political organiz.		Member nonpolitical organiz.		Non-member		Member political organiz.		Member nonpolitical organiz.		Non-member	
Nation	(%)	(No.)[b]	(%)	(No.)	(%)	(No.)	(%)	(No.)	(%)	(No.)	(%)	(No.)	(%)	(No.)	(%)	(No.)	(%)	(No.)
United States	79	(228)	70	(322)	54	(418)	65	(91)	60	(163)	46	(263)	87	(137)	81	(160)	68	(156)
Great Britain	80	(193)	69	(157)	56	(510)	83	(97)	61	(144)	52	(352)	74	(86)	77	(112)	62	(148)
Germany	60	(172)	52	(246)	37	(534)	59	(137)	48	(184)	34	(471)	94	(32)	65	(63)	57	(55)
Italy	77	(56)	49	(234)	34	(701)	68	(25)	45	(148)	29	(519)	85	(31)	55	(85)	48	(183)
Mexico	57	(103)	45	(139)	33	(765)	54	(79)	40	(101)	33	(697)	64	(24)	58	(36)	46	(67)

[a] I.e., those who received three highest scores on the subjective competence scale

[b] Numbers in parentheses refer to the bases upon which percentages are calculated.

tence scale; 69 per cent of the members of a nonpolitical organization are in these top three categories; while only 56 per cent of those who belong to no organization can be found in the highest categories of the scale. In Italy 77 per cent of the members of politically oriented organizations score high on the scale, in contrast with 49 per cent of those who belong to nonpolitical organizations, and 34 per cent of those who belong to no organization.

Both subjective competence and the frequency of organizational membership are related to educational attainment. Thus it is important to note that this relationship between membership and sense of ability to influence the government persists when educational level is held constant. Only among British respondents with higher education is there a reversal of the trend: those respondents who are members of a nonpolitical organization score slightly better on the subjective competence scale than do the respondents who are members of a political organization. But the expected pattern is quite strong among British respondents in the lower educational group, and on both educational levels elsewhere.

Table X.6 presents striking confirmation of the hypothesis about the impact of organizational membership on political attitudes. Such membership is indeed related to a citizen's self-confidence. The individual who belongs to an organization, compared with one who does not, is more likely to feel competent to influence the government. The table shows that the kind of organization one belongs to also makes a difference. Those who are members of a politically related organization are more likely to feel competent in their relations with the government than are those who belong to a nonpolitical organization. But the most striking finding is the contrast between those who are members of organizations that they do not perceive as being political and those who are members of no organization. In all nations, on both levels of education, those who are members of a nonpolitical organization are more likely to feel subjectively competent than are those who belong to no organization. This, then, appears to confirm the fact that latent political functions are performed by voluntary associations, whether these organizations are explicitly political or not. Those who are members of some organization, even if they report that it has no political role, have more political competence than those who have no such membership.

A similar pattern appears if we consider political discussion. Members of politically oriented organizations report more often than the other respondents that they discuss politics. This is to be expected, and it appears in all five nations and on both levels of education (with the exception of the Mexican respondents with higher education, where there is a slight reversal). And, as with the data on subjective competence, the individual who is a member of a nonpolitical organization is more likely to report he discusses politics than is the individual who belongs to no organization. Thus in Germany: 88 per cent of those who belong to a political organization discuss politics, in contrast with 70 per cent of the members of a nonpolitical organization. And both these percentages contrast with the figure that represents the frequency of such discussion among nonmembers: 47 per cent. Organizational membership, apparently, even if explicitly nonpolitical, makes it more likely that an individual will have a sense of ability to participate in politics and that he will actually participate in political discussion.

Organizational membership also seems to expand an individual's range of political opinion. If we compare members of politically oriented organizations, members of nonpolitical organizations, and nonmembers, according to their willingness to express opinions on a variety of political questions, we find that members of political organizations are most likely to express a wide range of political opinions; members of nonpolitical organizations and nonmembers followed in order. In Italy, for example, 68 per cent of the members of some politically oriented organization answered all six questions used to measure range of opinion, in contrast with 36 per cent of those who were members of a nonpolitical organization, and 20 per cent of those who belonged to no organization at all.[6]

Membership in an organization, political or not, appears

[6] See Chapter II for a description of the questions that are involved.

therefore to be related to an increase in the political competence and activity of the individual.[7] The member, in contrast with the nonmember, appears to approximate more closely what we have called the democratic citizen. He is competent, active, and open with his opinions.

Active and Passive Membership. One reason why organizational membership might be expected to effect political competence and activity is that the members of such organizations receive training for participation within the organization, and this training is then transferable to the political sphere. According to this argument, a member of an organization will have greater opportunity to participate actively within the organization than he would have within the larger political system. Organizations are, in a sense, small political systems, and both the skill in participation and the expectation that one can participate increase the individual's competence vis-à-vis the political system. Furthermore — and this is one of the most important effects imputed to organizational membership — training within these organizations means that there are alternate channels of recruitment into politics. If opportunities to participate in organizations did not exist, all such training for participation would have to take place within the political system itself, and would be dominated by the more general norms of that system. The existence of alternate channels means that the recruitment into political activity will not be as closely controlled by incumbent elites. In this way organizational participation leads to greater pluralism.

But we cannot assume that membership in a voluntary association necessarily involves active participation by the member. Many of these organizations are large and complex; to the individual member, perhaps they are as large and complex, with as distant centers of power, as his nation. Many of these organizations are centrally controlled, and allow little room for individual participation. Membership may offer very little training for political participation. A member of a large,

[7] This relationship between group membership and political efficacy and activity is reported in some of the studies carried on by the Survey Research Center, and in other community studies. See Robert E. Lane, *Political Life,* p. 188.

centrally organized trade union, for example, may feel as passive a participant in his organization as does a subject in a large, authoritarian nation; and he may in fact have as little voice.

To trace the impact of organizational membership on political attitudes, therefore, it is important to consider the extent to which individuals take active roles in their organizations. The gross membership figures tell us nothing about this participation. In order to have some estimate of the extent to which membership involves active participation, those respondents who reported membership were asked if they took any active role within their organization: in particular, whether they had ever held any form of official position, high or low, in a local branch or in some central office.

The data (see Table X.7) bring out more striking differences among countries than did the figures on gross membership. In the United States 26 per cent of the respondents report that they have held some such position in an organization. In Britain the proportion, though lower (13 per cent), is substantially above that in the other countries (7 to 8 per cent). This suggests that the effect of voluntary associations upon the nature of citizenship may differ significantly from one country to another. In some countries there is a relatively large stratum of individuals who more or less actively participate in the decision making of voluntary associations; elsewhere, organizational membership may be relatively formal and lacking in

TABLE X.7 *Respondents who report having been officers in organizations; by nation*

Nation	*Percentage of total population* (%)	(*No.*)*	*Percentage of organization members* (%)	(*No.*)
United States	26	(970)	46	(551)
Great Britain	13	(963)	29	(453)
Germany	7	(955)	16	(419)
Italy	7	(995)	23	(291)
Mexico	8	(1,007)	34	(242)

* Numbers in parentheses refer to the bases upon which percentages are calculated.

participatory opportunities. Organizations in which there is some opportunity for the individual to take an active part may be as significant for the development of democratic citizenship as are voluntary organizations in general.

These considerations add another link to our discussion of the nature of participation in the five countries. In particular, they point to a sharp distinction between the nature of participation in Germany, on the one hand, and Great Britain and the United States, on the other. All three countries are relatively high on organizational membership, especially among males. Yet the differences in the proportions of members who are active participating members (as measured by whether or not they have ever held an official position) are sharp. If we look at the second column of Table X.7 (the proportion of members who have held some official position), we see that 46 per cent of American members and 29 per cent of British members have held some official position in one of the organizations to which they belong, while only 16 per cent of the German members have had experience in active participation. (In fact, the percentage of active group members is lower in Germany than in Mexico or Italy — although in the latter two countries we are dealing with a much smaller population of group members.) Here again is a reflection of the tendency for participation in Germany to be widespread but not intense. It tends to be formal and involves little direct individual commitment and activity. Formal organizations in Germany, like those in Britain and the United States, are widespread and important in policy determination. But they differ in the degree to which they afford opportunities for their members to participate in decisions. Once again we find that in Germany the structures of a democratic system are well developed, but they do not yet play significant roles in the perspectives and behavior of citizens. They are elements of a democratic political structure; they are not yet assimilated into a democratic political culture.

The differences in the frequency of participation within organizations are highlighted if we consider which members are likely to be active. In general, as the data in Tables X.8 and X.9 indicate, males and those with higher education are more

TABLE X.8 *Organization members who have ever been officers; by nation and sex*

Nation	*Total* (%)	(*No.*)*	*Male* (%)	(*No.*)	*Female* (%)	(*No.*)
United States	46	(551)	41	(309)	52	(242)
Great Britain	29	(453)	32	(304)	22	(149)
Germany	16	(419)	18	(298)	9	(121)
Italy	23	(291)	24	(193)	19	(98)
Mexico	34	(242)	43	(146)	18	(96)

* Numbers in parentheses refer to the bases upon which percentages are calculated.

TABLE X.9 *Organization members who have ever been officers; by nation and education*

Nation	*Total* (%)	(*No.*)*	*Prim. or less* (%)	(*No.*)	*Some sec.* (%)	(*No.*)	*Some univ.* (%)	(*No.*)
United States	46	(551)	31	(156)	44	(245)	64	(150)
Great Britain	29	(453)	23	(241)	31	(176)	64	(22)
Germany	16	(419)	12	(321)	24	(79)	38	(16)
Italy	23	(291)	13	(173)	36	(91)	38	(26)
Mexico	33	(242)	30	(181)	39	(44)	52	(17)

* Numbers in parentheses refer to the bases upon which percentages are calculated.

likely to be active in their organizations than are female members and members with less education. An exception occurs in the United States, where female organizational members are more likely to be active participants than are men.[8]

It is of particular interest that the German pattern of frequent organizational membership, coupled with infrequent participation within the organization, is relatively uniform among all the German subgroups. Though German males are members of organizations as frequently as are British or

[8] A similar relationship was found in a study by John C. Scott ("Membership and Participation in Voluntary Associations," *American Sociological Review,* XXII [1957], pp. 315-26). He found that male respondents in a New England town were more likely than female respondents to belong to an organization. But among the organizational members, women were more likely to be officers than men. One reason for this may be the smaller size of the organizations to which women belong.

American males, and though Germans in particular educational groups are members as frequently as are their British or American counterparts, in no subgroup in Tables X.8 or X.9 do we find German respondents as frequently active within their organizations as are American and British respondents. Compare, for example, male respondents in the three countries. German males are as likely as British or American males to be members of voluntary associations: the proportions who report membership are 68 per cent in the United States and 66 per cent in Britain and Germany. On the other hand, 41 per cent of American male members and 32 per cent of the British male members report that they have been active in their organizations, whereas only 18 per cent of the German male members report such participation. Similar contrasts can be found in Table X.9 among the various educational groups, and can be observed as well within the various occupational groups.

The extent to which organizational membership involves some sort of active participation within that organization appears to vary significantly from nation to nation, and within nations among sex and educational groupings as well. Not all members take an active role in their organization. Furthermore, the extent to which an individual is active in the organization seems to be related to his political perspectives, as suggested clearly in Table X.10. Again we use the subjective competence score to measure this relationship (though measures of political activity would give similar results). Organizational members who have held active positions in their organizations are more likely than rank-and-file members to receive high scores on this scale. In Italy, for instance, 76 per cent of these respondents who report some active participation within their organization score in the top three categories of our scale of subjective competence, in contrast with 48 per cent of the more passive organizational members. However, even passive membership, when compared with nonmembership, appears to be associated with an increased sense of political competence. Whereas 48 per cent of the passive members score in the top three categories of the subjective competence scale, only 34 per cent of the nonmembers are in the higher levels. And the pattern for Italy is apparent in all nations, for individuals on

Table X.10 *Percentage of respondents who scored highest in subjective competence*[a] *by the extent of their activity in organizations; by nation and education*

	Total						Primary or less						Secondary or more					
	Active member		*Passive member*		*Non-member*		*Active member*		*Passive member*		*Non-member*		*Active member*		*Passive member*		*Non-member*	
Nation	(%)	(*No.*)[b]	(%)	(*No.*)	(%)	(*No.*)	(%)	(*No.*)	(%)	(*No.*)	(%)	(*No.*)	(%)	(*No.*)	(%)	(*No.*)	(%)	(*No.*)
United States	82	(253)	66	(298)	54	(418)	68	(98)	55	(166)	46	(263)	85	(165)	80	(132)	69	(156)
Great Britain	84	(130)	69	(320)	55	(510)	86	(56)	66	(184)	52	(352)	84	(69)	73	(127)	62	(148)
Germany	72	(65)	55	(353)	37	(534)	69	(39)	50	(282)	35	(471)	80	(25)	74	(69)	55	(55)
Italy	76	(66)	48	(224)	34	(701)	53	(32)	44	(150)	29	(519)	74	(43)	56	(73)	49	(183)
Mexico	68	(83)	42	(159)	33	(765)	63	(56)	39	(124)	32	(697)	76	(27)	49	(33)	46	(67)

[a] I.e., those who received three highest scores on the subjective competence scale.

[b] Numbers in parentheses refer to the bases upon which percentages are calculated.

both educational levels and for men and women. Apparently both the type of organization one belongs to and the intensity of one's activity within it are related to one's political attitudes. Yet organizational membership per se appears to have a residual effect on political competence and activity. The passive member as well as the member of a nonpolitical organization still differ from the individual who reports no such membership.[9]

These findings strongly support the proposition associated with the theory of mass society that the existence of voluntary associations increases the democratic potential of a society. Democracy depends upon citizen participation, and it is clear that organizational membership is directly related to such participation. The organizational member is likely to be a self-confident citizen as well as an active one. We can also specify somewhat more precisely the impact on political competence of various types of organizational membership. Membership in a *politically oriented* organization appears to lead to greater political competence than does membership in a nonpolitical organization, and *active* membership in an organization has a greater impact on political competence than does passive membership. This fact is important because it helps explain the differential effect of organizational membership among the nations. Lipset, using data from a variety of surveys, points out that the frequency of voluntary association membership is

[9] In 1948 the American military government in Germany conducted a survey among German youth to evaluate how effective the newly formed youth organizations were in the inculcation of democratic attitudes. They found that there was relatively little difference between youth club members and nonmembers in their adherence to democratic attitudes. For instance, 58 per cent of the youth club members and 55 per cent of the nonmembers believed it was better for a club to have a leader elected by majority rule rather than appointed. In contrast, 72 per cent of the club members whose own club leaders were elected favored election of leaders, in comparison with 48 per cent of the club members whose own leaders were appointed. Apparently the nature of the authority structure in the youth club had a greater effect on youth attitudes than did the fact of membership per se. See Office of Military Government for Germany (US), Opinion Survey Report No. 99, March 5, 1948, "A Report on German Youth." The survey of youth is based on 2,337 interviews with respondents between the ages of 10 and 25 years.

about as great in such stable democracies as the United States, Britain, and Sweden as it is in the relatively less stable democracies of Germany and France — a finding that seems to challenge the idea of a connection between stable democracy and organizational membership.[10] Our data for the United States, Britain, and Germany confirm that the rates of membership are similar for the three nations. But our findings also indicate that organizational membership may have quite different implications among the three nations. In Britain and the United States organizational membership much more frequently involves active participation within the organization than it does in Germany, where relatively few members appear to take an active part. And, as our data further show, the degree of activity within an organization has an effect upon political attitudes. The active member is more likely to be the competent democratic citizen.[11]

Multiple Membership. One other aspect of organizational participation must be considered to round out our picture of the differing patterns of participation and the impact of that participation on political attitudes among the nations. This is the number of organizations to which individuals belong. If one considers merely the frequency of membership and nonmembership among the nations, one finds some striking differences, yet this does not indicate the full extent of the differences in the amount of organizational participation. Nations differ, not only in the frequency with which respondents report membership, but also — and perhaps even more strikingly — in the frequency with which individuals report membership in more than one organization. This fact is illustrated in Table X.11. In the United States about one-third of our total sample are members of more than one organization and, indeed, 9 per cent of the sample are members of four or more organiza-

[10] See Lipset, *Political Man,* p. 67.

[11] We have no data that are comparable for Sweden or France, the other two nations cited by Lipset; but description of French voluntary associations strongly suggest that, like the German and unlike the American and British, they tend to be highly centralized and to allow little opportunity for active participation. See in particular Arnold Rose, *Theory and Method in the Social Sciences,* Minneapolis, 1954, p. 74, and M. Crozier, "La France, Terre du Commandement," *Esprit,* XXV (1957), 779-98.

tions. In Britain 16 per cent of the total sample are members of more than one organization. The figure falls off to 12 per cent of the total in Germany, 6 per cent in Italy, and 2 per cent in Mexico. Though on many measures of participation Great Britain and the United States were quite similar, on the question of organizational membership the impressions of many observers prove correct. Organizational participation in the United States, both in the total number who are members and the number who are members of several organizations, is much higher than that of any other country. This is reflected in the proportion of the total sample who are multiple members, as well as in the proportion of organization members who are members of more than one organization. In the United States 55 per cent of organizational members belong to more than one organization. The other figures are: Britain, 34 per cent; Germany, 27 per cent; Italy, 20 per cent, and Mexico, 8 per cent.

TABLE X.11 *Respondents who belong to one or more organizations; by nation*

Percentage who	*U.S.*	*U.K.*	*Germany*	*Italy*	*Mexico*
Belong to one organization	25	31	32	24	23
Belong to two organizations	14	10	9	5	2
Belong to three organizations	9	4	2	1	0
Belong to four or more organizations	9	2	1	*	*
Total percentage of multiple members	32	16	12	6	2
Total percentage of members	57 (970)[a]	47 (963)	44 (955)	30 (995)	25 (1007)

[a] Numbers in parentheses refer to the bases upon which percentages are calculated.

The number of organizations to which an individual belongs also affects his political competence. Organizational membership appears to have a cumulative effect; that is, membership in one organization increases an individual's sense of political competence, and membership in more than one organization leads to even greater competence. Those who belong to an organization show higher political competence than those who are members of no organization, but the members of more than one organization show even higher competence than those whose affiliation is limited to one.

What we have shown so far is that voluntary associations do play a major role in a democratic political culture. The organizational member, compared with the nonmember, is likely to consider himself more competent as a citizen, to be a more active participant in politics, and to know and care more about politics. He is, therefore, more likely to be close to the model of the democratic citizen. We have also shown that it makes a difference which type of organization an individual belongs to; political organizations yield a larger political "dividend" than do nonpolitical organizations. And it makes a difference how active an individual is within his own organization: the active member displays a greater sense of political competence than does the passive member. But perhaps the most striking finding is that any membership — passive membership or membership in a nonpolitical organization — has an impact on political competence. Membership in some association, even if the individual does not consider the membership politically relevant and even if it does not involve his active participation, does lead to a more competent citizenry. Pluralism, even if not explicitly political pluralism, may indeed be one of the most important foundations of political democracy.

CHAPTER XI

Political Socialization and Civic Competence

THE THEORY OF POLITICAL SOCIALIZATION

RECENT DISCUSSIONS of the process involved in the formation of adult political attitudes suggest a complex set of relationships.[1] The earlier psychocultural approach to the subject regarded political socialization as a rather simple process. Three assumptions were usually made: (1) the significant socialization experiences that will affect later political behavior take place quite early in life; (2) these experiences are not manifestly political experiences, but they have latent political consequences — that is, they are neither intended to have political effects nor are these effects recognized, and (3) the socialization process is a unidirectional one: the more "basic" family experiences have a significant impact upon the secondary structures of politics but are not in turn affected by them. Thus the

[1] See, for example, the various criticisms of the "authoritarian personality" studies, especially: Richard Christie and Marie Jahoda (eds.), *Studies in the Scope and Method of the Authoritarian Personality,* Glencoe, Ill., 1954. The chapters by Edward A. Shils, Herbert H. Hyman and Paul B. Sheatsley, and Harold D. Lasswell are particularly relevant. See also Herbert Hyman, *Political Socialization,* Glencoe, Ill., 1959; Sidney Verba, *Small Groups and Political Behavior,* Princeton, N.J., 1961, pp. 29 ff.; Gabriel A. Almond and James S. Coleman, *The Politics of the Developing Areas,* Princeton, N.J., 1960, pp. 26-33.

source of German attitudes toward authority was said to lie in the structure of authority in the German family and the expectations that derived from experiences with that authority structure; American and Russian political behavior could be traced to such early, nonpolitical experiences as patterns of weaning or toilet training.[2]

This approach to an explanation of political attitudes was too simple. One could not make unambiguous connections between early socialization experiences and politics; the gap between the two was so great that it could be closed only by the use of somewhat imprecise analogies and a rather selective approach to evidence. But though it was wrong in its specific statements about political behavior (at least its more incautious adherents were wrong), this approach was a fruitful beginning. A number of the assumptions were correct and did suggest new insights into the sources of political attitudes. Attention was focused on pre-adult experiences as a source of political attitudes. It was also suggested that authority pattern in pre-adult social situations played a crucial role in the formation of political predispositions. In general, nonpolitical human relations became a source for understanding political relations.

Where this approach to political attitude formation went wrong was in narrowing the focus of these assumptions. Nonpolitical experiences in childhood may play an important part in later political attitudes and behavior, but the impact of these experiences on politics continues throughout the adolescent and adult years. In fact there is some evidence that later experiences have a more direct political implication. Early socialization experiences significantly affect an individual's basic personality predispositions and may therefore affect his political behavior, but numerous other factors intervene between these earliest experiences and later political behavior that greatly inhibit the impact of the former on the latter. Such basic dimensions of political behavior as the degree of activity or involvement in politics or the individual's partisan

[2] For examples of this approach, see the works by Schaffner, Mead, and Gorer cited above in Chapter I, note 6.

affilation seem to be best explained in terms of later experiences.[3]

Another valuable insight of the psychocultural approach was that the nonpolitical authority patterns to which an individual is exposed have an important effect on his attitudes toward political authority. The authority patterns in the family are his first exposure to authority. And it is likely that his first view of the political system represents a generalization from these experiences.[4] But to think of the political system as the family writ large — as was essentially the view of those who saw the roots of the German authoritarian tradition within the German family — is too simple. In the first place, as will be pointed out below, certain characteristics of family authority patterns make generalization to the political realm somewhat difficult. Furthermore, there are a host of other nongovernmental authority patterns to which the individual is exposed: in school, on the job, in the various organizations to which he belongs. And these other patterns, particularly those closer in time and in kind to the political system, may have greater importance for political behavior than have the patterns in the family.[5]

Like the emphasis on family authority patterns, the importance attached to nonpolitical experiences carrying latent political consequences represented a significant, but too narrow, insight. The latent political socialization that is involved in, say, experiences with family authority patterns may cre-

[3] For a discussion of the factors that can intervene between early socialization experiences and political behavior, see Nathan Leites, "Psychocultural Hypotheses About Political Acts," *World Politics,* I (1948), pp. 102ff.

[4] Hess and Easton point out that the child's first image of the President represents a transfer from family experience, but he begins to differentiate between political and family roles as he grows older. See Robert D. Hess and David Easton, "The Child's Image of the President," *Public Opinion Quarterly,* XXIV (1960), pp. 632-44.

[5] See Harry Eckstein, *A Theory of Stable Democracy,* Princeton, N.J., 1961. Data to be presented later in this chapter will support Eckstein's point that the authority patterns closer to the political realm have a greater significance for political attitudes.

ate certain predispositions toward political attitudes within the individual; his receptivity to particular types of political relationships may be increased. But this is obviously an inadequate explanation of his political attitudes, for there are other forms of political socialization. There is, for instance, manifest political socialization — the intentional teaching of political attitudes in the family and in school. Perhaps of greater importance is the unintentional exposure of a child to material that is explicitly political — the views he hears expressed about politics or political leaders, explicitly political views that are communicated to him without the express intent of forming his political attitudes. It is likely, for instance, that a good deal of the transfer of partisan allegiance from generation to generation does not depend upon the intentional teaching of political views, but upon the fact that children hear their parents discussing politics and adopt the views they hear. Or more general attitudes, such as respect or lack of respect for government, might be formed in this way. Wylie, for instance, reports that children in the French village he studied ". . . constantly hear adults referring to government as the source of evil and to the men who run it as instruments of evil. There is nothing personal in this belief. It does not concern one particular government composed of one particular group of men. It concerns government everywhere and at all times — French governments, American governments, Russian governments, all governments. Some are less bad than others, but all are essentially bad." [6] Such unintentional exposure to political attitudes may be a major way in which *incivism* is passed on from generation to generation.

Attitudes toward politics may therefore be formed by exposure to the political attitudes of others, whether the attitude formation is intentional or unintentional. And this for-

[6] Lawrence Wylie, *Village in the Vaucluse*, p. 208. It is interesting to note that this political lesson is effective despite the fact that it directly contrasts with the teachings in the civics textbooks. It suggests that the explicitly political material that the child hears informally and that represents the real political attitudes of adults is more significant than the formal education he receives.

mation on the basis of political experience must be added to the attitude formation that occurs through the transfer of attitudes from the nonpolitical to the political realm.

There is one last respect in which the theory of political socialization needs expansion. The flow of influence is not necessarily unidirectional. Not only may the authority patterns of family or school or occupation influence the political system, but it is also possible for the standards applied to the political system to influence authority patterns in these other areas. In the United States, for instance, the norms of *political* democracy are often used as arguments in favor of further democratization of school and employment relationships. Though much of this may have little effect on actual practice, it probably has more than a simple rhetorical significance.[7]

In expanding our view of political attitude formation from one that concentrated on early, latent political socialization, we gain in completeness of explanation, but clearly lose in neatness and simplicity. The sources of political attitudes appear to be many. They include early socialization experiences and late socialization experiences during adolescence, as well as postsocialization experiences as an adult. They include both political and nonpolitical experiences, experiences that are intended by others to have an effect on political attitudes as well as those that are unintended. Clearly many types of experience can affect basic political attitudes, and these experiences can come at a variety of times. Having thus complicated our model of political socialization, we face the problem of simplifying it again. If political attitudes are not derived from simply one source, we can at least attempt to find what sources appear most significant and for what sorts of people, and what combinations of experiences are most closely associated with particular types of political attitudes. It is this problem of specifying the impact of various types of nonpo-

[7] The large body of literature concerned with the democratization of the German schools gives one the distinct impression that these authors think the schools ought to be democratic because this is what is appropriate for a democratic political system. See W. Stahl, *Education for Democracy in West Germany,* New York, 1961.

litical experiences on political attitudes that we shall deal with in this chapter.

Of course, phrased as it is, the problem is complex and probably insoluble. We shall deal with it by concentrating on only a few types of nonpolitical authority patterns that might be expected to influence political attitudes: those patterns in the family, school, and work place. First, we shall briefly describe some differences among the five nations in the frequency with which respondents report that they were able to participate in family and school decisions as children, and, in later life, at their places of work. We shall also examine the differences among educational and generational groups within each nation — differences that suggest important changes in participation opportunities over time. Second, we shall try to determine whether and to what extent those forms of social participation are related to political participation.

The essential question is whether there is a close relationship between the roles that a person plays in nonpolitical situations and his role in politics. Is there some strain toward homogeneity in these roles? This question suggests why the authority patterns within nonpolitical social groups may be the crucial variables to consider. These authority patterns represent, as it were, the political structures of these nonpolitical groups: if they are not identical to the authority and participatory patterns of government, they resemble them in form. They can, for instance, be more or less democratic; that is, they may allow the individual more or less opportunity to participate in decisions. Thus in concentrating on authority patterns in family, school, and job, we are concentrating on a set of relationships analogous to some basic political relationships.

There are a number of reasons why one might expect the authority patterns to which the individual is exposed outside of the political realm to have some influence on his attitudes toward politics. In the first place, the role that an individual plays within the family, the school, or the job may be considered training for the performance of political roles. He is likely to generalize from the former roles to the latter. If in most social situations the individual finds himself subservient to some authority figure, it is likely that he will expect such an authority relationship in the political sphere. On the other hand, if outside the political sphere he has opportunities to participate in a wide range of social decisions, he will probably expect to be able to participate in political decisions as well. Furthermore, participation in nonpolitical decision making may give one the skills needed to engage in political participation: the skills of self-expression and a sense of effective political tactics.

Because of the tendency to generalize from one social sphere to the other, we may reasonably expect some strain toward homogeneity among the authority relations to which an individual is exposed. But we do not expect complete homogeneity. There is a wide gap between family, school, and occupational participation and political participation. In the first place, an individual who has had ample opportunities to participate in a wide range of nonpolitical situations may live within a political system that affords few opportunities to participate. He may have the propensities for civic participation but little opportunity to perform a civic role. Conversely, his prepolitical experiences may give little encouragement for participation, but other social or political characteristics may lead him into participation. Furthermore, participation in the more intimate situations of the family, the school, and the job (particularly in the family and perhaps the school) may differ markedly from participation in politics. The authority patterns within the smaller units may take a different form from those in politics and thereby inhibit the degree to which he will generalize from one social situation to the other. The authority patterns of smaller, more intimate units tend to be informal. Decisions may "emerge" from the group without ever having been "decided" in any formal sense. The channels of influence are less clearly articulated. Because of this, the political socialization that occurs within more intimate social units may be inadequate training for the performance of civic activities within the larger, secondary political system. Therefore, institutions closer to the political realm and in which authority patterns become more similar to authority patterns in the political system may be more crucial for the formation of political attitudes.[8]

The above discussion suggests that the major difference between nongovernmental and governmental authority patterns may be a structural one: political decision making is a more formal process, yet the opportunities for political participation may not differ from those afforded by the nonpolitical social systems. But if, instead of looking at the *actual* amount of homogeneity, we look at the individual's subjective attitudes toward authority — that is, the extent to which he *thinks* there is such homology — we may expect to find a greater similarity between political and nonpolitical authority patterns. Though the individual may not have that much control over whether or not the structure of politics affords him many actual opportunities to participate, his expectations of whether or not he is able to participate (what we have called his "subjective competence") ought to be more amenable to influences from outside of the realm of politics.

Before describing some of the data relevant to this question, a few caveats are in order. As with much of our data on political participation, we shall be dealing in this chapter with respondents' reports on how much they were able to participate in decisions in the family, the school, and the job. And the relationship we are interested in is that between perceived ability to participate in these areas and perceived ability to participate in politics. We do not ask whether a man who participated in family decisions is more likely to participate in politics; we ask the more modest question of whether the man who *remembers* that he was able to participate in the family currently *believes* he is able to participate in politics. However, since the expectation that one can participate appears to be a major factor in leading to actual participation, our findings will be relevant, though not conclusive, in answering the question of the impact of nonpolitical authority experiences

[8] For a discussion of the differences between decision-making patterns in small primary groups and larger secondary groups, see Sidney Verba, *Small Groups and Political Behavior,* chapter II. For a further discussion of this point, see below.

on political behavior. Another warning is in order regarding the problem of participation within the family and the school. In these cases we are asking respondents to remember the pattern of authority relations as they existed in what is often the rather distant past. Many of these reports must, therefore, be considered at best the approximations of past relationships. This problem of memory does not arise in regard to current job participation.

As pointed out earlier, the patterns of interpersonal relations within the family, the school and, to a lesser extent, the job are likely to take forms different from those within the political system. They are likely to be less formal. Decision making in such situations does not involve membership in formal parties or participation in a formal election system; it is more likely to consist of an expectation that one will be consulted, if only tacitly, before decisions are made; or that one is free to express one's point of view when decisions are being considered. Democracy in the more intimate primary group is expressed in the tone of relations and in implicit norms. If this form of participation affects political attitudes, it does so in the form of latent political socialization: that is, its explicit purpose is not to inculcate standards of political participation. However, political socialization may be explicit as well as implicit. Parents or teachers may explicitly attempt to teach norms of political behavior. The impact of this explicit civic training will be considered as well.

EARLY PARTICIPATION IN DECISIONS

Participation in Family Decisions. The two most significant institutions for the socialization of the child are the family and the school. In both, authority patterns are important and salient. Within the family and the school the child is first exposed to authority relationships. And though the authority patterns of both are necessarily hierarchical, involving relations between adults and children, the institutions may vary substantially in the extent to which they allow some freedom for children to participate. This participation may begin implicitly at a very early age. But since we felt that patterns of activity closer in time to political participation would be of greater significance and more reliably remembered, we decided to ask about participation within the family during adolescence. Respondents were asked if they could remember how much influence they had had in family decisions that concerned them when they were about sixteen. The results are reported in Table XI.1. In all countries but Italy, more than half of the respondents remember having some influence in family decisions, and in Italy the proportion is close to one-half. Respondents in the United States and Britain most frequently report (73 per cent and 69 per cent, respectively) that they had some influence over family decisions; German, Italian, and Mexican respondents in roughly equal frequency report that they had no influence.

Respondents were also asked if they had had opportunities to complain about decisions. Had they felt free to complain if decisions were made that they did not like? And could they remember actually complaining? Within the informal structure of the family this freedom to dissent may be considered a form of participation. In general, British and American respondents report the greatest ability to participate in family decisions in this way. British respondents report more frequently than others that they remember feeling free to complain, whereas the American respondents report somewhat more frequently than others that they remember actually complaining. At the other extreme, about one-half of the Mexican respondents report that it was better not to complain and

TABLE XI.1 *Remembered influence in family decisions; by nation*

Percentage who remember they had	*U.S.*	*U.K.*	*Germany*	*Italy*	*Mexico*
Some influence	73	69	54	48	57
No influence	22	26	37	37	40
Don't know, don't remember, and other	5	5	9	15	3
Total percentage	100	100	100	100	100
Total number of cases*	970	957	955	995	923

* On tables reporting data about remembered family experiences, those respondents who were not raised within a family (in an institution, for instance) are omitted.

that they in fact did not complain. The frequencies with which German and Italian respondents report family participation lie between those of the United States and Britain, on the one hand, and Mexico, on the other.

Participation in School. The data on participation within the family roughly parallel much of the data previously reported on participation within politics: a relatively greater frequency of participation in Britain and the United States, intermediate participation in Germany, and somewhat lower participation in Italy and Mexico. On the other hand, the data on remembered participation in the schools show a sharp contrast between the United States and the other four countries. This is true for informal participation within the school. When asked whether they felt free to complain of unfair treatment or if they ever actually complained, American respondents report most often that they felt free to complain and that they had actually complained.

TABLE XI.2 *Freedom to participate in school discussions and debates; by nation*

Percentage who remember they	*U.S.*	*U.K.*	*Germany*	*Italy*	*Mexico*
Could and did participate	40	16	12	11	15
Could but did not participate	15	8	5	4	21
Could not participate	34	68	68	56	54
Don't know and other	11	8	15	29	10
Total percentage	100	100	100	100	100
Total number	969	963	953	907	783

But the sharpest difference in school participation is observed if one considers more formal opportunities to participate. Here the distinction between education in the United States and education elsewhere is immediately apparent. Respondents were asked whether children in their school were given the opportunity to discuss and debate political and social issues. If they reported that there were such discussions, then they were asked if they themselves took part. The results to these two questions are reported in Table XI.2. In the United States 40 per cent of the respondents report that there were such discussions and that they took part. In the other nations the percentage so reporting is much smaller, ranging from 16 per cent in Britain to 11 per cent in Italy. Clearly, the amount of explicit training for political participation in the schools is much higher in the United States than elsewhere.

Class and Early Participation. Our data suggest that authority patterns in the family and the school vary substantially among different social groups. In all five nations the frequency with which respondents report that they were able to participate in decisions within the family or at school — both their freedom to complain about decisions and the actual complaining they remember doing — rises with level of education. The data must be interpreted with great caution; yet they do suggest strongly that experience with family authority patterns differs among the social classes. Those of higher social status are more likely to participate in family decisions. If such experience facilitates the growth of democratic political competence in later life, one of the many reasons for the generally lower political competence of those with low educational attainment may be that these people are usually raised in families that do not nourish the expectation that one can make one's voice heard in decisions.

A similar class difference is observable in school participation. Respondents with higher education remember informal participation (complaining about unfair treatment) and formal participation (classroom discussion) much more frequently than do those of lower educational attainment. For example, 25 per cent of the Italian respondents who did not get beyond primary school report that they remember complaining about unfair treatment, in contrast with 44 per cent of those who reached secondary school. And the differences are as sharp within each of the nations. Even more striking are the differences among social groups in the frequency of remembered formal participation in classroom discussions. In each nation the frequency of remembered participation is about three or four times as great among respondents with some secondary education as it is among those with only primary education.

The implications of these data are significant. If experience with nongovernmental patterns of authority is indeed a source of political attitudes, then the sharp differences in political attitudes that one observes among respondents from various social backgrounds may originate in their early experiences with authority. We shall return to this question below.

One further point must be made about the distribution of school and family participatory experiences among those with varying educational backgrounds. In our earlier discussion of the national differences in the frequency with which respondents report remembered opportunities to participate within the family, we found a rough parallel between the frequencies of reported ability to participate in politics and remembered participatory family experiences. Both were most frequent in the United States and Britain and least frequent in Italy and Mexico. And within the schools we found the contrast between the United States and the other four nations to be the clearest pattern. But if one considers the data on the relationship between education and opportunities to participate, it becomes clear that much of the difference in school and family experiences is due to the differing distributions of educational attainment among the nations. The national differences in remembered family participation are only faintly mirrored if one compares respondents with no more than primary school education, and not mirrored at all among those with higher education. The remembered informal participation in schools also shows little systematic national difference within each educational group. It is, in fact, only with formal participation in school debates that any sharp national difference persists — and this is the clear contrast between the frequency of participation in the United States and in other nations.

Thus those with higher education in all five nations seem to receive somewhat greater opportunities to participate in nonpolitical situations than do those with lower educational attainment. And when one considers respondents of similar educational backgrounds, cross-national differences in opportunities to participate become insignificant.

Age and Early Participation. Perhaps even more significant than the differences among social classes in the degree to which individuals have opportunities to participate in family and school decisions are the differences among generations. Our data strongly suggest that patterns of family and school participation have been changing, and, what is most important, that they have been changing in the same direction in all five nations. The older the respondent, the less likely he is to report opportunities to participate. In almost every instance the groups over fifty years of age report school and family participation least frequently. Despite the wide disparities in the recent histories of these nations, the differences in their social structures and in overall levels of participation and competence, all five appear to be experiencing a similar secular trend toward a less authoritarian school and family system.[9] Furthermore, these changes appear to be somewhat independent of the political system. This is at least the inference one can draw from the fact that there has been a relatively steady change in patterns of family authority — especially in Germany — since the early part of the century despite the obvious great political and social vicissitudes. On the other hand, school authority patterns in Italy and Germany do not show evidence of as steady a change since the early part of the century, a fact that suggests that these patterns are more likely to be affected by the political system.

What we may be observing in this general trend toward greater participation in the school and family are certain aspects of the industrialization, urbanization, and modernization processes in Europe and the United States. The last century has seen a dramatic shift from agricultural to industrial employment, from rural to urban residence, and a sharp rise in educational levels. This has meant by and large a shift from the extended, patriarchal family to the nuclear family,

[9] The fact that older respondents are more likely to have forgotten whether or not they could participate does not seem to be the reason for age differences in reported participation. For this pattern of age differences holds even if we consider the proportion who remember being able to participate of those respondents who were able to remember if they participated or not. Thus the age differential obtains even when we control for the factor of worse memory among older respondents. Furthermore, older respondents report more frequently than the younger that they remember *not* being able to participate.

the emancipation of women, and the development of greater individual autonomy. The striking point about these general changes in patterns of social authority and individual participation is that they do not immediately, or even necessarily, spill over into the political sphere. They do, however, have political consequences. We shall return to these below.

Job Participation. Thus far we have looked at nonpolitical participation in the early lives of our respondents. But though much of the politically relevant experience with authority patterns occurs in the preadult years, it is also likely that these experiences continue beyond childhood. Opportunities to participate in adult life, as well as preadult opportunities in family and school, can affect one's expectations of chances to participate politically. In particular, participation at work ought to have a significant effect on the individual's belief in his ability to participate politically. Though job participation comes later in life than participation in family and school, and therefore at an age when the individual's attitudes are probably less malleable, the very fact that it is contemporary with political participation suggests that disparities between the patterns of authority would lead to greater strains to bring them into harmony with each other.

How much opportunity do individuals have to participate in decisions at their place of work? Though this question could be asked only of those respondents who were employed in some enterprise where there was someone in authority over them, the question had this advantage over those about the family and the school: it was not retrospective. Respondents were asked, not about experiences in the past, but about their current job situation. One can therefore attribute greater reliability to these responses.

Table XI.3 reports the responses to this question. British and American respondents report most frequently (80 per cent and 78 per cent, respectively) that they are consulted when decisions are made on the job. At the other extreme, Mexican and Italian respondents least often report that they are consulted (though in both countries the percentages are more than half). In Germany the proportion of respondents who report consultation lies in between. A similar pattern

TABLE XI.3 *Consulted about job decisions; by nation*

Percentage saying they are consulted	*U.S.*	*U.K.*	*Germany*	*Italy*	*Mexico*
Sometimes or often	78	80	68	59	61
Rarely or never	21	19	29	36	38
	1	—	3	5	—
Total percentage	100	100	100	100	100
Total number*	428	470	369	314	277

* Smaller bases because not all respondents had people in authority over them in their jobs.

is found in connection with a question on the extent to which respondents say they feel free to protest on the job if a decision is made of which they do not approve. Again the freedom to participate is most frequently reported in the United States and Britain, followed by Germany. In this case, however, there is a sharp difference between Mexico and Italy, with the Italian respondents much less frequently saying that they feel free to participate.

The pattern of perceived ability to participate on the job is rounded out by data on the extent to which respondents report they actually have complained about decisions. Such complaints are reported most frequently in the United States and Britain, and are somewhat less common in Italy and Germany. Mexican workers report the smallest frequency of complaining.[10]

The opportunity to participate at work is also unevenly distributed throughout the various occupations. Some occupations, apparently, allow a wider scope than others for worker participation. In general, the higher the status of the occupation, the more likely the individual is to be consulted on decisions. In all five nations skilled workers report more frequent consultation than do unskilled workers, and white-collar workers report either more frequent consultation than skilled workers (in Germany, Mexico, and Italy) or about as

[10] Mexicans frequently say that they would feel free to protest — yet they rarely do so. This may be another manifestation of the aspirational character of the Mexican pattern of participation: a high belief in one's efficacy, not matched by actual experience in participation.

much consultation (the United States and Britain). And those in professional or managerial positions (who nevertheless have someone in a position of authority over them) report even more frequent consultation. It is clear, thus, that the nature of the occupation has a similar effect in each nation on the participatory opportunities that are afforded. This holds true, not only for consultation by supervisors, but for individuals' feelings of freedom to protest decisions they do not like.

Whatever the reason for the increase in participatory opportunities as one ascends the occupational scale, the implications for political participation are clear. In the first place, those in higher-status jobs are more likely to receive the sort of training in participation that we have suggested may be related to political participation. And second, economic advance and a shift in the distribution of the labor force toward a higher proportion of skilled, white-collar, technical and managerial personnel may be accompanied by the development of a more competent citizenry. What this implies for the development of democratic political participation is not self-evident, however. Increased work-place participation creates a strain and a potential competence to which political systems tend to respond; but the response may take forms other than increased opportunities for real political participation.

The data on differences in occupation status suggest an important qualification about the national differences in the frequencies of work-place participation. As with family and school participation, it appears that work-place participation is in part a function of the distribution of occupational types in each nation, as well as a function of national "style." The national differences within each matched occupational group often appear to be quite a bit smaller than for the entire samples. But this is particularly so on the level of the white-collar occupations. Among white-collar workers and those in professional or management positions, opportunities to participate are fairly uniform in all nations. On the blue-collar levels of skilled and unskilled workers, sharp national differences persist. This suggests that on the higher-status occupational levels — whether because of the demands of the job or because democratic ideologies are more widespread here — a uniform cross-national pattern of participation exists. The effects of national affiliation are more apparent on lower occupational levels.[11]

The materials thus far presented suggest that participation in family, school, and job is related to patterns of political participation in each nation. In general, respondents in the two nations where frequency of political participation seems to be highest (the United States and Britain) also report most frequently that they were able to participate in nonpolitical decisions. And respondents in Italy and Mexico, where the overall levels of political participation tend to be low, generally report the least frequent participatory experience in nonpolitical situations. However, the data also suggest that the relationship between political and nonpolitical participation may be more complicated. For instance, British respondents report levels of school participation that are somewhat similar to those in Germany, Italy, and Mexico, and quite different from that in the United States. On the other hand, the clearest parallel to the data on political participation exists in the data on job participation. Those nations with the most political participation also appear to afford the greatest opportunities for work-place participation, the distinction being especially sharp on the blue-collar level. This latter point is important, for the data on job participation represent the only evidence on nonpolitical participation contemporaneous with adult political participation. The data on family and school participation are often information about the distant past. This suggests that the patterns of authority perceived by an individual as most similar are those adult patterns of authority, political and nonpolitical, to which he is contemporaneously exposed — thus democracy in both may develop simultaneously. Let us consider these questions more directly.

[11] For a similar point in relation to educational level, see Chapter XII below.

SOCIAL PARTICIPATION AND CIVIC COMPETENCE

Family Participation and Civic Competence. Our main interest in nongovernmental patterns of authority — those of the family, school, and place of work — is in the effect that these patterns have on the political attitudes and behavior of those who have been exposed to them. Specifically, we want to know if a sense of ability is in some way transferred from the more limited sphere of participation in nonpolitical decisions to the larger one of participation in politics; or, to put it in another way, is the member of a democratic family more likely to be a democratically competent citizen?

In order to assess the impact that participation within the family has on later political competence, we divided our respondents into three groups: those who consistently reported that they had had participatory opportunities in the family; those who consistently reported that they had had no such opportunity, and those who remember more mixed patterns of participation.[12] These were then compared according to their scores on our scale of "subjective political competence" — that is, according to their belief as to their ability to influence the government. This subjective perception is intimately related to political behavior, to positive identification with the political system, and to the acceptance of democratic attitudes. If, then, participation within the family can foster a sense of political competence, we can safely say that such nonpolitical participation will have some effect on the extent of democratic political orientations within a nation.

As the data in Table XI.4 indicate, there is a connection between remembered ability to participate in family decisions and current political competence. In all five nations those who remember consistently being able to express them-

[12] Grouped together as family participants are respondents who report that they had some influence on family decisions, that they would have felt free to protest a decision they did not like, and that they remember actually protesting. Nonparticipants report that they had no influence, that they did not feel free to protest, and that they do not remember protesting. Those with a mixed pattern of participation answered some of the items positively and some negatively — for instance, that they had some influence on family decisions but did not feel free to complain.

TABLE XI.4 *Percentage who scored highest in subjective competence*[a] *among respondents who report varying degrees of participation in family decisions; by nation and education*

	Total						*Primary or less*						*Secondary or more*					
	Partic.		*Mixed*		*Nonpartic.*		*Partic.*		*Mixed*		*Nonpartic.*		*Partic.*		*Mixed*		*Nonpartic.*	
Nation	%	*No.*[b]	%	*No.*	%	*No.*	%	*No.*	%	*No.*	%	*No.*	%	*No.*	%	*No.*	%	*No.*
United States	70	(377)	67	(462)	47	(89)	58	(144)	56	(264)	42	(73)	77	(233)	80	(198)	69	(16)
Great Britain	70	(359)	63	(479)	51	(93)	67	(186)	59	(313)	45	(71)	73	(165)	70	(154)	76	(17)
Germany	52	(233)	50	(449)	42	(164)	46	(163)	45	(381)	42	(153)	66	(67)	75	(65)	[45	(11)]
Italy	46	(242)	41	(462)	34	(169)	35	(132)	37	(311)	31	(143)	59	(109)	50	(149)	52	(25)
Mexico	50	(126)	41	(598)	26	(199)	51	(85)	39	(524)	24	(191)	48	(41)	57	(73)	c	

[a] I.e., those who received three highest scores on the subjective competence scale

[b] Numbers in parentheses refer to the bases upon which percentages are calculated.

[c] Too few cases

selves in family decisions tend to score highest in subjective political competence. In the United States, where the scores on the subjective competence scale tend to be highest, 70 per cent of the respondents who report that they were able to participate in the family are in the highest three groups on the subjective competence scale, whereas 47 per cent of those who report that they were not able to participate are in these highest three groups. Similarly, in Mexico, where the scores on subjective competence are generally lowest, 50 per cent of those who participated in the family are in the three highest groups of the subjective competence scale, in contrast with 26 per cent of those who could not participate in the family. And the same pattern may be observed in the other three nations.

Since experiences with family authority patterns as well as sense of political competence vary with education, it is important to consider this relationship with matched educational groups. When we separate those with secondary education or better from those with no more than primary school instruction, an interesting qualification to our earlier generalization becomes apparent. The relationship between remembered ability to participate within the family and subjective political competence persists among those with lower educational attainment (though in Italy and Germany only to a slight extent), but not among those in the higher educational group. In all five countries family participation is generalized to political participation among those with primary school education. But among those with higher education there is little apparent connection between the two variables.

This finding suggests an important qualification to any hypothesis about the extent of generalization between family experience and political participation. Apparently, the degree to which such generalization takes place depends on other factors. The fact that generalization from family to polity does not apply to those on higher education levels suggests that family participation may be of least significance among those who ordinarily would be expected to have most subjective political competence. Among those with higher education, political competence develops for a number of reasons. For one thing, these people will have greater skill than others in political participation; they will be more likely to have been taught norms that foster political participation. Furthermore, the general social expectation is that those with higher educational attainment will be politically competent. And, of course, they are more likely to mingle with others who consider themselves politically competent. If, then, their family training is not such as to foster participation, there are other factors that can substitute for it.

On the other hand, those with lower educational attainment are both less likely to have learned participatory skills or the norm that one ought to participate and less likely to find themselves in situations where they are expected to be politically competent. And where there is no presumption in favor of political competence, generalization from the family level can have, as it were, greater marginal effect. If political participation receives support outside the family sphere, family participation becomes less crucial as a determinant of political involvement. The effect that family participation has on political competence is not a universal one and may be offset by other factors.[13]

School Participation and Civic Competence. Much of what has been said about the impact that family participation has

[13] Another interpretation of the results must be mentioned here. It is possible that some of the relationship between family participation and sense of political competence is an artifact of the interview situation. The questions about political competence were asked near the beginning of the interview, those on family participation near the end. Yet respondents may have upgraded or downgraded their memories of family experiences to match their reports of their current competence in politics. One would expect this to have happened especially among those whose memories of family experiences are dimmest; and this might explain the closer relationship between political and family competence among those in the older age groups and perhaps among those with lower educational attainment. (The age group data are reported in the unabridged edition of this book.)

If this were the case, it would cast doubt on the validity of our connection between experience with nonpolitical authority and political attitudes. Some data reported in the unabridged edition (p. 357, footnote 20) however, suggest that this relationship cannot be explained away as an artifact of the interview.

on the sense of political competence may be said about the impact of school participation. The opportunity to participate within the school appears to have a definite effect upon one's position on the subjective competence scale. But the variety of types of participation within the school — particularly the difference between informal participation (protesting a decision) and formal participation (taking part in classroom discussions) — allows us to look somewhat more closely at the way in which participation in the school affects political competence.

Consider first the effect of remembered ability to participate informally in decisions in the school. In order to group our respondents according to the extent to which they report they were able to protest decisions, we divided them (on the basis of their responses to three questions) into three groups: those who consistently answered that they could participate in this way; those who consistently answered that they could not so participate, and those who gave mixed responses.[14] In many ways this parallels our grouping of respondents according to the extent of their family participation. And in many ways the data on informal school participation resemble those on informal family participation. As Table XI.5 indicates, those who remember that they were able to protest effectively within the school are most likely to be high on the scale of subjective competence. And to take again the nations with the highest and lowest overall rates of subjective political competence: in the United States 75 per cent of those who report that they were able to participate within

[14] The three questions were:

"*1.* If you felt you had been treated unfairly in some way or disagreed with something the teacher had said, did you feel free to talk to the teacher about it, a bit uneasy about it, or was it better not to talk to the teacher?

"*2.* Would it have made any difference?

"*3.* Do you remember ever doing this?"

Those who said they felt free to protest, that it might have made a difference, and that they remember protesting are listed as participants. Those who replied negatively to the three items are the nonparticipants. The remainder of the respondents are in the mixed category. Those who could not remember have been omitted from the table.

TABLE XI.5 *Percentage who scored highest in subjective competence*[a] *among respondents who report varying degrees of informal school participation; by nation and education*

Nation	Total						Primary or less						Secondary or more					
	Partic.		*Mixed*		*Nonpartic.*		*Partic.*		*Mixed*		*Nonpartic.*		*Partic.*		*Mixed*		*Nonpartic.*	
	%	*No.*[b]	%	*No.*	%	*No.*	%	*No.*	%	*No.*	%	*No.*	%	*No.*	%	*No.*	%	*No.*
United States	75	(252)	67	(496)	54	(158)	66	(100)	58	(257)	42	(109)	80	(152)	77	(239)	78	(49)
Great Britain	70	(187)	66	(462)	56	(265)	68	(102)	62	(274)	53	(187)	74	(79)	73	(177)	63	(73)
Germany	53	(186)	49	(436)	44	(229)	48	(133)	45	(361)	44	(229)	67	(52)	73	(70)	57	(23)
Italy	51	(128)	46	(385)	32	(478)	43	(60)	42	(236)	28	(393)	59	(68)	53	(146)	54	(84)
Mexico	52	(177)	45	(376)	24	(205)	49	(118)	43	(319)	24	(197)	56	(59)	55	(57)	c	

a I.e., those who received three highest scores on subjective competence scale

b Numbers in parentheses refer to the bases upon which percentages are calculated.

c Too few cases

the school are in the top three categories of the subjective competence scale, in contrast with 54 per cent of those who report that they could not participate; while in Mexico 52 per cent of the school participants are in the top three subjective competence categories, in contrast with 24 per cent of the nonparticipants.

But as with the data on participation in the family, it is important to consider the educational groups separately. If one looks at the relationship between school participation and political competence within higher and lower educational groups, a result strikingly similar to that found in regard to family participation appears. Informal participation within the school appears to be more closely associated with political competence among those with limited education than among those who achieved somewhat higher education. The distinction between those with primary school education and those with secondary education or more is not as sharp as it was in connection with family participation, but the distinction is clear nevertheless. In all five countries the extent of school informal participation is associated with a high score on the subjective competence scale among those in the lower educational group. Among those with higher education, on the other hand, the relationship between school participation and political competence is either not a direct one (as in Mexico, Italy, and the United States), or is weaker than the one among primary-school respondents (as in the other two nations).

Again as with family participation, this phenomenon may reflect the relative absence of other factors that might foster political competence among those with lower education. School training in participation has a greater marginal effect than it would have if there were — as there are among those with higher education — other factors that could substitute for this training.

In general, as with family participation and political competence, there does appear to be some relationship between school experiences and political attitudes, but the relationship is not a strong one. School participation seems to affect the sense of political competence among some groups more than among others. Our earlier hypothesis — that the impact of nonpolitical participation upon political competence is greatest among those who, for other reasons, would be expected to be less politically competent — receives some support from a comparison of educational groups.

Thus far we have considered the effect of rather informal participation within family and school on the sense of political competence. We have been concerned in both social situations with the respondent's remembered ability to protest an unfair decision. But in connection with school participation we are also interested in the effect of more formal opportunities to participate. Does experience in classroom discussion and debate increase the probability that an individual will feel subjectively competent to influence the government? Our data indicate that one can answer with a qualified "yes." In the United States, Britain, Germany, and Mexico, on both levels of educational attainment, and in Italy among those with primary education, remembered participation in school discussions and debates is related to an increased sense of political efficacy. Those respondents who remember that they could and did participate in these discussions tend to score higher on the scale of subjective competence than do those respondents who remember that they could not participate. In the United States, for instance, 76 per cent of those who say that they could and did participate in school discussions score in the upper half of the subjective competence scale, in contrast with 63 per cent of those who report that they had no such opportunity. And in Mexico the respective percentages are 59 and 39.

One interesting point is apparent in connection with participation in school debates. In general, the respondents who score the lowest on the subjective competence scale are not those who report that they had no opportunity to participate in discussions and debates. Rather, those who report that there were such opportunities but that *they did not take advantage of them* tend to score as low as or lower than those who had no such opportunities. In the United States and Germany on both educational levels, in Mexico on the lower educational level, and in Italy on the higher educational level, those who report that they could have but did not participate receive generally lower scores on the subjective competence scale than those who were not afforded such opportunities.

This fact suggests a qualification to our earlier findings. We are dealing here with more than the impact of the objective situation within the school upon a later sense of political competence. The reason why those who did not take advantage of the opportunities to participate are even lower in their level of subjective political competence than are those who were not even given the opportunity may well lie in certain individual characteristics that affect both the respondent's participation in the school and his sense of political competence. Given the opportunity to participate, those who did not do so are likely to be nonparticipants for personal reasons. Perhaps it is lack of self-confidence or skill; perhaps there are social reasons, such as membership in a relatively less privileged group. These reasons may be independent of the participation opportunities in the school.

The data on formal opportunities to participate suggest, therefore, that some of the generalization phenomena we observe — that is, the apparent transfer of participatory experience in family and school to the political sphere — may not result from the impact of a participatory family or school system on political attitudes. Rather, the degree of participation in the school and the family, as well as the level of subjective competence in political matters, may *both* derive from the same psychological or social factors. This qualification about the meaning of our findings is apparent in the data on formal school participation. But it may apply even more strongly to the previously reported data on the impact of remembered informal participation on political competence. Whether or not a child feels free to protest or actually does protest in family or school is not determined solely by the adult-created authority structure of the family or school. Rather, family or school participation and political self-confidence may both be affected by the extent to which the child has a strong ego.

Thus our data on the impact of family and school participation on later political attitudes suggest, at best, that there is some connection. But how strong the connection is, under what circumstances it is more or less close, and the process by which the connection is made are questions that cannot yet be answered.

So far, we have been concentrating mostly on the latent effects of family and school experiences upon political competence. We have been discussing the effects on political attitudes, not of direct formal teaching, but of the generalization from experiences in family or school to politics. Even in the case of the opportunity for formal discussion in the classroom, the significant aspect was the discussion itself, not the subject matter of the discussion. One may ask, however, whether direct teaching, too, might not have significant effects on political attitudes.

We can compare those respondents who report that time was spent in their school in teaching about politics and government with those who report that they were not so taught. The data suggest that manifest teaching about politics can increase an individual's sense of political competence, but that this depends upon the content of the teaching. In the United States, Britain, and Mexico, those who were taught about politics are more likely than the others to score high on the subjective competence scale. The pattern in Germany and Italy is quite different. In Germany those with primary education are somewhat more likely to feel politically competent if they were taught about politics in the school, whereas those with secondary education or better are somewhat less likely to feel highly competent politically if they remember such teaching. In Italy those with primary school education are somewhat less likely to feel politically competent if they remember political teaching, whereas this teaching apparently makes no difference among those with higher education. Though there is a relatively clear connection between manifest political teaching and political competence in the United States, Britain, and Mexico, there is no clear connection in the two nations whose educational systems were dominated for much of the life span of our respondents by anti-democratic philosophies. This contrast suggests strongly that manifest teaching about politics can have an impact, and this impact will depend a good deal on the content of what is taught.

Job Participation and Political Competence. The data so far presented suggest that there is some relationship between family and school experiences and an individual's later political attitudes. But as we have suggested, the formation of political attitudes continues after the individual becomes an adult and enters his political role. Attitudes change, new experiences can have political effects. If early authority experiences can affect political attitudes, so can authority experiences in later life. Individuals are exposed to a wide range of these experiences, be it in the family, in church, voluntary association, or at work. Can these later relationships and experiences affect an individual's sense of political competence? If, for instance, an adult has the opportunity to participate in decisions in his contemporary nonpolitical relationships, will he generalize from these experiences and believe that he can participate in his public life? Conversely, will those who are given little opportunity of mastery over decisions in their day-to-day lives generalize this to a belief in their lack of political ability?

These questions are similar to those we raised about participatory opportunities in the family and the school. Essentially we are interested in the extent to which a democratic political system depends upon democratic substructures in the society. Do democratic political orientations (which include the attitude that one can be a participant in political decisions) depend upon opportunities to participate in nonpolitical social relationships? Of crucial significance here are the opportunities to participate in decisions at one's place of work. The structure of authority at the work place is probably the most significant — and salient — structure of that kind with which the average man finds himself in daily contact. Furthermore, this form of participation may have a heightened effect on political participation because authority patterns in the work place, though probably a mixture of formal and informal authority, have a larger formal component than, say, authority patterns within the family.

As reported earlier, there is some parallel between the frequency with which respondents report that they can participate in decisions made at work and the frequency with which respondents are politically competent. And the data in Table XI.6 indicate that this parallel does indeed reflect a relationship between the extent of opportunities to participate in job decisions and the extent of subjective political competence. In each nation those who report that they are consulted about decisions on their job are more likely than the others to score high on the scale of subjective political competence. And the same relationship exists between informal job participation (freedom to protest) and sense of political competence. Those respondents who report that they feel free to protest decisions are more likely to feel subjectively competent to influence the government.

Unlike many of the relationships between family and school participation and political competence, the relationships between competence on the job and subjective political competence remain strong even within matched educational groups. Whereas the impact of family or school participation on political competence appeared to decrease among those with higher educational attainment, the impact of job participation remains strong on both educational levels. And as Table XI.6 indicates, though there are differences in the degree to which individuals in various types of occupation can participate in decisions on the job, this participation has a positive effect on political competence among occupations at all levels. Among unskilled workers, skilled workers, and white-collar workers (the only occupational strata with enough cases to make this analysis feasible, those who report that they are consulted in decisions at their place of work, compared with those who are not consulted, report higher levels of subjective political competence. This is the case in all nations but Mexico, where the relationship between the two forms of participation is less clear.

It is, of course, impossible to conclude that there is a unidirectional flow of influence from patterns of participation on the job to patterns of participation in politics. It is quite likely that opportunities for job and political participation have a reciprocal effect on each other: that is, the relation-

Table XI.6 *Percentage who scored highest in subjective competence[a] among respondents who report varying degrees of formal participation in job decisions; by nation and occupation*

	Total[b]				*Unskilled*				*Skilled*				*White collar*			
	Consulted on the job		*Not consulted*		*Consulted*		*Not consulted*		*Consulted*		*Not consulted*		*Consulted*		*Not consulted*	
Nation	%	*No.*[c]	%	*No.*	%	*No.*	%	*No.*	%	*No.*	%	*No.*	%	*No.*	%	*No.*
United States	75	(334)	62	(94)	70	(70)	53	(32)	73	(71)	69	(16)	82	(93)	63	(27)
Great Britain	71	(372)	52	(98)	74	(88)	54	(41)	71	(140)	50	(30)	75	(65)	[60	(15)]
Germany	58	(253)	38	(116)	55	(42)	26	(42)	52	(61)	44	(32)	61	(62)	[46	(13)]
Italy	57	(181)	35	(130)	49	(45)	31	(67)	74	(31)	[40	(15)]	55	(76)	52	(21)
Mexico	51	(170)	45	(107)	26	(17)	43	(18)	48	(74)	53	(46)	47	(55)	45	(23)

[a] I.e., those who received three highest scores on subjective competence scale

[b] The total columns refer to job holders of all kinds. The occupational breakdown into unskilled, skilled, and white collar has been selective and does not include all job holders in the total columns.

[c] Numbers in parentheses refer to the bases upon which percentages are calculated.

ship between perceived ability to participate on the job and perceived ability to participate in politics may represent, not merely a generalization from the work place to the political sphere, but a generalization in the other direction as well. Demands to participate in job decisions are often justified by the political norms of democratic participation. And the individual whose political experience includes chances to participate in decisions will be less likely to accept unquestioningly the authority relationships at his place of work. In any case, our data suggest a tendency toward homogeneity between job and political authority patterns: those who are oriented to participate in one area will be oriented to participate in the other. Whether job participation leads to democratic political orientations, or vice versa, is difficult to tell; but the evidence is strong that these two develop closely together and mutually support each other.

The Cumulative Effect of Participatory Experiences. There is evidence that the impact of participation in nonpolitical decision making — at home, school, and job — is cumulative. The individual who has consistent opportunities for nonpolitical participation — compared with someone whose ability to participate in one nonpolitical area is not matched by an ability to participate in another nonpolitical area — is more likely to generalize this to political participation.

Consider the respondents who report that they had the opportunity to participate in family or school decisions. One would assume that this opportunity to participate will probably be generalized into subjective political competence, if it is not thwarted by experience with authority situations in which one cannot participate. This hypothesis is supported by the data in Tables XI.7 and XI.8. In Table XI.7, individuals who could and could not participate in family decisions are then divided into those who can and cannot participate in decisions on the job. The results are clear. Among those who report that they were able to take part in family decisions, those who can also take part in job decisions are more likely to score high in subjective political competence than are those whose ability to participate in family is not matched by a present ability to participate in job decisions. In Britain, for instance, 75 per cent of those whose family participation is matched by participatory opportunities at work score in the highest three cells of the subjective competence scale, in con-

TABLE XI.7 *Percentage who scored highest in subjective competence*[a] *among respondents who report varying degrees of participation in family and job decisions; by nation*

	Family participants				*Family nonparticipants*			
	Job partic.		*Job nonpartic.*		*Job partic.*		*Job nonpartic.*	
Nation	(%)	(*No.*)[b]	(%)	(*No.*)	(%)	(*No.*)	(%)	(*No.*)
United States	77	(242)	70	(61)	70	(80)	45	(31)
Great Britain	75	(270)	58	(64)	64	(92)	37	(30)
Germany	61	(144)	38	(52)	59	(81)	37	(49)
Italy	60	(120)	44	(70)	50	(48)	24	(41)
Mexico	56	(72)	52	(44)	43	(97)	45	(62)

[a] I.e., those who received three highest scores on subjective competence scale.

[b] Numbers in parentheses refer to the bases upon which percentages are calculated.

TABLE XI.8 *Percentage who scored highest in subjective competence*[a] *among respondents who report varying degrees of participation in school discussions and job decisions; by nation*

	School participants				*School nonparticipants*			
	Job partic.		*Job nonpartic.*		*Job partic.*		*Job nonpartic.*	
Nation	(%)	(*No.*)[b]	(%)	(*No.*)	(%)	(*No.*)	(%)	(*No.*)
United States	83	(195)	67	(55)	63	(126)	56	(34)
Great Britain	77	(163)	34	(32)	67	(192)	57	(61)
Germany	67	(110)	38	(39)	53	(125)	36	(69)
Italy	57	(67)	42	(33)	55	(116)	38	(78)
Mexico	57	(60)	52	(40)	38	(82)	51	(90)

[a] I.e., those who received three highest scores on subjective competence scale.

[b] Numbers in parentheses refer to the bases upon which percentages are calculated.

trast with 58 per cent of those respondents whose family participation is not backed up by job participation. And as Table XI.8 indicates, the same cumulative effect exists in connection with school and job participation. Those who could participate in school decisions and can now participate in job decisions are more likely to be politically competent than are those whose school participation is not supported by later job participation. Taking Britain as our example again, we find the relationship even more striking. Seventy-seven per cent of the respondents who report being able to participate both in school and job decisions are in the top three groups of our subjective competence scale, in contrast with 34 per cent of those who were able to participate in the school but cannot participate on the job. This relationship however, holds for only four out of five of the nations. The Mexican data show little of this cumulative effect.

CONCLUSION

A major element of a democratic political orientation is the belief that one has some control over political elites and political decisions. This belief has many roots. An individual might base his estimate of his capacity to influence the government upon direct experience with that government. Opportunities to participate in decisions might convince him of his competence, while thwarted influence attempts might lead to the opposite conclusion. Or he might base his subjective competence on more indirect evidence about the operations of the political system. He might observe others attempting to influence politics and learn from their experience; or he might learn from the estimates that he hears others make of the extent to which the "ordinary man" can influence politics. In these ways he will form his political beliefs from his observation of politics or from his exposure to others' views of politics.

Without denying the importance of the political system itself as a source of individuals' attitudes toward that system, this chapter has attempted to seek some of the nonpolitical sources of the belief that one has a voice in governmental affairs. One such source is experience with authority figures outside the governmental sphere. From these experiences the individual generalizes to politics. If in all his social relationships he is afforded no opportunity to participate meaningfully in decisions, he may derive from this a general belief in his incapacity to control any decisions, including political decisions. On the other hand, if he finds authority figures in social situations amenable to influence, he may come to believe that authority figures in politics will also be amenable to his influence.

The data presented in this chapter suggest that there is indeed a generalization from the nonpolitical sphere to the polity. If an individual has had the opportunity to participate in the family, in school, or at work, he is more likely than someone who did not have the same opportunities to consider himself competent to influence the government. But this conclusion must be presented with some caution. As we pointed out in this chapter, the relationship between nonpolitical participatory experience and political attitudes is by no means unambiguous. It appears stronger among some groups than among others. And many respondents manifest a sense of political competence though they had little participatory experience outside of politics, while others are not politically competent despite social experiences that should have furthered such competence. This lack of a strong, unambiguous relationship is not surprising. There is, after all, quite a gap in time between the ability to participate within the family and one's ability to participate in politics. The authority structures differ in nature, and this might impede generalizations from the primary group to the political system. Furthermore, each type of political system interacts differently with the expectations that an individual brings with him from nonpolitical experiences. No matter what opportunities he has to participate outside of politics, his generalization from these experiences to politics will be inhibited in a political system that is recognized as authoritarian. The difference between nonpolitical and political authority patterns may cause some strain or discontent, but the differences may not lead to a sense of competence. Experience with nonpolitical authority patterns may affect an individual's political attitudes by creating a set of predisposed responses to stimuli. The individual who has had opportunities for nonpolitical participation, compared with someone who has not had these opportunities, will be more likely to choose a participatory response *if* a political situation arises in which there is some chance to participate. An individual who has had a voice in family, school, or job decisions is more likely to accept the belief that he is a competent citizen *if* there is any other basis for the belief. Nonpolitical experiences with participation increase the individual's availability for an active political role and increase the likelihood that he will believe in his political influence.

The data in this chapter, however, allow us to go a bit further in specifying the way in which nonpolitical experiences create predispositions. Three points may be made about the effects of nonpolitical authority patterns on political attitudes: these effects are *cumulative,* other *social factors may substitute* for them, and they appear to be in a *rank order of importance.*

The cumulative effect that nonpolitical participation has upon political participation was suggested in Tables XI.7 and XI.8. And certainly this kind of effect is to be expected. If one finds oneself consistently in social situations where one has a voice over decisions, this is more likely to result in a general sense of competence than if the experience with participation in one area is not matched by similar experiences in other areas.

Second, other social factors may substitute for experience within the school or family. In particular, our data suggest that education on the secondary level or above can replace family participation, and to some extent school participation, as a factor leading toward political competence. This implication may be drawn from the fact that among those with education beyond the primary school, experiences with school participation have little impact on political competence, and experiences with family participation have no impact. Those with higher education, this suggests, do not need the push toward a sense of political competence that participatory family and school experiences might provide, for there are so many other factors that operate to make them politically competent.

But though a higher level of education may be able to substitute for family or school participation, it is interesting to note that job participation, though it can reinforce that which is learned in the family and the school, cannot replace it. This is seen in Tables XI.7 and XI.8. Even among those who have the opportunity to participate on the job (the respondents in the first and third columns of these two tables), it makes a difference whether or not they were previously able to participate in the family and the school. Though they have current opportunitites to participate, if they could not participate in the family or in the school, they are less subjectively competent in politics than are those who could participate previously. And this is true in all the nations.

Why is it that a higher level of education can substitute for family or school participation, whereas work-place participation cannot do so? If we may speculate, the reason may lie in the fact that education above the primary level represents a many-sided experience that can, in a large number of ways, increase an individual's potentiality to participate. The processes whereby higher educational attainment affects political competence are varied: they may be intellectual processes, as when one learns a set of skills useful for participation; they may be the inculcation of participatory norms through direct teaching of those norms; they may involve social pressures, as when educational attainment places one in a social situation in which one is expected to participate. These processes are different from those by which one generalizes from family and school authority patterns to politics; and they may, therefore, be little affected by what experiences the individual has had with family and school participation. Even if his nonpolitical participation is such that it would tend to counteract the factors that foster participation derived from his educational level, the fact that these are different types of influences on his level of participation would minimize the conflict between them.

Somewhat different is the relationship between school and family participation, on the one hand, and work-place participation, on the other. Work-place participation does not have as broad an effect upon one's sense of political competence as educational attainment does; it is a much narrower factor, which does not produce as basic a set of changes in one's intellectual capabilities, values, or social situation. Furthermore, it acts upon political competence in much the same way that experience in participation in the family or school does: through a process of generalizing one's capabilities from one field to the other. It is likely then that work-place participation, insofar as its effects tend to be in the opposite direction from the effects of school or family participation, will conflict with the other experiences. It will therefore be more likely to dampen the effect of family or school participation than to replace them.

The last point that must be made is that the impact of nonpolitical participation on political attitudes differs from one nonpolitical area to another. There appears to be a rank order in the strength of connection between nonpolitical types of participation and political competence: the connection becomes stronger as one moves from family to school to job participation. When we considered the relationship between family participation and sense of political competence within high and low educational groups, we found that it weakened somewhat among those with primary education or less and disappeared among those with more than primary education. Between school participation and sense of political competence, on the other hand, the relationship is not weaker on the lower educational level; and though it is weaker in all nations on the higher level, a positive relationship still persists within three of the five nations. In contrast to the situation with family and school participation, the relationship between job participation and political competence remains strong on both educational levels — even among those with secondary education or better. And we might add here, since it is relevant to the general argument that will be made, that the generalization of participatory experiences from voluntary association to the polity shows a similar relationship. As was pointed out in Chapter X, those who are active participants in voluntary associations are more likely than passive members to be politically competent; and this relationship is apparent on both educational levels.

This rank order in the strength of the relationship between the various modes of nonpolitical participation and political attitudes suggests an important specification of the way in which nonpolitical participation affects political attitudes. The individual's experiences at work and in voluntary associations differ basically from those in the family and the school in that they are closer — in time as well as structure — to the polity. Job and group memberships are contemporaneous with political participation. More important, perhaps, is the fact that the mode of participation within the work place or voluntary association comes closer in form to political modes of participation than does participation within the family or the school. Authority patterns in the work place and voluntary association are mixtures of formal and informal patterns. The bases of the authority hierarchy include incumbency of formal positions within the organization as well as technical and "human relations" skills. This is in many ways similar to patterns of political authority; in any case, more similar than are the patterns in the family or the school. In the latter two institutions authority patterns are "naturally" hierarchical, depending to a large extent on age differentials. Furthermore, especially in the family, the patterns of authority tend to be informal and implicit. In terms of formality of authority patterns, the school, rather than the home, more closely approximates the political system. And there exists in the school, in comparison to the family, a closer connection between participation and sense of political competence.

There are several reasons for this rank order. In the first place, as Eckstein has suggested, the closer a social structure is to the political system, the more likely there is to be a strain toward congruence between the two authority patterns.[15] If the social structure and the political system are close, it is difficult for the individual to segregate his roles in the two systems. But if, as with the family and, to a lesser extent, the school, they are relatively remote from the political system, he may with less strain be able to isolate his nonpolitical experiences with authority from his political experiences with authority.

The hierarchical connection between nonpolitical author-

[15] Eckstein, *op. cit.*, means by the "closeness" of a structure to the political system both its closeness in time and its closeness in the extent to which the structure is involved in political and governmental affairs. But the extent to which systems are similar in the degree of formality of authority patterns and in the criteria for authority positions is also relevant.

ity patterns and attitudes toward political authority suggests another conclusion: that in a relatively modern and diversified social system socialization in the family and, to a lesser extent, in the school represents inadequate training for political participation. As Eisenstadt has suggested, in societies in which the main adult roles are non-familial — that is, where they are universalistic, functionally specific, and achievement-oriented — roles learned within the particularistic, diffuse, and ascriptive family will not be harmonious with later adult roles. The performance of these roles within the family will not ensure the attainment of full social maturity, nor will they prepare the child adequately for participation within the larger social system.

In situations of this sort, other socializing agencies will come to play significant roles,[16] especially, it seems, in relation to the political system. In a society with a specialized political system, the transfer from family to polity is difficult, and there is likely to be less congruence between the two than in societies with less specialization in the performance of political functions.[17] Our data tend to support these generalizations. Family experiences do play a role in the formation of political attitudes, but the role may not be central; the gap between the family and the polity may be so wide that other social experiences, especially in social situations closer in time and in structure to the political system, may play a larger role. Furthermore, these other experiences may also interact with family or school experiences. Sometimes they may dampen or

[16] S. N. Eisenstadt, *From Generation to Generation,* Glencoe, Ill., 1956, Chap. I. A similar argument is made by Helmut Schelsky, *Die Skeptische Generation: Eine Soziologie der Deutschen Jugend,* Düsseldorf-Köln, 1957, Chaps. II and III.

[17] See Robert A. Levine, "The Role of the Family in Authority Systems: A Cross-cultural Application of the Stimulus-generalization Hypothesis," *Behavioral Science,* V (1960), pp. 291-96. Levine finds that among the Gussi of Kenya — a stateless political system with segmentary patrilineages — there is a high degree of generalization of attitudes from the family to the political system. In contrast with modern systems, says Levine, the transfer in Kenya occurs because the scope and norms of the political system resemble those in the family. Thus the shift from family to political participation involves fewer discontinuities than in modern political systems.

heighten the effects of that early socialization training. At other times — the experience with higher levels of education was our example here — they may substitute for it.

This discussion suggests that it may be difficult to draw the implications of one of the major findings in this chapter: that patterns of participation have been changing relatively uniformly over time in the direction of greater opportunities for participation in family and school. This change will increase the individual's "availability" for political participation. But whether or not this will lead to an increase in effective political participation is problematic.

CHAPTER XII

Profiles of Nations and Groups

In previous chapters we have presented our data dimension by dimension. We began with knowledge and awareness of the various aspects of government and politics in our five countries; then we turned to political emotion and involvement, the sense of political obligation and competence, and social attitudes and experiences in other authority contexts that might have effects on political attitudes. Our concern was not only to describe differences among our countries, but also to discern what relations existed among these attitude dimensions.

It may be useful at this point to draw our *demographic* findings together, to present summaries of national and group tendencies. In our examination of the political orientations of sub-national groups, we are in two respects limited by our data. First, reliable comparisons of demographic subgroupings would have required a larger sample. With our sample of approximately 1,000 in each country, we rapidly run out of cases as we introduce controls to determine whether a particular attitude difference results from a demographic characteristic other than the one under examination. The second limitation is more serious: the substance of our interview stressed attitudes toward the structure of political systems, rather than policy orientations or social attitudes and styles of life.[1] Subcultural differences are ideological as well as structural, and they are associated with social ideologies and life patterns; thus we shall be able to develop the relationship between demographic groups and political subcultural tendencies in only a limited way. Briefly, we shall only be able to show the extent to which educational and social class groups, men and women, and religious groups constitute political subcultures within the framework of our parochial–subject–citizen classification.

NATIONAL PATTERNS

Italy: An Alienated Political Culture. The picture of Italian political culture that has emerged from our data is one of relatively unrelieved political alienation and of social isolation and distrust. The Italians are particularly low in national pride, in moderate and open partisanship, in the acknowledgment of the obligation to take an active part in local community affairs, in the sense of competence to join with others in situations of political stress, in their choice of social forms of leisure-time activity, and in their confidence in the social environment.

If we consider Italian political history, these tendencies are not surprising. Before unification Italy had experienced centuries of fragmentation and external tyranny in which allegiant subject and citizen orientations could not develop. In the brief century of their national history Italians have learned to associate nationalism with humiliation, and constitutionalism and democracy with ineffectiveness. The liberating experiences — the *Risorgimento* and the resistance to Fascism in World War II — were incomplete and deeply divisive in their effects. Thus Italians tend to look upon government and politics as unpredictable and threatening forces, and not as social institutions amenable to their influence. The political culture of Italy does not support a stable and effective demo-

[1] This qualification must be made for our national as well as subnational findings. Our study as a whole stresses orientation to the structure and process of policies, rather than the substance of public policy.

cratic system; but these characteristics are quite understandable in the light of her political history.[2]

We may add two more features to this description of the Italian political culture. Italian national and political alienation rests on social alienation. If our data are correct, most Italians view the social environment as full of threat and danger. Thus the social fabric sustains neither an allegiant political culture nor an allegiant pattern of political participation. And perhaps as sobering is the fact that the Italians are the most traditional of our five peoples in their attitudes toward family participation. The norms of the patriarchal family still persist among a large proportion of Italians. Though the younger age groups have experienced participatory family socialization patterns more frequently than have the older groups, these differences between generations are of a smaller order than in the United States, Britain, and Germany.

The striking economic improvements in recent years in Italy hold out some prospect of changes in social structure and political culture. Rapid industrial development will certainly weaken traditionalism, and rising standards of living, assuming equitable distribution, may increase social trust and confidence in the political system. But the present pattern is of a predominantly alienated political culture.

This alienation may or may not be accompanied by belief in some revolutionary alternative to the present Italian political system. Italian Communists may, by our definition, be viewed as participants: they are aware of and involved in politics and they have an active sense of their own political competence — despite the fact that they would cease being participants in the same sense if their political party came into power. This is also true of the supporters of the Fascist right, insofar as they take an active part in public affairs. It is paradoxical that the majority of politically involved and informed Italians are opposed to the contemporary constitu-

[2] For a detailed discussion of Italian political culture, see Joseph LaPalombara, *Interest Groups in Italian Politics,* Princeton, 1964, Chap. IV.

tional and democratic regime, and that the bulk of the support for this regime comes from Italians who are oriented as subjects or as parochials. We saw in Chapter IV that Italy's largest political party, from which her governments have been drawn since World War II, rests in considerable part on the votes of politically uninvolved Catholic women.

Mexico: Alienation and Aspiration. What have been most striking in the Mexican pattern of political culture are the imbalances and inconsistencies. Mexico is lowest of all five countries in the frequency with which impact and significance are attributed to government and in its citizens' expectations of equal and considerate treatment at the hands of the bureaucracy and police. At the same time, the frequency with which Mexicans express pride in their political system is considerably higher than that of the Germans or Italians. And the objects of this pride tend predominantly to be the Mexican Revolution and the presidency. Furthermore, what sense of participation there is appears to be relatively independent of a sense of satisfaction with governmental output. As was pointed out in Chapter VIII, those Mexicans with a high sense of subjective competence are no more likely than those with low competence to evaluate specific governmental performance favorably, though they are more likely to express general system affect. In Mexico, then, participant orientation appears to have outrun subject orientation, and the role of participant tends to be isolated from a sense of allegiance in the subject sense.

Much of this isolation and imbalance may be explained by Mexican political history. Before 1910 the Mexican political system was primarily an exploitative, extractive one. Prerevolutionary parochialism was based on tradition; more, it represented a protective reaction against an exploitative central regime, and against predatory local chieftains and guerrilla bands. Thus historical experience and personal memory sustain an alienation from governmental authority, and these specific memories are consistent with contemporary authority trends in the various institutions of Mexican society.

The Mexican Revolution of 1910 represented a break with the past, for the government began to affect the population materially and favorably. But corruption and authoritarianism persist. The result, according to Scott, is an ambivalence in authority reactions. Mexicans have had direct experience with bureaucratic authority, and they reject that authority as corrupt and arbitrary. At the same time, there exists the myth of the benign Revolution and *presidencialismo,* the institutional charisma that the Mexican presidency has acquired in recent decades.[3]

There is another striking inconsistency in the Mexican data: high frequencies in subjective political competence are coupled with the lowest frequencies of all five countries in political performance (as measured by political information scores, voluntary association membership, and political activity). On the one hand, Mexicans have been exposed to a revolutionary ideology that places a high value on political participation. Exposure to these norms may create a tendency toward overestimating the competence of the self; a tendency to confuse aspiration with performance. On the other hand, the high rate of social mobility in Mexico, the discontinuous patterns of socialization associated with it, and the value conflicts that result from it create a high incidence of personal-identity crises comparable to the situation described by Pye in his Burmese study.[4] The personality aspects of this mobility are value conflict and a fragile self-esteem that typically produces over- and underestimation of the self. This may account for the inconsistency in Mexican responses: high self-appraisal of competence, coupled with cognitive inadequacy and political inexperience.

[3] Robert E. Scott, "Mexico," in Sidney Verba and Lucian W. Pye, eds., *Political Culture and Political Development,* Princeton, 1965. On the basis of social psychological and anthropological studies, Scott argues that the majority of Mexicans are oriented to the political system as subjects. But the Mexican subject orientation is ambivalent: it is characterized by both strong dependency needs and rejective and rebellious tendencies. Scott describes this ambivalence as one that pervades all authority relations in Mexican society — family, school, work group, and governmental-political system. The authority syndrome involves an exploitative and dominative exercise of power by those in authority positions, and a rebellious-dependency reaction by those in subordinate roles.

[4] Pye, *Politics, Personality, and Nation Building.*

Nevertheless, these civic aspirational tendencies in Mexican political culture are important evidence that the democratic aspiration of the Mexican Revolution and the political elite is meaningful to the population. The norms have begun to take root among large numbers of Mexicans. And increasingly the Mexican political system offers opportunities for political experience that may begin to consolidate these aspirations.

Germany: Political Detachment and Subject Competence. Germany is a technologically advanced nation with a highly developed and widespread educational and communications system. It had a bitter and traumatic political history before the founding of the present republic: a humiliating defeat in World War I, an abortive experiment in democracy, the Nazi dictatorship, the devastation and national division at the end of World War II. Both her technological advance and her traumatic history are reflected in Germany's political culture.

The high level of development in the communications and educational fields is reflected in the fact that most Germans are aware of and well informed about politics and government. In a number of ways they take part in the political system. The frequency of voting is high, as is the belief that voting is an important responsibility of the ordinary man. And their level of exposure to political material in the mass media of communications is high. Furthermore, German political culture is characterized by a high level of confidence in the administrative branches of government and a strong sense of competence in dealing with them.

Yet the contemporary political culture also reflects Germany's traumatic political history. Awareness of politics and political activity, though substantial, tend to be passive and formal. Voting is frequent, but more informal means of political involvement, particularly political discussion and the forming of political groups, are more limited. Germans are often members of voluntary associations, but rarely active within them. And norms favoring active political participation are not well developed. Many Germans assume that the act of voting is all that is required of a citizen. And Germany is the only nation of the five studied in which a sense of administrative competence occurs more frequently than a sense of political competence. Thus, though there is a high level of cognitive competence, the orientation to the political system is still relatively passive — the orientation of the subject rather than of the participant.

Germany's traumatic political history affects other important characteristics of the political culture. Though there is relatively widespread satisfaction with political output, this is not matched by more general system affect. Germans tend to be satisfied with the performance of their government, but to lack a more general attachment to the system on the symbolic level. Theirs is a highly pragmatic — probably overpragmatic — orientation to the political system; as if the intense commitment to political movements that characterized Germany under Weimar and the Nazi era is now being balanced by a detached, practical, and almost cynical attitude toward politics. And the attitudes of the German citizen to his fellow political actors are probably also colored by the country's political history. Hostility between the supporters of the two large parties is still relatively high and is not tempered by any general social norms of trust and confidence. And the ability of Germans to cooperate politically also appears to have serious limitations.

The United States: A Participant Civic Culture. The pattern of political culture found in the United States approximates what we have labeled the civic culture. There are several significant components in this cultural pattern. In the first place, the role of the participant is highly developed and widespread. As our data show, respondents in the United States, compared with those in the other four nations, are very frequently exposed to politics. They report political discussion and involvement in political affairs, a sense of obligation to take an active part in the community, and a sense of competence to influence the government. They are frequently active members of voluntary associations. Furthermore, they tend to be affectively involved in the political system: they report emotional involvement during political campaigns, and they have a high degree of pride in the political system. And their attachment to the political system includes both generalized system affect as well as satisfaction with specific governmental performance.

The civic culture, though, is a mixed and incorporative culture. The participant role is highly developed, but the more passive roles of subject and parochial persist, and are fused with the political system. That these other orientations temper the performance of the participant role can be shown by the fact that primary affiliations are important in setting the political style of participation in the United States. They are both an influence resource, providing individuals with what we have called a reserve of influence, and an important link in the political communications process. Moreover, the ability to cooperate with one's fellow citizens, which the use of informal groups as a political resource reflects, appears to depend upon a more general social trust and confidence that permeate the political system. This social trust is also seen in the "open" pattern of partisanship in the United States. Though there is emotional involvement in the outcome of elections, this does not mean complete rejection of one's political opponent.

The civic culture, then, is characterized by balance among the parochial, subject, and participant roles. But though the American political culture comes close to this balance, the data suggest that there is some imbalance in the direction of the participant role. As was suggested in Chapter VII, participant orientation in the United States appears better developed than subject orientation and to some extent dominates it. Subject competence seems to depend upon political competence; those Americans who feel competent in bureaucratic authority contexts are likely to be those who feel competent in political contexts. In the specific measures of subject competence — expectations of consideration by bureaucratic and police authority — the Americans drop to third place among our five countries, below Britain and Germany. This cultural imbalance, we have suggested, is the result of American historical experience with governmental and bureaucratic authority — an experience that began with distrust and revolution against the British Crown, and that has been consolidated by the American tendency to subject all governmental institutions, including the judiciary and bureaucracy, to direct popular control.

Great Britain: A Deferential Civic Culture. The political culture in Great Britain also approximates the civic culture. The participant role is highly developed. Exposure to politics, interest, involvement, and a sense of competence are relatively high. There are norms supporting political activity, as well as emotional involvement in elections and system affect. And the attachment to the system is a balanced one: there is general system pride as well as satisfaction with specific governmental performance.

Furthermore, the British political culture, like the American, fuses parochial and subject roles with the role of participant. Primary groups are relatively open to the political process and available as influence resources, and the political culture is permeated by more general attitudes of social trust and confidence. Open patterns of partisanship predominate. To some extent, the British political culture represents a more effective combination of the subject and participant roles. As suggested in Chapter VII, the development of the participant orientation in Britain did not challenge and replace the more deferential subject orientations, as was the tendency in the United States. Despite the spread of political competence and participant orientations, the British have maintained a strong deference to the independent authority of government. Thus the British political culture, like the American, approximates the balanced civic culture; but the balance is weighted somewhat differently from that in the United States. If in the latter country there tends to be too much weight placed on the participant role, in Britain the deferential subject role is more strongly developed and widespread.

EDUCATION AND POLITICAL CULTURE

Throughout this study we have reported differences among several educational groups. As in most other studies of political attitudes, our data show that educational attainment appears to have the most important demographic effect on political attitudes. Among the demographic variables usually investigated

— sex, place of residence, occupation, income, age, and so on — none compares with the educational variable in the extent to which it seems to determine political attitudes. The uneducated man or the man with the limited education is a different political actor from the man who has achieved a higher level of education.

There are a number of reasons for this. One reason, of course, is that educational differences are associated with differences in other social characteristics. Individuals who have achieved higher education, compared with those who have not, are likely to have higher incomes, to be in higher-status occupations, to be males, and so on — and all these characteristics tend in the same attitudinal direction. But even when these additional factors are controlled, respondents of lower and higher education still differ substantially in political attitudes. The main reason for this is probably that education has so many different kinds of effects. For one thing, people do *learn* in schools: they learn specific subjects as well as skills useful for political participation. And they learn the norms of political participation as well. Much of this learning may be through direct teaching; some of it may be more indirect. Not only does education influence political perspectives, it also places the individual in social situations where he meets others of like educational attainment, and this tends to reinforce the effect of his own education.

The way in which education affects an individual's political attitudes was discussed in Chapter XI. Here we concentrate, not on the process by which education acts upon political orientation, but on the specific ways in which those who have achieved education differ in their political orientations from those who have not. For this purpose, it is useful to have data from more than one nation. We can ask whether there are uniform differences among educational groups observable in all nations, or whether the nations differ in this respect. Does education create differing political subcultures in each nation, and, if so, does the educated subculture differ in the same way from the uneducated subculture in all the nations?

Since most of the data pertaining to education have been presented in other parts of the text, we need only summarize those findings here. Three types of differences between the political orientations of the more and the less educated respondents can be discerned. First, there are those political orientations that are strongly affected by higher education — and affected the same way in all five nations. Second, there are some political attitudes that change relatively little from one educational group to another. Here, too, there is cross-national uniformity, but the uniformity lies in the absence of differences in attitude among educational groups. Third, there are some political orientations upon which educational level has a different effect from nation to nation. In some nations those with higher education have a higher frequency of a particular orientation; in other nations it is those with lower education who have the higher frequency of the same orientation; or in one nation educational groups differ in their frequency of the particular orientation, while in other nations they will not so differ.

It is of great interest, and among the most important facts we discovered, that most of the relationships between education and political orientation are of the first type: educational groups differ from one another substantially, and in a similar way, in each nation. The manifestations of this cross-national uniformity are the following concerning the more educated individual:

(1) he is more aware of the impact of government on the individual than is the person of less education (Chapter II);

(2) he is more likely to report that he follows politics and pays attention to election campaigns than is the individual of less education (Chapter II);

(3) he has more political information (Chapter II);

(4) he has opinions on a wider range of political subjects; the focus of his attention to politics is wider (Chapter II);

(5) he is more likely to engage in political discussion (Chapter III);

(6) he feels free to discuss politics with a wider range of people (Chapter III). Those with less education are more

likely to report that there are many people with whom they avoid such discussions;

(7) he is more likely to consider himself capable of influencing the government; this is reflected both in responses to questions on what one could do about an unjust law (Chapter VI) and in respondents' scores on the subjective competence scale (Chapter VIII).

The above list refers to specifically political orientations, which vary in the same way in all five nations. In addition, our evidence shows that the more educated person:

(8) is more likely to be a member — and an active one — of some organization (Chapter X); and

(9) is more likely to express confidence in his social environment: to believe that other people are trustworthy and helpful (Chapter IX).

In all nine relationships the differences between those with relatively little education and those who are more highly educated are substantial. In all the nations, in almost all the cases, those with no more than primary education and those with some university training differ by at least twenty percentage points, and often by substantially more, in the frequency with which a particular attitude is held. The attitude dimensions affected in this way are ones that common sense and previous research would lead us to expect: information about politics and awareness of the activities of the government, for example. Yet the findings deserve some emphasis, for they illustrate that, despite national differences in political history and the current context of politics, and despite wide differences in the educational and social systems, strikingly uniform cross-national patterns can be found.

In each of these nations, it would seem, the educated classes possess the keys to political participation and involvement, whereas those with less education are less well equipped. In each nation the educated classes are more likely to be aware of politics (to be aware of the impact of government, to have information about government, to follow politics in the various media); to have political opinions on a wide range of subjects; and to engage in political discussions. The more highly educated are also more likely to consider themselves competent to influence the government and free to engage in political discussions. This set of orientations, widely distributed among those with high education and much less widely distributed among those with low education, constitutes what one might consider the minimum requirements for political participation. More complex attitudes and behavior depend upon such basic orientations as awareness of the political system, information about it, and some exposure to its operations. It is just this basic set of orientations that those of limited education tend not to have.

It is interesting, furthermore, that the orientations that distinguish the educated from the relatively uneducated tend, with one exception, to be affectively neutral. So far we have not shown either that educated individuals necessarily support the political system more, or that they are more hostile to it. We have merely shown that they are more aware of it. Nor do we know the content of the political discussions that go on on the higher educated level: we know only that there are more such discussions on that level than on any other. The educated individual is, in a sense, available for political participation. Education, however, does not determine the content of that participation.

Though educational differences in political orientation show a striking cross-national uniformity, this does not imply that differences among nations disappear when one considers matched educational groups. As we have pointed out, respondents on various educational levels within each nation differ from one another in the same way as the total samples of the populations differ from one another. The primary-educated Mexican is still different from the primary-educated German or Briton. But perhaps the most striking point is that within each nation the same relationship between those with more and less education obtains. Within each nation the more educated segment is more fully involved in the political system, is more fully a participant in politics. The less educated segment is less likely to take a full participating role.

But there is evidence that educational level does affect the *degree* of difference among the nations. On all the measures of political cognition or participation listed above — awareness of governmental impact, exposure to politics, political information, range of political opinions, subjective political competence, political participation — respondents on the higher educational levels tend to be more similar to one another than are the respondents on the lower educational levels. In general, the range between the nation in which political participation is most frequent (United States) and the one in which it is less frequent (Italy) is greatest among respondents with little education and least among those with higher education. Thus the university-educated respondents in Italy may differ from the university-educated respondents in the United States, but they are more like each other than are the Italians and Americans who did not get beyond primary education.

That higher education tends to reduce national differences suggests that the nature of political culture is greatly determined by the distribution of education. We have seen in Chapter XI that education can substitute for family participation and, to some extent, for school participation as well; that is, the subjective competence of the more educated individual is less dependent on family or school participation than is the competence of the less educated individual. And the more highly educated segments of all five nations show a cross-national uniformity in political orientation. Educational systems vary, yet there is a certain uniformity in the educational experience; thus these people share a common experience. Those with less education share less of a common cross-cultural experience with one another and are more affected by the particular history and culture of their own national systems. To say that education replaces national differences is of course an exaggeration; national differences persist, as we have said, even among the highly educated; moreover, the generalization being made here applies only to specific political orientations. Nevertheless, the highly educated participate in politics, no matter what their nation; participation by the less educated depends more heavily upon nation.

The highly educated show another cross-national uniformity: compared with the less educated, they participate more frequently in voluntary associations. We would expect this from educated respondents as they pursue professional activities or certain kinds of leisure activity. But beyond that, the finding demonstrates the way in which the potentialities for political participation can accumulate within this segment of society. Not only does education itself increase political participation; it also places the individual in an organizational situation which further heightens his participation.

We referred above to one exception in this first class of orientations that are uniformly affected by education: trust and confidence in the social environment. We have to qualify our comment that only cognitive awareness and political competence are increased by education in all five countries, for educated people appear to have trust in the social environment. And insofar as this trust is an important precondition of the capacity to join with others to effect political goals, we may stress even further the importance of education as a factor affecting democratic capabilities. It may not be too much to say that it produces a protocivic tendency. (We shall show below, however, that certain crucial components of the civic culture are not affected by education.)

We turn now to the second class of political orientations: those which the relatively uneducated share with the more educated in all five nations. One example of such an attitude was reported in Chapter V. There we saw that the norm that one ought to be a participant in the local community is found somewhat more frequently within the highly educated segments of society than among those with lower education, but this difference is relatively small compared with the other differences listed above. Similarly, we reported in Chapter IV that the frequency with which individuals say favorable things about opposition party supporters does increase with education, but again the increase is neither consistent nor great. Both the more and less educated parts of each nation have relatively similar evaluations of opposition party supporters. And in the example of the strategy of influence, in particular the belief that one can cooperate with others in attempting to influence the government (dis cussed extensively in Chapters VI and IX), there is almost no difference among the educational levels. Within each nation, local competents on all educational levels showed roughly the same frequency of cooperative competence. These three dimensions that are relatively unaffected by education — the norm that one ought to participate, the strategy to be employed in participating, and the degree of antagonism between the supporters of political parties — are not neutral political orientations. As political orientation becomes loaded with affective and evaluative content, we begin to find relatively great uniformity within each nation, and less difference among the educational subgroups. Of particular interest is the fact that interparty antagonism and cooperative competence do not differ as much among the educational levels as does the more neutral, interpersonal activity of engaging in political discussion.

In subjective and cognitive competence, then, the more educated respondents in each nation exist more fully within the political system. But when it comes to norms of political behavior or feelings about politics or partisanship, the various educational groups within each nation are more like one another. To illustrate this point, we shall consider those attitudes in our survey in which education seems to have a different impact from one nation to another. We found this inconsistent pattern in three dimensions:

1. In the United States and Britain those who are relatively more educated are more likely to express pride in the political aspects of their nation than are those with somewhat less education; a similar but smaller difference exists in Mexico; in Germany and Italy, however, there is no such difference between the education groups (Chapter III).

2. The sense of administrative competence — the extent to which individuals think they will be treated fairly and have their point of view considered — varies hardly at all between the educational groups in the United States and Britain; it varies slightly more in Germany, and substantially in Mex-

ico and Italy (Chapter III). Despite a uniform pattern in each nation (in each case those with higher education are more likely to have a sense of administrative competence), the variation and the degree of difference between the upper and lower educational levels suggests that the relationship belongs in this third group of political orientations: where the national differences between the educational groups are not uniform.

3. The relationship between the affective tone of election campaigns and educational attainment presents a mixed cross-national pattern (Chapter IV). In the United States, Britain, and Mexico, the more highly educated express more general satisfaction with their electoral participation, and also more frequently express the other three feelings we asked about: anger at election campaigns, enjoyment of election campaigns, and the feeling that these campaigns are silly or ridiculous. In Germany those with higher education more frequently express anger at election campaigns; but in their expression of satisfaction, as well as in the other two affective orientations to elections, they do not differ in any systematic way from those with lower education. In Italy, on the other hand, though anger, enjoyment, and the feeling that elections are silly increase in frequency as one moves up the educational ladder, the sense of satisfaction at electoral participation does not increase in this way.

In summary, we can say that in all five countries the less educated strata of the population tend to constitute subject and parochial subcultures. Pure parochials, in the sense defined in our classification, are rarely encountered among the respondents in our five countries. The overwhelming majority have had some exposure to governmental authority. The closest approximation of parochialism occurs among uneducated women particularly in Italy and Mexico. And here it is more normative and affective than cognitive. That is, in these countries, and to some extent in the others, political awareness and involvement are not considered appropriate to the female role. Hence we encounter uneducated women who know vaguely of the existence of government and politics, but who are uninvolved with them and take their indifference for granted.

The uneducated in our five countries who are oriented to government and politics are frequently oriented as subjects rather than as citizens. They tend more frequently to recognize the impact of government and to expect equal treatment by bureaucratic authority than to engage in political discussion or follow politics and election campaigns. But here there are national differences of some importance. In the United States, Britain, and Germany, large proportions of the uneducated (though much smaller than the educated) are oriented toward political input as well as governmental output. In other words, there are substantial numbers of citizens among them. In Italy and Mexico, on the other hand, the uneducated are far less frequently oriented toward politics and political participation. They tend to be subjects in their orientation, and at the level of illiteracy they approach parochialism.

But we have been speaking thus far only of the cognitive and competence dimensions, in which education has fairly uniform effects from country to country. If we look at these dimensions where education has little or no effect, or where its effects differ from country to country, we must qualify the propositions we have made regarding the parochial and subject tendencies among the uneducated. Thus in the United States and Britain the uneducated tend to share with the educated a common affective and normative allegiance to the political system, even though they differ sharply in the incidence of awareness and subjective competence. In Germany and Italy the uneducated tend to share with the educated a normative and affective alienation from the political system. The Mexican pattern is more complex, resembling the American and British in some respects, and the German and Italian in others.

WOMEN AND POLITICAL ORIENTATION

Some of the advocates of feminine suffrage a few decades ago made exaggerated claims about the consequences of granting equal political rights to women. A polity that included women as active participants would, they said, abolish poverty, protect family life, and raise educational and cultural standards; an international society made up of nations in which women had the suffrage would not tolerate war. Certainly these expectations have not been realized. Wherever the consequences of women's suffrage have been studied, it would appear that women differ from men in their political behavior only in being somewhat more frequently apathetic, parochial, conservative, and sensitive to the personality, emotional, and esthetic aspects of political life and electoral campaigns.[5]

Our data, on the whole, confirm the findings reported in the literature. In each of the countries we studied, men showed higher frequencies and higher intensities than women in practically all the indices of political orientation and activity that we employed. However, when we compare one country with another, it is quite clear that the feminine political patterns differ. We suggest that these differences have important implications for the functioning of political systems, and that these implications are not simply of the parochial, apathetic, conservative, and "emotional" sort referred to in the literature. Even if these patterns persist, and in all likelihood they will, they are probably not the most important consequences of the enfranchisement of women.

The Open and the Closed Family. In Chapter IX we showed that leisure activities differ among the five countries. Americans and Britons report much more frequently than Germans, Italians, and Mexicans that they spend their free time in organized or social activities. What is most interesting is the fact that these relatively higher frequencies seem to derive from the rate of social interaction among American and British women (see Table XII.1). Thus the percentages of men who choose political, community, religious, and social

[5] See Robert E. Lane, *Political Life*, pp. 209ff.; Maurice Duverger, *The Political Role of Women;* Fred W. Greenstein, "Sex-Related Political Differences in Childhood," *The Journal of Politics*, XXIII (1961), pp. 353ff.; M. Dogan and J. Narbonne, *Les Françaises Facent à la Politique*, Paris, 1955; Gabriele Bremme, *Die Politische Rolle der Frau in Deutschland.*

forms of free-time activity are similar in the United States, Britain, and Germany — whereas it is the American and British women who most frequently report these types of leisure activities. In Italy and Mexico neither men nor women seem to want to interact or actually to interact with others in their community.

TABLE XII.1 *Percentage who choose outgoing leisure activities*[a]; *by nation and sex*

	Total		*Male*		*Female*	
Nation	(%)	(*No.*)[b]	(%)	(*No.*)	(%)	(*No.*)
United States	40	(970)	24	(455)	54	(515)
Great Britain	30	(963)	22	(460)	37	(503)
Germany	16	(955)	18	(449)	13	(506)
Italy	7	(995)	6	(471)	9	(524)
Mexico	11	(1,007)	8	(355)	13	(652)

[a] For text of question, see Ch. IX.

[b] Numbers in parentheses refer to the bases upon which percentages are calculated.

Needless to say, these figures do not cover the whole gamut of social interaction. The respondents were asked to exclude their occupational and family interests. Nevertheless, the findings are striking. They suggest a type of family in the United States and Britain that is open to the community, and open via both men and women. When we recall that the proportion of respondents in the United States and Britain who trust other people and have confidence in the safety of social relations is much higher than it is in Germany, Italy, and Mexico, we may add a significant item to the social interaction pattern. The higher rate of social interaction in the United States and Britain seems to be associated with a sense of safety and responsiveness in the community — a sense that is shared equally by American and British men and women.

Political Participation and Awareness. It remains to show that the relative "openness" of the American and British family is associated with the political orientations and roles of American and British women. We may begin with some of our indices of political activity. Table XII.2 records the proportions of male and female respondents in the five countries who report that they discuss politics. If we look at the total columns, it is clear that, though in all five countries men more frequently than women say they discuss politics, in the United States and Britain the differences in frequency are rather small. Around two-thirds of the women in each country say they discuss politics; Germany, Mexico, and Italy follow in order of frequency. At the level of primary education or less, the differences between the sexes are more pronounced in all five countries. Nevertheless, well over half of

TABLE XII.2 *Percentage who discuss politics; by sex and education*

	Total				*Primary or less*				*Secondary or more*			
	Male		*Female*		*Male*		*Female*		*Male*		*Female*	
Nation	(%)	(*No.*)*	(%)	(*No.*)	(%)	(*No.*)	(%)	(*No.*)	(%)	(*No.*)	(%)	(*No.*)
United States	83	(455)	70	(515)	73	(248)	57	(269)	95	(207)	83	(246)
Great Britain	77	(459)	63	(503)	74	(277)	56	(340)	83	(182)	75	(163)
Germany	77	(442)	46	(499)	74	(352)	42	(440)	88	(90)	74	(59)
Italy	47	(471)	18	(524)	36	(293)	13	(403)	64	(178)	37	(121)
Mexico	55	(355)	29	(652)	49	(285)	26	(592)	77	(67)	56	(60)

* Numbers in parentheses refer to the bases upon which percentages are calculated.

the less well-educated American and British women report that they discuss politics, as compared with 42 per cent of the German, 26 per cent of the Mexican, and 13 per cent of the Italian women.

At the level of secondary education or higher, the proportions of women who discuss politics in the United States, Britain, and Germany reach or exceed three-quarters. The increase in Mexico is substantial; whereas in Italy, though the increase from primary to secondary is large, only a little more than one-third of the educated feminine population report that they talk politics. The German figures are of particular interest. At the level of secondary education, German women discuss politics as frequently as British women and only a little less frequently than the American. However, German women in general feel more restricted in their political communications.[6]

[6] See Table XIII.13, Unabridged Edition, p. 391.

Although American and British men and women resemble each other in their sense of freedom to discuss politics, almost two-thirds of the German women report feeling severely restricted, as compared with 48 per cent of the German men. The Italian pattern is similar to the German, whereas the Mexican falls in the middle of the five nations.

What this would seem to suggest is that in the United States and Britain, where women report high rates of social interaction in their communities, and where they report almost as frequently as men that they feel free to discuss politics, the family becomes part of the system of political communications. In Italy, on the other hand, the general rate of political discussion is low, and particularly low among women; here, too, it would appear that when men engage in political discussion, they tend to do so outside the home: in the café, on the street, or in their places of work. In Germany and Mexico, which seem to present an intermediate pattern, educated women in particular engage in political discussion at a relatively high rate. In Germany the rate of political discussion among educated women is as high as it is among American and British women; the rate among uneducated German women is substantially below that of their American and British counterparts.

Our hypothesis, that American and British families tend to be involved in the political communications system, is supported by our data on voluntary association membership. More than two-thirds of the American men and almost half of the American women in our sample are members of voluntary associations (civic organizations, interest groups, church groups, social groups, and the like). One-quarter or more of the American men and of the women have at some time been officers of voluntary associations. In Britain proportionately fewer women are members of organizations, and only a small percentage have ever been officers of such groups. In Germany the differences between men and women in their organizational activity are greater than in Britain, while in Italy and Mexico the proportion of female organizational members is lowest of all.

In all five countries the percentages of organizational members increase with education. The German frequencies for both men and women exceed the British and are almost as high as the American. It is a striking finding that 34 per cent of educated American women have at some time been officers of voluntary associations. In Italy and Mexico, organizational membership is quite low even among the better educated women (27 per cent).[7]

TABLE XII.3 *Percentage who acknowledge duty to participate in local community; by sex and nation*

	Total				*Primary or less*				*Secondary or more*			
	Male		*Female*		*Male*		*Female*		*Male*		*Female*	
Nation	(%)	(*No.*)*	(%)	(*No.*)	(%)	(*No.*)	(%)	(*No.*)	(%)	(*No.*)	(%)	(*No.*)
United States	52	(455)	50	(515)	37	(248)	42	(269)	70	(207)	59	(246)
Great Britain	43	(459)	36	(503)	43	(277)	33	(340)	42	(182)	43	(163)
Germany	31	(442)	16	(499)	29	(359)	16	(440)	40	(90)	22	(59)
Italy	14	(471)	6	(524)	9	(293)	5	(403)	22	(178)	12	(121)
Mexico	31	(355)	24	(652)	29	(285)	22	(592)	39	(67)	36	(60)

* Numbers in parentheses refer to the bases upon which percentages are calculated.

In the dimension of simple political cognition (political information, awareness of public affairs), compared with that of participation, we have a reversal in the ranking of national female performance, as well as in the ranking of nations. Just as Germans in general rank higher in political cognition than do the British, so do German women exceed British women in frequency of cognition. On the other hand, the Italian pattern persists in the cognitive dimension, even among educated Italian women. Six out of ten educated Italian women report that they never or infrequently follow politics and political campaigns — a proportion almost twice that of their Mexican counterparts.[8]

Political Responsibility and Competence. Sex differences in political obligation and competence fall into a pattern that tends to support our earlier hypothesis about the role of women in Britain and the United States. Thus Table XII.3

[7] See Table XIII.4, unabridged edition, p. 392.

[8] Chapter 13, Tables 5 and 6, Unabridged Edition, p. 393.

shows that almost equal proportions of American men and women say that ordinary people have an obligation to participate actively in the public affairs of their local communities. In Britain the over-all percentage is somewhat lower and the difference between men and women somewhat greater. But in Germany the female frequency drops to half that of the male. German women acknowledge political obligations in the local community less frequently than do Mexican women. The sense of local civic obligation among Italian men and women has an extremely low frequency; indeed, it appears to be almost nonexistent among Italian women.

Education clearly increases the frequency of political obligation in all five countries. But in this dimension, too, the

TABLE XII.4 *Percentage who report subjective political competence (local and national); by nation and sex*

	Local				*National*			
	Male		*Female*		*Male*		*Female*	
Nation	(%)	(*No.*)*	(%)	(*No.*)	(%)	(*No.*)	(%)	(*No.*)
United States	81	(455)	83	(515)	77	(455)	72	(515)
Great Britain	83	(459)	72	(503)	70	(459)	56	(503)
Germany	72	(442)	53	(499)	49	(442)	27	(499)
Italy	62	(471)	41	(524)	38	(471)	19	(524)
Mexico	62	(355)	46	(652)	46	(355)	33	(652)

* Numbers in parentheses refer to the bases upon which percentages are calculated.

evidence supports our hypothesis that relatively educated American and British men and women have similar frequencies, whereas in Germany and Italy substantial differences persist among secondary-educated men and women. In Germany 22 per cent of the secondary-educated women, as compared to 40 per cent of the secondary-educated men, acknowledge political obligation in the local community. In Italy the figure for males is 22 per cent; for females, 12 per cent. The Mexican pattern is very similar to the British, with 39 per cent of the educated males and 36 per cent of the educated females acknowledging local obligations.

If we examine the responses to our questions on the sense of competence to influence local and national governments, several points may be made (Table XII.4). In all five countries women as well as men more frequently feel locally competent than nationally competent; and this difference is especially noticeable among women. But despite this universal trend, almost three-fourths of the American female respondents express a sense of national competence. In Germany, though 53 per cent of the women express local competence, only 27 per cent express national competence; and the Italian figures are, respectively, 41 per cent and 19 per cent. Mexican women express national competence somewhat more frequently than do German women. As these data suggest, the view that female political competence tends to be limited to the local community seems to be true of the continental European countries, but much less true of the United States and Britain.

Education raises the frequency of subjective political competence at both the local and national levels in all five countries. And it raises it for both males and females. The majority of the better-educated women in all five countries express a sense of competence to influence their local governments. But the Italian percentage of locally competent, educated women is lowest of all: 52 per cent (n: 121), as compared with 87 per cent (n: 246) for educated American women, 83 per cent (n: 163) for the British, 82 per cent (n: 159) for the German, and 68 per cent (n: 60) for Mexican educated women. Women's sense of competence to influence the national government also increases universally with education. However, the better-educated Italian women express national political competence infrequently (25 per cent, n: 121). In the dimension of local and national competence, educated German women show frequencies almost as high as those of American and British women.

Feelings Toward Nation and Politics. Here we have measures of emotional involvement in politics for men and women. One of these measures, discussed in detail in Chapter III, is pride in nation. There we pointed out that the incidence of pride in the political aspects of the nation was high in the United States and Britain, fairly high in Mexico, and very low in Germany and Italy. The female patterns resemble the overall national patterns. Thus 91 per cent (n: 515) of the American women express political pride, as compared with 61 per cent (n: 563) of the British women, 26 per cent (n: 652) of Mexican women, 15 per cent (n: 499) of German women, and 3 per cent (n: 523) of Italian women.

We are able to ascertain an apathy rate from our series of questions on feelings during election campaigns. If we define as politically apathetic those who report none of the three feelings of enjoyment, anger, and contempt during election campaigns, the following pattern emerges (Table XII.5): in all five countries the female apathy rate is higher than the male. In Germany it is almost double the male rate; in Mexico both proportions are high and more nearly equal; in Italy the rates are very high for both men and women, with almost two-thirds of the women manifesting apathy. In the United States 14 per cent of the women and 9 per cent of the men are apathetic; in Britain the percentages are 32 for women and 20 for men.

Education reduces the rate of apathy among women in all countries. Nevertheless, apathy is characteristic of almost one-half of the secondary educated Italian women (n: 121), as compared with 29 per cent (n: 163) of the better-educated

TABLE XII.5 *Percentage who report no feelings about election campaigns; by sex and nation*

Nation	*Male* (%)	*(No.)**	*Female* (%)	*(No.)*
United States	9	(455)	14	(515)
Great Britain	20	(459)	32	(503)
Germany	24	(442)	44	(499)
Italy	46	(471)	62	(524)
Mexico	30	(355)	48	(652)

* Numbers in parentheses refer to the bases upon which percentages are calculated.

women in Britain, 24 per cent (n: 59) of those in Germany, 22 per cent (n: 60) of those in Mexico, and 10 per cent (n: 246) of those in America.

Women and the Political System. In summary, we may say

that American women and, to a somewhat lesser extent, British women tend to be active and involved in their communities, both in an informal and in an organizational sense. They are trustful of their social surroundings, politically informed, observant, and emotionally involved in the political scene. They acknowledge the obligation to participate actively in local political affairs, they feel competent to exercise influence over their government, and they take pride in the political characteristics of their nations. Except in the dimension of political awareness and knowledge, German women manifest lower frequencies than do American and British women. But except in the dimensions of social interaction, pride in nation, and local community obligation, educated German women manifest frequencies similar to those of American and British women. Mexican women show an uneven pattern: relatively low in the dimensions of participation and knowledge, they equal or surpass the German female rates in the obligation and national competence dimensions, and they are relatively high in national pride. The Italian feminine pattern is almost consistently low in all the political dimensions discussed here.

If we consider these data from the point of view of the political systems in the five countries, it is evident that we have to revise older theories of the role of women in democracy. These theories have tended to treat the sex differential in the same way that they treat other demographic categories, such as income, occupation, education, and the like. What they have overlooked is the fact that the great majority of adults are married; that they create families, raise children, and help to socialize these children into their adult roles and attitudes. Thus the political characteristics of women affect the family as a unit in the political system and affect the way in which the family performs the political socialization function. In all five countries, of course, the overwhelming majority of politicians, civil servants, and political activists are men. But it makes a great deal of difference whether women tend to live outside the political system in an intramural family existence, which is generally the case in Italy and among the relatively uneducated German and Mexican women, or within the political system, which tends to be the case in the United States and Britain. Duverger's comment that women ". . . have the mentality of minors in many fields and, particularly in politics, they usually accept paternalism on the part of men. The man — husband, fiancé, lover, or myth — is the mediator between them and the political world" [9] is an essentially continental European comment, and even here Duverger may be commenting more on the past and present than on the future.

Although our data do not permit us to demonstrate it directly and explicitly, we are suggesting that in the United States and Britain the family tends to be a part of the political system, that events and issues in the polity tend to be transmitted into the family via both marriage partners, and that political discussion tends to be frequent and reciprocal, rather than male-dominated. Furthermore, we suggest that the problems of family life, the needs of women and children are more directly and effectively transmitted into the polity through this kind of politically open family. The esthetic quality and emotional tone of political life are probably also affected by the political competence and activity of women in the United States and Britain. We would suggest, too, that a family that is open to reciprocal discussion of political issues provides a type of political socialization that enables children to develop *within the family itself* a sense of political competence and obligation, and to learn to tolerate the ambiguities of politics and political controversy.

From this point of view, politically competent, aware, and active women seem to be an essential component of the civic culture. The significance of the political emancipation of women is not in the suffragette's dream of women in cabinets, parliaments, at the upper levels of the civil service, and the like; nor is it in Duverger's conception of the dependent minor. March has shown that there tends to be a division of labor between husbands and wives in the kinds of issues on

[9] Duverger, *op. cit.*, p. 129. For comments on Duverger, and an analysis of differences in the socialization of American boys and girls, which affect male and female adult political patterns, see Greenstein, *op. cit.*, p. 370.

which they take the initiative.[10] Greenstein has shown that American boys are more politically aware and informed than girls,[11] and he suggests how differential political socialization in the family produces these sexual differences. He also points out, correctly, that there are inherent limitations in the adult female role, which set an outer boundary to political participation for the great majority of women. What a purely American study would not bring to light is the fact that, by comparison with continental European women, American and British women tend to "live in" the community and the polity; and this has considerable significance for the functioning of the polity. We have only suggested what these consequences may be.

OTHER DEMOGRAPHIC PATTERNS

The many studies of voting behavior, party preference, and attitudes on political issues have shown that these patterns depend heavily on social position: occupation, income, and social status. The sorts of attitudes we have been concerned with — political awareness, competence, activity, and affect — are also influenced by socio-economic status. Individuals with lower income or with lower-status jobs are less likely to be involved in politics, to be well informed, to be active. However, though economic position does have a general cross-national effect on attitudes, this effect is neither as clear nor as strong as that of education. When education is held constant, differences among economic groups decline. Still, a fairly uniform relationship does remain: the man higher in the economic hierarchy, just like the more educated man, is more likely to be politically competent and active.

The relation between religion and political attitudes is more complex. Lenski, in his detailed analysis of differences in attitudes and behavior among religious groups in the Detroit area, makes the point that Catholics tend to be more traditional in their social orientations than Protestants and Jews.

10 James G. March, "Husband-Wife Interaction Over Political Issues," *The Public Opinion Quarterly,* XVIII (1953-54), pp. 461-70.

11 *Op. cit.,* pp. 365ff.

They are less frequently achievement oriented, and morally and intellectually less autonomous. They are more conservative on matters of social and religious morality. In the field of public policy, he reports, Catholics tend to be more "welfare" oriented than Protestants, and they give less support to civil rights.[12]

In the dimensions covered in our survey, there is some slight support for Lenski's thesis that Catholics are more traditional than Protestants, yet the differences are so small as to be negligible. Far more important is the finding that in the three of our countries where both denominations are present in substantial numbers — the United States, Britain, and Germany — Protestants and Catholics have similar structural political orientations. In other words, the two denominations do not constitute political subcultures in the structural sense of the term. Certainly in all three countries there is a strong relation between denominational and party preference. And had our study included public policy, morality, and value questions, then greater differences would probably have come to light.

Other demographic characteristics, such as age, region, and city size have been treated only in specific contexts in our study. We are unable to treat them more systematically because of the priorities of our research design. We were concerned primarily with national rather than subcultural patterns, and with attitudes toward the political system rather than public policy. Investigation of the phenomena of political subcultures and of their relationship to demographic characteristics requires a research design of its own.

[12] Gerhard Lenski, *The Religious Factor*, Garden City, New York, 1961, chaps. 4 and 8.

CHAPTER XIII

The Civic Culture and Democratic Stability

THUS FAR WE have concentrated upon one aspect of political systems: that which we call political culture. The bulk of this book has dealt with the similarities and differences in the patterns of political attitudes found in the five nations. We have attempted to describe these similarities and differences as well as to explain them; to relate political attitudes to the structure of politics and to general attitudes toward people and society. In all this the political culture has been the focus of our attention. When other aspects of the political system have been brought into the discussion, it has usually been because of their impact on the political culture. But an important question remains to be dealt with: what is the impact of a political culture on the political system of which it is a part?

The five nations we have studied are democracies, though quite different from one another in their characteristics and their political histories. We shall therefore consider the way in which political culture affects democratic government; more specifically, we shall ask how far it goes toward creating and maintaining stable and effective democracy. Is there a democratic political culture — a pattern of political attitudes that fosters democratic stability, that in some way "fits" the democratic political system? To answer this question we must look at the political culture in the two relatively stable and successful democracies, Great Britain and the United States. As we have said, the political cultures of these two nations approximate the civic culture. This pattern of political attitudes differs in some respects from the "rationality-activist" model, or the model of political culture which, according to the norms of democratic ideology, would be found in a successful democracy. Civics texts would have us believe that the problem facing the citizen in a democracy is, to quote the title of a recent book in the field, *How to Be an Active Citizen.*[1] According to this rationality-activist view, a successful democracy requires that citizens be involved and active in politics, informed about politics, and influential. Furthermore, when they make decisions, particularly the important decision of how to cast their vote, they must make them on the basis of careful evaluation of evidence and careful weighing of alternatives. The passive citizen, the nonvoter, the poorly informed or apathetic citizen — all indicate a weak democracy. This view of democratic citizenship stresses activity, involvement, rationality. To use the terminology we have developed, it stresses the role of the participant and says little about the role of the subject or parochial.

Recent studies of political behavior call the rationality-activist model into question, for it is becoming clear that citizens in democracies rarely live up to this model. They are not well informed, not deeply involved, not particularly active; and the process by which they come to their voting decision is anything but a process of rational calculation.[2] Nor does this model accurately represent the civic culture we have found in Britain and the United States. It is true — and this point is both substantively important as well as indicative of the usefulness of comparative data — that the informed, involved, rational, and active citizen is more frequently found in the

[1] Paul Douglass and Alice McMahon, *How to Be an Active Citizen,* Gainesville, Fla., 1960.

[2] See, for instance, Berelson *et al., Voting,* chap. XIV; Campbell *et al., The American Voter,* chap. X, and Julian L. Woodward and Elmo Roper, "Political Activity of American Citizens," *American Political Science Review,* XLIV (1950), pp. 872-85.

successful than in the unsuccessful democracies. The characteristics of the rationality-activist model of democratic citizenship are indeed components of the civic culture; but the point to be stressed here is that they are only *part* of that culture.

The civic culture is a mixed political culture. In it many individuals are active in politics, but there are also many who take the more passive role of subject. More important, even among those performing the active political role of the citizen, the roles of subject and parochial have not been displaced. The participant role has been added to the subject and parochial roles. This means that the active citizen maintains his traditional, nonpolitical ties, as well as his more passive political role as a subject. It is true that the rationality-activist model of the citizen does not imply that participant orientations replace subject and parochial ones; but by not mentioning the latter two roles explicitly, it does imply that they are irrelevant to the democratic political culture.

Actually, these two orientations do more than persist: they play an important part in the civic culture. In the first place, the parochial and subject orientations modify the intensity of the individual's political involvement and activity. Political activity is but one part of the citizen's concerns, and usually not a very important part at that. The maintenance of other orientations limits the extent of his commitment to political activity and keeps politics, as it were, in its place. Furthermore, not only do the parochial and subject orientations persist side by side with the participant orientations, but they penetrate and modify the participant orientations. Primary affiliations, for instance, are important in the patterns of citizen influence. In addition, a diffuse set of social attitudes and interpersonal attitudes tends to affect the content of the political attitudes — to make them less intense and divisive. Penetrated by primary group orientations and by general social and interpersonal attitudes, political attitudes are not solely the results of articulated principle and rational calculation.

How can we explain the discrepancy between the ideals of the rationality-activist model and the patterns of political attitudes we actually find, even in the more stable and successful democracies? One possible explanation, and the one most often found in the literature on civic education, is that this discrepancy is evidence for the malfunctioning of democracy. Insofar as people do not live up to the ideal of the active citizen, democracy is a failure. If one believes that the realities of political life should be molded to fit one's theories of politics, such an explanation is satisfactory. But if one holds to the view that theories of politics should be drawn from the realities of political life — a somewhat easier and probably more useful task — then this explanation of the gap between the rationality-activist model and democratic realities is less acceptable. From the latter point of view, one would probably argue that the gap exists because the standards have been set unreasonably high. Given the complexity of political affairs, given the other demands made upon an individual's time, and given the difficulty of obtaining information necessary for making rational political decisions, it is no wonder that the ordinary citizen is not the ideal citizen. In the light of an individual's nonpolitical interests, it might be quite irrational to invest in political activity the time and effort needed to live up to the rationality-activist model. It may just not be worth it to be that good a citizen.

But though a completely activist political culture may be a utopian ideal, there may be other, more significant reasons why an intricately mixed civic culture is found in the more successful democracies. The civic culture, which sometimes contains apparently contradictory political attitudes, seems to be particularly appropriate for democratic political systems, for they, too, are mixtures of contradictions. Harry Eckstein has suggested that a democratic political system requires a blending of apparent contradictions — he calls them "balanced disparities" — if it is to function effectively. On the one hand, a democratic government must govern; it must have power and leadership and make decisions. On the other hand, it must be responsible to its citizens. For if democracy means anything, it means that in some way governmental elites must respond to the desires and demands of citizens. The need to maintain this sort of balance between governmental power and governmental responsiveness, as well as the need to maintain other balances that derive from the power/responsiveness balance — balances between consensus and cleavage, between affectivity and affective neutrality — helps explain the way in which the more mixed patterns of political attitudes associated with the civic culture are appropriate to a democratic political system.[3]

Power and Responsiveness. The maintenance of a proper balance between governmental power and governmental responsiveness represents one of the most important and difficult tasks of a democracy. Unless there is some control of governmental elites by nonelites, it is hard to consider a political system democratic. On the other hand, nonelites cannot themselves rule. If a political system is to be effective — if it is to be able to initiate and carry out policies, adjust to new situations, meet internal and external challenges — there must be mechanisms whereby governmental officials are endowed with the power to make authoritative decisions. The tensions produced by the need to pursue the opposing goals of governmental power and governmental responsiveness become most apparent in times of crisis. Wars, for instance (hot or cold), have often shifted the balance so far in the direction of governmental power and authority as to cause concern about the preservation of democratic responsiveness. Yet if the balance is not so shifted, it is argued that democratic governments may succumb to external challenges.

Crises bring to the fore the problem of maintaining an adequate balance, but the problem exists in the day-to-day running of a democracy. How can a governmental system be constructed so that a balance is maintained between power and responsiveness? As E. E. Schattschneider has put it, "The

[3] The contradictory demands placed upon democratic political systems have been stressed in some as yet unpublished lectures by Professor Harry Eckstein, upon which this chapter draws. The authors are grateful for the opportunity to see his notes on this subject. That democratic systems are called upon to pursue apparently opposing goals is also stressed in Berelson *et al., op. cit.,* Chapter XIV, and in Parsons, "Voting and the Equilibrium of the American Political System," in Burdick and Brodbeck (eds.), *American Voting Behavior,* Glencoe, Ill., 1959.

problem is not how 180 million Aristotles can run a democracy, but how we can organize a community of 180 million ordinary people so that it remains sensitive to their needs. This is a problem of *leadership, organization, alternatives, and systems of responsibility and confidence.*" [4] In trying to resolve this problem, political scientists have usually spoken in terms of the structure of electoral conflict. An electoral system, designed to turn power over to a particular elite for a limited period of time, can achieve a balance between power and responsiveness: the elites obtain power, yet this power is limited by the periodic elections themselves, by the concern for future elections during the interelection period, and by a variety of other formal and informal checks. For a system of this sort to work, there must obviously be more than one party (or at least some competing elite group with the potentiality of gaining power) to make the choice among elites meaningful; and at the same time there must be some mechanism whereby an elite group can exercise effective power — perhaps by the giving of all power to the victorious party in a two-party system, or by the formation of workable coalitions among a group of parties. Most of the debate on the most appropriate electoral system for a democracy (proportional representation, single member districts, or some mixed form) has resolved around two questions: how to maximize the competing goals of power and responsiveness, and how to decide which goal deserves greater stress.[5] There has also been much concern over the proper organization of political parties to maximize both of these goals. This concern clearly motivated the members of the American Political Science Association's Committee on Political Parties, when, in their report, they called for a political party system that is ". . . democratic, responsible, and effective — a system that is accountable to

[4] E. E. Schattschneider, *The Semi-Sovereign People,* New York, 1960, p. 138. Italics in original.

[5] On this continuing debate, see, among others, Enid Lakeman and James D. Lambert, *Voting in Democracies,* London, 1955; F. A. Hermens, *Democracy or Anarchy,* South Bend, Ind., 1941, and M. Duverger, *Political Parties,* London, 1954.

the public, respects and expresses differences of opinion, and is able to cope with the great problems of modern government."[6]

The tension between power and responsiveness can be managed to some extent by the structure of partisan conflict. But our main interest is in the relationship between this tension and political culture, particularly the civic culture. Can the set of attitudes held by citizens help to maintain the delicate balance between the contradictory demands placed on a democratic system? This concentration upon the political attitudes of ordinary citizens does not imply a rejection of the important role of political structures or of elite attitudes and behavior. These are important as well, and we shall return to them below when we consider the way in which the attitudes of ordinary citizens and of elites interact.

The tension between governmental power and responsiveness has a parallel in the conflicting demands made upon the citizens of a democratic system. Certain things are demanded of the ordinary citizen if elites are to be responsive to him: the ordinary citizen must express his point of view so that elites can know what he wants; he must be involved in politics so that he will know and care whether or not elites are being responsive, and he must be influential so as to enforce responsive behavior by the elites. In other words, elite responsiveness requires that the ordinary citizen act according to the rationality-activist model of citizenship. But if the alternate pole of elite power is to be achieved, quite contradictory attitudes and behavior are to be expected of the ordinary man. If elites are to be powerful and make authoritative decisions, then the involvement, activity, and influence of the ordinary man must be limited. The ordinary citizen must turn power over to elites and let them rule. The need for elite power requires that the ordinary citizen be relatively passive, uninvolved, and deferential to elites. Thus the democratic citizen is called on to pursue contradictory goals; he

6 "Toward a More Responsible Two Party System," a report of the Committee on Political Parties, of the American Political Science Association, *American Political Science Review,* XLIV (1950), Special Supplement, p. 17.

must be active, yet passive; involved, yet not too involved; influential, yet deferential.[7]

NORMS, PERCEPTIONS, AND ACTIVITY

The data presented in this book suggest some ways in which these conflicting demands might be managed. The crucial cases for our analysis are clearly Britain and the United States, for if there is some pattern of attitudes that can allow this tension to be managed, one might expect it to act most effectively within the relatively more stable democracies. It is in these two nations that we found the closest approximation to the civic culture. Our data suggest that in two broad ways the civic culture maintains the citizen's active–influential role as well as his more passive role: on the one hand, there is in the society a *distribution* of individuals who pursue one or the other of the conflicting citizen goals; on the other hand, certain *inconsistencies in the attitudes of an individual* make it possible for him to pursue these seemingly conflicting goals at the same time. Let us first consider the inconsistencies within the individual.

As our survey showed, there exists a gap between the *actual political behavior* of our respondents, on the one hand, and their *perceptions of their capacities to act* and their *obligations to act,* on the other. Respondents in Britain and the

[7] It should be clear that the tension described here is not the same as that between the obligations of the citizen and the obligations of the subject, as discussed in Chapter I. There we dealt with the fact that the democratic citizen has a set of role expectations within the input structure of the political system. He is expected to participate in some ways in decisions. At the same time he has "subject" obligations toward the output aspects of the political system. He is expected to abide by decisions once they are made. This mixture, too, is part of the civic culture. But the tension described in this section is not between an individual's role in relation to the input structure (i.e., as citizen) and his role in relation to the output structure (i.e., as subject) — a tension that at least in theory appears fairly easy to resolve. Rather, the tension described here is between two modes of relating to the input structures. The citizen has both to be influential and to affect the course of policy; at the same time he must be noninfluential and allow political elites to make decisions independently. Thus the tension we are describing lies within the role of citizen.

United States manifest high frequencies of what we have called subjective political competence. As reported in Chapter VI, a large proportion considers itself able to influence the decisions of the local government, and a substantial, though not quite as large, proportion feels the same way about the activities of the national government. Yet this high estimation of one's competence as an influential citizen is certainly not matched by actual political behavior. In the first place, only a small proportion of those respondents who say they could influence the government report that they have ever attempted such influence. And even if those who think they could influence governmental decisions were to attempt to do so — which is unlikely — they would almost certainly not have the success that they believe they would have. It is clearly an exaggeration when 40 per cent of American respondents or 24 per cent of the British say that there is some likelihood that an attempt of theirs to influence the national legislature would be successful.

A similar gap exists between the sense of obligation to participate in political life and actual participation. As reported in Chapter V, a much higher proportion of respondents says that the ordinary man has some obligation to participate in the affairs of his local community than in fact does participate; and again the pattern is clearest in the United States and Britain. As one respondent, quoted in Chapter V, put it, "I'm saying what [one] ought to do, not what I do." And there is evidence that this position is far from rare. Certainly, the sense of obligation to take some part in one's community affairs is not matched by the importance attributed to such activity by respondents. The proportion saying that one has such obligations is in each nation much larger than the proportion that, when asked to report on its free-time activities, reports participation in community affairs. Fifty-one per cent of the American respondents report that the ordinary man ought to take some active part in the affairs of his community. But when asked what they do in their free time, only about 10 per cent of the American respondents mention such activities. And when Gillespie and Allport asked a somewhat differently phrased question of youth in the United States, only about one in five said that he expected community participation to be a source of satisfaction.[8] This suggests that though there is a widespread norm that one ought to participate within the community, active participation is far from the most significant activity to most people. It is not what most people do in their spare time, nor is it the major source of satisfaction, joy, and excitement.

These two gaps — between a high perception of potential influence and a lower level of actual influence, and between a high frequency of expressed obligation to participate and the actual importance and amount of participation — help explain how a democratic political culture can act to maintain a balance between governmental elite power and governmental elite responsiveness (or its complement, a balance between nonelite activity and influence and nonelite passivity and noninfluence). The comparative infrequency of political participation, its relative lack of importance for the individual, and the objective weakness of the ordinary man allow governmental elites to act. The inactivity of the ordinary man and his inability to influence decisions help provide the power that governmental elites need if they are to make decisions. But this maximizes only one of the contradictory goals of a democratic system. The power of the elites must be kept in check. The citizen's opposite role, as an active and influential enforcer of the responsiveness of elites, is maintained by his strong commitment to the norm of active citizenship, as well as by his perception that he can be an influential citizen. This may be in part a myth, for it involves a set of norms of participation and perceptions of ability to influence that are not quite matched by actual political behavior. Yet the very fact that citizens hold to this myth — that they see themselves as influential and as obligated to take an active role — creates a potentiality of citizen influence and activity. The subjectively competent citizen, as was pointed out in Chapter VI, has not necessarily attempted to influence the government, but he is *more likely* to have made such attempts

[8] James M. Gillespie and Gordon W. Allport, *Youth's Outlook on the Future,* New York, 1955, p. 57.

than is the citizen who does not consider himself competent.[9]

A citizen within the civic culture has, then, a reserve of influence. He is not constantly involved in politics, he does not actively oversee the behavior of political decision makers. But he does have the potential to act if there is need. This reserve of influence — influence potential that is inactive and uncommitted to the political system — was best illustrated by the data, presented in Chapter VI, on the ability of citizens to create political structures in time of need. The citizen is not a constant political actor. He is rarely active in political groups. But he thinks that he can mobilize his ordinary social environment, if necessary, for political use. He is not the active citizen: he is the potentially active citizen.

Yet the intermittent and potential character of the citizen's political activity and involvement depends upon steadier, more persistent types of political behavior. By living in a civic culture, the ordinary man is more likely than he would be otherwise to maintain a steady and high rate of exposure to political communications, to be a member of an organization, and to engage in informal political discussion. These activities do not in themselves indicate an active participation in the decision-making process of a society; but they do make such participation more possible. They prepare the individual for intervention in the political system; and more important perhaps, they create a political environment in which citizen involvement and participation are more feasible.

We have been saying that inconsistencies within attitudes and inconsistencies between attitudes and behavior, rather than the one-sided attitudes of the rationality-activist model, can maintain the tension between citizen activity and citizen passivity. But now we must ask whether these inconsistencies cause instability in the civic culture. Much of the recent theorizing about attitude formation emphasizes the strain toward consistency or consonance among the beliefs, attitudes, and behavior of an individual; there now exists a large body of data to support the theory that cognitive inconsistencies will produce a stress toward the reduction of those inconsisten-

[9] On the importance of the democratic myth, see, V. O. Key, Jr., *Public Opinion and American Democracy,* New York, 1961, p. 547.

cies.[10] But as we have seen, the balance between citizen influence and citizen passivity *depends upon the inconsistencies* between political norms and perceptions, on the one hand, and political behavior, on the other. This inconsistency, however, creates no undue strain within the citizen; for politics, as much of our data suggest and as the data from many other studies confirm, is not the uppermost problem in his mind. Compared with other concerns, politics is usually invested with relatively little affect or involvement. Thus inconsistencies among attitudes or between attitudes and behavior can be more easily tolerated, for they can be overlooked or ignored. As Rosenberg and Abelson have put it, ". . . potential imbalance will remain undiscovered by an individual unless he is motivated to think about the topic and in fact does so." [11] Because politics has little importance for them, few citizens are motivated to think about their influence or their political activities.

That politics has relatively little importance for citizens is an important part of the mechanism by which the set of inconsistent political orientations keeps political elites in check, without checking them so tightly as to make them ineffective. For the balance of inconsistent orientations would be more difficult to maintain if the issues of politics were always considered important by the citizens. If issues arise that individuals consider important, or if some relatively severe dissatisfaction with government occurs, the individual will be motivated to think about the topic and thus will be under greater pressure to resolve the inconsistency — to make attitudes and behavior consonant with each other. One way he may do this is to bring his behavior into line with norms and

[10] Some of the important literature developing this theory includes: Leon Festinger, *A Theory of Cognitive Dissonance,* Evanston, Ill., 1957; F. Heider, *The Psychology of Interpersonal Relations,* New York, 1958; C. E. Osgood, C. J. Suci, and P. H. Tannenbaum, *The Measurement of Meaning,* Urbana, Ill., 1957, and M. J. Rosenberg *et al., Attitude Organization and Change,* New Haven, Conn., 1960. See also the special issue of the *Public Opinion Quarterly* on attitude change, XXIV (Summer 1960), especially the articles by Zajonc, Cohen, Rosenberg, and Osgood.

[11] Milton J. Rosenberg and Robert F. Abelson, "Analysis of Cognitive Balancing," in Rosenberg *et al., op. cit.,* chap. IV, p. 121.

perceptions by becoming politically active. Thus the inconsistency between attitudes and behavior acts as a latent or potential source of political influence and activity.

To say that the civic culture maintains the balance between power and responsibility suggests a further point about democratic politics. It suggests why unresolved political issues of great importance eventually create instability in a democratic political system. The balance between activity and passivity can be maintained only if the issues of politics are relatively mild. If politics becomes intense, and if it remains intense because of some salient issue, the inconsistency between attitude and behavior will become unstable. But any relatively permanent resolution of the inconsistency is likely to have unfortunate consequences. If behavior is brought into line with attitudes, the amount of attempted control of elites by nonelites will create governmental ineffectiveness and instability. On the other hand, if attitudes change to match behavior, the resulting sense of impotence and noninvolvement will have damaging consequences for the democratic quality of the political system.

However, this does not suggest that all important issues damage a democratic political system. It is only when issues become intense and remain intense that the system may be made unstable.[12] If significant issues arise only sporadically

[12] It is important to stress the term *issues* used in this connection. Not all salient political events are issues, i.e., points of dispute. This model applies best to those political disputes in which individuals are involved and have relatively specific demands that they would like satisfied by the government. The content of some political events may be so distant from the individual that, though he may consider the events important, he is in no position to formulate demands relevant to them; thus even if the issue is significant, he will exert less pressure on political elites than he would on other issues. (Warren Miller has found that there is a closer relationship between the views of constituents and their Congressmen on such subjects as civil rights and welfare than on foreign policy. The relatively greater distance of foreign policy issues from the ordinary man might explain this. See Miller, "Policy Preferences of Congressional Candidates and Constituents," paper delivered at the meetings of the American Political Science Association, September 1961.)

Some political crises that are not issues — i.e., not subjects of disputes among the citizens of a nation or between the citizens and the elites — may

and if the government is able to respond to the demands stimulated by these issues, an equilibrium can be maintained between citizen influence and government influence. In ordinary times, citizens are relatively uninterested in what governmental decisions makers do, and the latter have the freedom to act as they see fit. However, if an issue becomes prominent, citizen demands on officials will increase. If officials can respond to these demands, the importance of politics will fall again and politics will return to normal. Furthermore, these cycles of citizen involvement, elite response, and citizen withdrawal may tend to reinforce the balance of opposites needed for democracy. Within each cycle, the citizen's perception of his own influence is reinforced; at the same time the system adjusts to new demands and thereby manifests its effectiveness. And the system may become generally more stable through the loyalty engendered by participation and effective performance.[13]

These cycles of involvement are an important way of maintaining the balanced inconsistencies between activity and passivity. If the constant involvement and activity associated with salient issues would eventually make the maintenance of the balance difficult, so, too, would the complete absence of involvement and activity. The balance can be maintained over time only if the gap between activity and passivity is not too wide. If the belief in one's political competence is not reinforced occasionally, it is likely to fade. Or, if the belief is maintained in a purely ritual manner, it will not represent

---

lead to an increased involvement in political affairs that is not coupled with increased demands for influence over decisions. Wars, for instance, may unite a population behind the elites and, by triggering off feelings of loyalty, lead to demands for strong leadership rather than for chances to participate in decisions. This type of situation may have unstabilizing consequences for democracy, although the consequences will be different from those spelled out above. In this case, the stress on loyalty and the demand for strong leadership may lead to a reduction of citizen control over governmental elites.

[13] For an example of such a cyclical pattern of disinterest-involvement-influence-withdrawal, see William K. Muir, Jr., *Defending the "Hill" Against Metal Houses,* 1955, cited in Dahl, *Who Governs?* chap. XVI. See Dahl, chap. XXVIII, for a general discussion relevant to our argument.

potential influence or be a check on decision makers. This, perhaps, is what characterizes the "aspirational" political competence observable in Mexico. Mexican respondents manifest relatively high levels of subjective political competence, especially in comparison to their very low levels of "administrative" competence, exposure to communications, and the like. Furthermore, they quite frequently mention group-forming strategies. But as we have seen, their sense of competence is not matched by experience in political action. There is a gap between the subjective perception of competence and actual political behavior, as there is in the United States and Britain. But the gap is much wider. In the United States, for instance, 33 per cent of those respondents who say they believe they can influence the local government have actually tried to do so, as have 18 per cent of the British local competents. But among the Mexican local competents, only 9 per cent report such experience. Thus the perception–behavior gap may be so wide as to make difficult the performance of the dual functions of furthering citizen control and maintaining citizen passivity. For the democratic "myth" to be an effective political force, it cannot be pure myth. It must be an idealization of real behavioral patterns. Where, as perhaps in Mexico, it has very little relation to reality, it cannot function as part of a balanced civic culture.[14]

We have so far dealt with the way in which activity and passivity may be balanced within the individual citizen. But this balance is maintained, not merely by the set of attitudes individuals have, but by the distribution of attitudes among different types of political actors in a system: some individuals believe that they are competent and some do not; some individuals are active and some are not. This variation in beliefs and activity among individuals also helps enforce the power-responsiveness balance. This can be seen if we consider the

[14] If the ordinary man's belief in his competence is to be reinforced, it may not be necessary for him to be personally involved in successful influence activity vis-à-vis the government. It may be enough simply that he be aware of others engaged in such activity. But the likelihood that an individual will see others attempting to influence the government will naturally depend upon how frequently people make such attempts.

equilibrium mechanism described above: an issue becomes salient, activity rises, and balance is restored by a governmental response that reduces the salience of the issue. One reason that an increasingly prominent issue and the consequent rise in political activity are kept from straining the political system is that the prominence of the issue rarely increases for all citizens at once. Rather, it is particular groups that show a rise in political activity, while the rest of the citizens remain inactive. In this way the amount of citizen activity at any one point in time is not so great as to strain the system.

The above discussion is based upon our data on the attitudes of ordinary citizens. But if a mechanism such as the one we postulate is to work, the attitudes of elites must complement those of nonelites. The decision maker must believe in the democratic myth — that ordinary citizens ought to participate in politics and that they are in fact influential. If the decision maker accepts this view of the role of the ordinary citizen, his own decisions serve to maintain the balance between governmental power and responsiveness. On the one hand, he is free to act as he thinks best because the ordinary citizen is not pounding on his door with demands for action. He is insulated by the inactivity of the ordinary man. But if he shares the belief in the influence potential of the ordinary man, his freedom to act is limited by the fact that he believes there *will* be pounding on his door if he does not act in ways that are responsive. Furthermore, if he shares the view that the ordinary man ought to participate in decisions, he is under pressure to act responsively because he believes that such citizen influence is legitimate and justified. Though our data cannot demonstrate this, there is reason to believe that political elites share the political culture of the nonelite; that in a society with a civic culture they, as well as nonelites, hold the attitudes associated with it.[15] Elites are, after all, part of the same political system and exposed to

[15] Yet there are important ways in which elites differ from the general population in their political attitudes; see chap. I, p. 27. Further, there are probably differences in autonomy between British and American political elites; see below, for some comments on these differences.

many of the same political socialization processes as are non-elite. And studies have shown that political and community leaders, as well as those of higher social status, are more likely than those of lower status to accept the norms of democracy.[16]

The consideration of elite attitudes suggests another mechanism whereby elite responsiveness can be enforced while the activity and involvement of the ordinary citizen remain low. The pattern of citizen influence is not always, or even predominantly, one of stimulus (the citizen or group of citizens make a demand) followed by response (the governmental elite acts to satisfy the demand). Rather, the well-known "law of anticipated reactions" may operate here. A good deal of citizen influence over governmental elites may entail no activity or even conscious intent of citizens. On the contrary, elites may anticipate possible demands and activities and act in response to what they anticipate. They act responsively, not because citizens are actively making demands, but in order to keep them from becoming active.[17]

Within the civic culture, then, the individual is not necessarily the rational, active citizen. His pattern of activity is more mixed and tempered. In this way he can combine some measure of competence, involvement, and activity with pas-

[16] Relevant here are our data on the effect of educational differences on the differences in attitudes among respondents. Also relevant is the finding in Samuel Stouffer's, *Communism, Conformity, and Civil Liberties,* New York, 1955, to the effect that community leaders are more tolerant and more accepting of democratic norms than are nonleaders. Several studies of German public opinion support this general finding. See, for instance, Erich Reigrotski, *Soziale Verflechtungen in der Bundesrepublik,* Part 2, and *Basic Orientation and Political Thinking of West German Youth and Their Leaders,* DIVO Institute Frankfurt am Main-Bad Godesberg, 1956.

Political leaders in democracies must express agreement with the democratic myth in public. Of course, much of this may be lip service. But the requirement that they give public support to this set of beliefs also puts pressure on them to accept the beliefs — unless hypocrisy is a conscious value among political elites. As the studies in cognitive dissonance have shown, the requirement that an individual make a certain kind of public declaration creates pressures to change his private beliefs in that direction. See Rosenberg *et al., op. cit.,* and Festinger, *op. cit.*

[17] See Chapter VII for a discussion of "anticipatory" and other forms of influence.

sivity and noninvolvement. Furthermore, his relationship with the government is not a purely rational one, for it includes adherence — his and the decision maker's — to what we have called the democratic myth of citizen competence. And this myth has significant consequences. For one thing, it is not pure myth: the belief in the influence potential of the average man has some truth to it and does indicate real behavioral potential. And whether true or not, the myth is believed.

THE MANAGEMENT OF AFFECT

We have discussed the way in which the civic culture balances involvement and activity with indifference and passivity. But the balance achieved by the civic culture goes further. Not only must involvement and activity be balanced by a measure of their opposites, but the *type* of political involvement and activity must itself be balanced. In particular, there appears to be a need for a balanced affective orientation to politics; or rather, there must be a balance between instrumental and affective orientations to politics. Politics must not be so instrumental and pragmatic that participants lose all emotional involvement in it. On the other hand, the level of affective orientation to politics ought not to become too intense.

There are several reasons why this balance, rather than a maximization of either pragmatism or passion, is needed in an effective democracy. In the first place, political commitment, if it is to be dependable, cannot be completely unemotional. Loyalty to a political system, if it is based on purely pragmatic considerations of the effectiveness of that system, represents, as Lipset has suggested, a rather unstable basis of loyalty, for it is too closely dependent upon system performance.[18] If it is to remain stable in the long run, the system requires a form of political commitment based upon more general attachment to the political system — a commitment we have called "system affect." Furthermore, as Eckstein suggests, a purely pragmatic and unemotional political involvement implies a politics of opportunism; a politics that will

[18] Lipset, *Political Man*, pp. 77-83.

probably lead to cynicism.[19] On the other hand, if an affective commitment to politics or to a particular political group is too intense, this can have unfortunate consequences for a democracy. In the first place, an intense emotional involvement in politics endangers the balance between activity and passivity, for that balance depends on the low salience of politics. Second, such intense involvement tends to "raise the stakes" of politics: to foster the sort of mass, messianic movements that lead to democratic instability.[20] Furthermore, the consequences can be harmful whether the commitment is to the system as a whole and the incumbent elites or only to particular subgroups in society. It is clear that intense commitment to particular political parties or groups can produce an unstabilizing level of fragmentation in the system. But even an intense commitment to the political system and to the incumbent elites is likely to have harmful effects. If citizens are to maintain some control over political elites, their loyalty to the system and to the elites must not be complete and unquestioning. Furthermore, the civic culture implies the maintenance of the more traditional parochial roles along with the role of citizen. The preservation of a sphere of activity that is outside of politics is important if one is to have the balanced participation of the civic culture.[21]

Participation in politics, this suggests, ought to be neither purely instrumental nor purely affective. The political par-

19 Eckstein uses as an example of this the politics of *Trasformismo* of pre-World War I Italy. See his *Theory of Stable Democracy*, p. 33.

20 See Kornhauser, *op. cit.*

21 This helps explain the way in which nonissue crises — that is, political events which, though considered important and salient by the population, do not involve citizen demands for influence over governmental decisions — may destroy the balance of the civic culture. It was suggested in note 11 that they destroy the balance by increasing demands for leadership and therefore shifting the balance away from elite responsiveness. Crises of this sort may upset the balance of the civic culture in another way: by increasing the amount of loyalty to the system to such a high level that it is considered "unpatriotic" to question the actions of elites. When this stage is reached, democracy is obviously in danger. Furthermore, a crisis such as a war may destroy the balance within the civic culture between the parochial and the citizen roles. Too much of life — including the nonpolitical sphere of relations — may become political.

ticipant ought to receive both instrumental and emotional gratifications from his participation. And this balanced involvement in politics again appears to characterize the civic culture in the two more successful democracies. As discussed in Chapter VIII, in the United States and Britain the more the respondent considers himself capable of participating in politics, the more likely he is to receive affective satisfaction from the political system and to evaluate positively the instrumental performance of that system. In contrast, the other three nations show patterns of unbalanced participation. In Germany and Italy the sense of ability to participate is accompanied by a higher evaluation of the instrumental effectiveness of the system but not by a deeper general commitment. In Mexico the opposite is true: sense of participation is accompanied by greater pride in the system but not a higher evaluation of its performance. In Italy and Germany, commitment to the political system is largely pragmatic, and is based on little emotional commitment. In Mexico there may be an unrealistic attachment to symbols, coupled with the absence of a belief in instrumental rewards of politics.

CONSENSUS AND CLEAVAGE

Our data suggest another way in which the political cultures of the more successful democracies are characterized by a balanced type of commitment. As was reported at various places throughout this volume, respondents in the United States and Britain more frequently than respondents in the other three nations express pride in their political system and feel satisfaction when voting. They are more likely to report interest in politics and actually to discuss politics. And they are more likely to report some emotional involvement in political campaigns. All these indicate a comparatively high level of political involvement. Yet the political involvement in these two countries is tempered in intensity by its subordination to a more general, overarching set of social values. As the data in Chapter IX suggest, attitudes of interpersonal trust and cooperation are more frequent in the United States and Britain than in the other nations. More important, these general social attitudes penetrate into the realm of politics. The role of social trust and cooperativeness as a component of the civic culture cannot be overemphasized. It is, in a sense, a generalized resource that keeps a democratic polity operating. Constitution makers have designed formal structures of politics that attempt to enforce trustworthy behavior, but without these attitudes of trust, such institutions may mean little. Social trust facilitates political cooperation among the citizens in these nations, and without it democratic politics is impossible. It probably also enters into a citizen's relation with political elites. We argued earlier that the maintenance of elite power was essential in a democracy. We would now add that the sense of trust in the political elite — the belief that they are not alien and extractive forces, but part of the same political community — makes citizens willing to turn power over to them.

Furthermore, these general social attitudes temper the extent to which emotional commitment to a particular political subgroup leads to political fragmentation. This general set of social attitudes, this sense of community over and above political differences, keeps the affective attachments to political groups from challenging the stability of the system. Furthermore, it acts as a buffer between the individual and the political system, and thereby reduces the "availability" (in Kornhauser's use of the word) of the ordinary citizen for involvement in unstabilizing mass movements.[22] These norms — particularly those which say that political criteria are not to be applied to all situations — place a limit on politics. They indicate that certain social relationships are not to be dominated by political considerations. And in this way they allow the individual to maintain a certain degree of independence from the political system.

This brings us to a further balance that must be maintained within a democratic political system: that between consensus and cleavage.[23] Without some meaningfully structured cleavage in society, it is hard to see how democratic politics can operate. If democracy involves at some point a choice among alternatives, the choice must be about some-

[22] *The Politics of Mass Society,* chap. 2.

[23] The significance of this balance is also stressed by Eckstein, Berelson, and Parsons. See the references in note 3 above.

thing. If there were no cleavage, if people did not combine into meaningfully opposed political groupings, this would suggest ". . . a community in which politics was of no real importance to the community,"[24] and one in which the alternation of political elites meant little. Too much agreement would mitigate against the enforcement of elite responsiveness. Yet if cleavage went too far, ". . . a democratic society . . . would probably be in danger of its existence. The issues of politics would cut so deeply, be so keenly felt, and, especially, be so fully reinforced by other social identifications of the electorate . . ." as to threaten democracy.[25] There must be what Parsons has called a "limited polarization" of society.[26] If there is no consensus within society, there can be little potentiality for the peaceful resolution of political differences that is associated with the democratic process. If, for instance, the incumbent elite considered the opposition elite too threatening, it is unlikely that the incumbents would allow a peaceful competition for elite position.

This balance between consensus and cleavage is managed within the civic culture by a mechanism similar to the one that managed the balance between activity and passivity; that is, an inconsistency between norms and behavior. This is illustrated by the data presented on attitudes toward primary group membership and partisan affiliation (reported in Chapters V and X). On the one hand, as all studies of voting behavior indicate, primary groups tend to be homogeneous in the partisan sense; families, friendship groups, workplace groups tend to be composed of people of like political views. And, what may be more important evidence for their partisan homogeneity, if there is some heterogeneity of political views within the group, there will be pressure toward attitude change to produce homogeneity.[27] This homogeneity attests

24 Berelson *et al., op. cit.*, p. 319

25 *Ibid.*

26 Parsons, in Burdick and Brodbeck, eds., *American Voting Behavior*, p. 92.

27 This homogeneity is partly due to the fact that members of a primary group tend to share similar social characteristics that affect their vote. They tend to be members of the same class, residential area, and so forth.

to the existence of cleavage in the political system. If partisan affiliation were not closely correlated with primary group affiliations, it is hard to see how there could be any basis for meaningful political competition, for partisan affiliation would then be unimportant as well as unrelated to basic social groupings in society. On the other hand, the cleavage produced by this correlation between primary group affiliation and partisan affiliation is tempered in the United States and Britain by the consensual norm (discussed in Chapters IV and IX) that one's primary group *ought not* to be politicized. Though one's most intimate associates tend to be of like political affiliation (and if they are not, there will be pressure for attitudes to change until they are), this cleavage is balanced by a general social norm that places some relationships (in theory, if not in practice) above politics. Again, the civic culture allows a balance between apparently contradictory demands through the mixture of a set of norms (that primary groups be nonpartisan) and actual behavior (that primary groups are indeed homogeneous in the partisan sense) that are themselves in contradiction one with the other.

This is but one example of the way in which the civic culture manages cleavage in society. In general, this management of cleavage is accomplished by subordinating conflicts on the political level to some higher, overarching attitudes of solidarity, whether these attitudes be the norms associated with the "rules of the democratic game" or the belief that there exists within the society a supraparty solidarity based on nonpartisan criteria.[28]

This balance, furthermore, must be maintained on the elite as well as the citizen level. Though our data are not relevant here, it is quite likely that similar mechanisms operate on the elite level as well. The elaborate formal and informal rules of etiquette in the legislatures of Britain and the

---

But even when these characteristics are held constant, the political composition of the primary group has a strong residual effect on the individual's political attitudes; see Berelson *et al., op. cit.,* pp. 88-93 and 137-38; and Herbert McCloskey and Harold E. Dahlgren, "Primary Group Influence on Party Loyalty," *American Political Science Review,* LIII (1960), pp. 757-76.

[28] See Parsons, *op. cit.,* p. 100.

United States, for example, foster and indeed require friendly relations (or at least friendly words) between the supporters of the opposing parties. And this tempers the intensity of partisanship. It is not that partisanship is destroyed as a significant force; rather, it is kept in its place by more general norms of social relationships.

In sum, the most striking characteristic of the civic culture as it has been described in this volume is its mixed quality. It is a mixture in the first place of parochial, subject, and citizen orientations. The orientation of the parochial to primary relationships, the passive political orientation of the subject, the activity of the citizen, all merge within the civic culture. The result is a set of political orientations that are managed or balanced. There is political activity, but not so much as to destroy governmental authority; there is involvement and commitment, but they are moderated; there is political cleavage, but it is held in check. Above all, the political orientations that make up the civic culture are closely related to general social and interpersonal orientations. Within the civic culture the norms of interpersonal relationships, of general trust and confidence in one's social environment, penetrate political attitudes and temper them. The mixture of attitudes found in the civic culture, we have argued in this chapter, "fits" the democratic political system. It is, in a number of ways, particularly appropriate for the mixed political system that is democracy.

POLITICAL CULTURE AND STABLE DEMOCRACY

That the civic culture is appropriate for maintaining a stable and effective democratic political process can best be appreciated if we consider the impact of deviations from this model. We can begin by considering again the United States and Britain. We have argued that these two nations most closely approximate the model of the civic culture, but that in important respects they differ from each other in the way in which they approximate the model. Both nations achieve a balance of the active and passive roles of the citizen, but whereas in the United States the balance appears to be weighted somewhat in the direction of the active, participant pole, in Britain it tends somewhat in the direction of the subject, deferential pole. Although in the United States the development of participant orientations has tended to overshadow the subject role, in Britain strong subject orientations have persisted despite the development of more active participant orientations. Though the British citizen became an active participant, he did not lose his respect for the independent authority of government to the extent that this occurred in the United States.

The kind of balance between active and passive orientations is in turn reflected in the way in which the political system balances governmental power and governmental responsiveness. In Britain the persisting deferential and subject orientations foster the development of strong and effective governments and the maintenance of an efficient and independent administrative structure. Americans, on the other hand, tend to be uneasy with a powerful government — and their uneasiness is reflected in the institutional structures of government as well as in the strain of immobility that often pervades the American political process. On the other hand, one can argue that the balance in Britain is tilted too far in the opposite direction. It is possible that deference to political elites can go too far, and that the strongly hierarchical patterns in British politics — patterns that have often been criticized as limiting the extent of democracy in that nation — result from a balance weighted too heavily in the direction of the subject and deferential roles.

In comparison with Great Britain and the United States, Germany, Italy, and Mexico have relatively lower levels of social and interpersonal trust. More important, what social trust there is does not penetrate into political relationships, which tend to represent a separate and autonomous realm of attitudes. The absence of general social attitudes that penetrate the political realm inhibits the ability of citizens to cooperate with each other in their relations with the government. Thus their ability to influence the government in time of need — in particular, their ability to create *ad hoc* political structures for this purpose — is limited. Furthermore, their lack of ability to cooperate politically reflects a more general inability to enter political bargains, to collaborate, and to aggregate interests. The society divides up into closed and relatively hostile camps; or to use our terminology, the balance between consensus and cleavage appears to be heavily weighted toward the latter. In these three nations, and especially in the first two, where the pattern of fragmentation coincides with partisan affiliation, the political culture seems to be unbalanced in the direction of political cleavage. This is not to argue that Germany and Italy may not be moving toward a reduction of political fragmentation. Certainly in Germany the current political party system represents a much lower level of fragmentation and interparty hostility than existed under the Weimar Republic. But at present the balance appears to lie in the direction of cleavage rather than consensus, and this in turn affects the operation of the political system.

Perhaps the most significant deviations from the civic culture occur in the political participation and commitment in these three nations. In the ideal civic culture the activity and involvement of the citizen are balanced by a measure of passivity and noninvolvement. Similarly, the commitment itself is balanced, combining a commitment to the actual operation and performance of the government as well as to the political system per se. But in Germany, Italy, and Mexico, there are important deviations from these ideal patterns, and the deviations differ from one country to another.

In Germany a passive subject orientation persists and has not yet been balanced by a participant orientation. Our German respondents appear more at ease in dealing with the output side of governmental activity, where government becomes administration rather than politics. Political activity tends to be more formal than informal — exposure to mass media, voting, formal but inactive membership in voluntary associations. Within these dimensions the activity levels are high, but they are not matched in frequency by more informal political discussions or group-forming influence strategies. Furthermore, the commitment to the system is heavily oriented to the output of the system. Those who consider themselves competent to participate in political decisions are more likely to be satisfied with governmental output, but their more general attachment to the system, or what we call system affect, is not likely to be any higher. And in general, though the satisfaction with governmental operations is relatively high, the attachment to the system is much lower. In Germany, then, the balance of the political culture is weighted in the direction of the subject role and of passive forms of participation. The government is viewed largely as an agency of administration. And the attachment to the political system is closely related to the ability of the government to satisfy pragmatic needs.

The response patterns in Italy are similar to those in Germany in certain important respects. As in Germany, the type of commitment to the political system is closely related to governmental output without being balanced by system affect. But Italian response patterns differ from the German, for the sense of subject allegiance is not present. If the German does not fully participate as an influential citizen in the input side of government, he does consider himself capable of acting effectively as a subject within an administrative context. The Italian, on the other hand, is more likely to be thoroughly alienated both as participant and as subject.

In some respects the Mexican political culture represents the most interesting imbalanced pattern of commitment and involvement. In this country the role of allegiant subject is least well developed. The Mexicans are more alienated from governmental output than are respondents in any of the other four nations — especially in terms of administrative output. Yet this alienation does not involve the more consistent pattern of alienation found in Italy. There is a relatively high level of system affect, especially connected with the symbols of the Mexican Revolution. Furthermore, there is a participant orientation toward the input side of the political system. But the type of participant orientation is what we have called an aspirational one. The level of subjective political competence is relatively high, but is unmatched by performance. This gap between perceived ability to influence the government and actual experience with such influence is also a feature of the civic culture, but the gap in Mexico is much wider than in the United States and Britain. And the relatively high level of political information, exposure to mass media and political communications upon which the American and British sense of political competence rest is also missing in Mexico. In Mexico, therefore, the balance between subject and participant orientations is heavily weighted in the direction of the participant. And the orientation to participation is not a balance of aspiration and performance where the former supports the latter, as in the civic culture; instead, it is a concentration on aspiration in which the performance remains unfulfilled.

Germany, Italy, and Mexico deviate from the civic culture in three different ways, but in each country the deviations create a political culture incongruent with an effective and stable democratic political system. In Germany the lack of commitment to the political system that is relatively independent of system output suggests that the stability of the system may be in doubt if the level of output becomes less satisfactory. There is little capital of "system affect" to draw upon if governmental performance should weaken. Furthermore, weakness of the participant role in Germany, especially the lack of an informal participatory culture, suggests that too much reliance is placed upon hierarchical leadership. Though the formal political institutions of democracy exist in Germany and though there is a well-developed political infrastructure — a system of political parties and pressure groups — the underlying set of political attitudes that would regulate the operation of these institutions in a democratic direction is missing.

In Mexico relatively high levels of system affect are coupled with a lack of experience with political input and an almost total rejection of political output. But the aspirational aspect of the Mexican political culture suggests a potentiality for a civic culture, for the orientation to participation is present. But if the German political system lacks the capital of system affect that might allow it to weather crises, the Mexican system may be described as living off its capital of system affect. Unless the output performance of the system can match the aspirations of the citizens (and what is relevant is not the objective level of output, but the evaluation of its adequacy by the citizens), then the Mexican pattern, too, may have within it the seeds of instability.

Italy suggests an even higher level of instability. Though Germany and Mexico have some of the components of the civic culture, Italy lacks both the passive output satisfaction of the Germans and the aspirational input satisfaction of the Mexicans. The potential for the development of a civic culture would appear lowest here.

These considerations ought not to be taken as predictions of the future of the three political systems. We are spelling out differing potentialities, but we have concentrated on too narrow an aspect of the political system to allow prediction. To a considerable extent the future of these nations will be affected by the nature of their political cultures, but other factors will also have important consequences. International events, which have been outside our purview, will certainly have significant effects both on the political cultures of these nations and on their performance and stability. The future of German democracy rests in part on tendencies within the political culture, but it rests as well on the resolution of the East–West conflict; and Italy's political future is not unaffected by these tensions. And certainly since the advent of Castroism in Cuba, the impact of the external environment upon Mexico's political culture and structure has become especially important. The political cultures of these nations will play important roles in mediating these external impacts, but the weight of these impacts make it difficult for us, as students of political culture, to predict the future.

THE SOURCES OF THE CIVIC CULTURE

This study began with a concern for understanding the development of political democracy. Our concern was occasioned by the large number of nations in which the realization of such a political system is an overt yet difficult goal. We refer, not only to the new nations of the world, but to many older nations that have for a long time been attempting to create a stable pattern of democratic institutions. The statesmen who attempt to create political democracy often concentrate upon the creation of a formal set of democratic governmental institutions and the writing of a constitution. Or they may concentrate upon the formation of a political party to stimulate the participation of the masses. But the development of a stable and effective democratic government depends upon more than the structures of government and politics: it depends upon the orientations that people have to the political process — upon the political culture. Unless the political culture is able to support a democratic system, the chances for the success of that system are slim.

The civic culture appears to be particularly appropriate for a democratic political system. It is not the only form of democratic political culture, but it seems to be the one most congruent with a stable, democratic system. It may therefore be useful to consider how it is transmitted from generation to generation. The first point that may be made is that it is not taught, in any complete sense of the term, in the schools. Civics training in the United States stresses a kind of citizen behavior that is closer to the rationality-activist model than to the civic culture. This is an important component of the civic culture, but it is only one component. In Great Britain, where there is also a close approximation of the civic culture, there is relatively little explicit attempt to inculcate either the pattern of norms and behavior associated with the civic culture or the pattern associated with the rationality-activist model. There is little explicit philosophy concerning what makes a "good British subject" and how children ought to be trained for their role as citizens. The point is not that the explicit training in the schools plays no role in the creation of a civic culture; it is, rather, that it may play only a minor role.

That the civic culture is not transmitted solely by explicit indoctrination is not surprising. Its attitudes and behavior combine in a complicated, subtle way; it is a culture that is characterized to some extent by inconsistencies and the balancing of opposites. One important component of the civic culture is the set of attitudes concerning confidence in other people — a diffuse, partially inconsistent pattern that does not lend itself readily to explicit teaching. How, then, can it be transmitted from generation to generation?

Our consideration of political socialization in Chapter XI suggests an answer. The civic culture is transmitted by a complex process that includes training in many social institutions — family, peer group, school, work place, as well as in the political system itself. Furthermore, the types of experience within these institutions vary. Individuals learn political orientations through intentional teaching, as in a school civics class; but they also learn through overtly political experiences that are not intended to be lessons in politics, as when the child overhears parents discussing politics or when he observes the action of the political system. Or the training in political orientations may be neither explicit nor political in content, as when the individual learns about authority from participating in authority structures in the family or the school or when he learns about the trustworthiness of others from his early contact with adults.

So broad a pattern of political socialization provides an excellent way to inculcate the subtleties that comprise the civic culture. Insofar as some of the teaching is implicit, inconsistencies among orientations can be passed on without recognition. And insofar as many types of political training occur simultaneously, one may learn different aspects of the political culture from different sources. This kind of learning can minimize the strain that might result if orientations toward activity and passivity (to take one example of the opposing political attitudes of the civic culture) were introduced from a single source. Thus through his own participation in family and school and through the manifest teaching of the norms of political participation, the child may learn to expect opportunities to participate in decisions. Yet at the same time, his exposure to the necessarily hierarchical patterns of authority in family and school will temper this expectation of mastery over his political environment. Similarly, what he learns in civics textbooks about the need for political activity and for a politics of idealism will be tempered by what he observes of the actual political behavior and attitudes of adults. And this mixed set of orientations developed in childhood will be further modified by later, direct experiences with politics. His expectations and norms about participation will interact with the opportunities that the political system offers for participation, with the importance he himself places on particular issues, and with the demands that other roles place upon him.

A major part of political socialization, then, involves direct exposure to the civic culture and the democratic polity themselves. In this way each new generation absorbs the civic culture through exposure to the political attitudes and behavior of the preceding generation.

The preceding discussion, on the problem of transferring the civic culture from generation to generation, applies mostly to those nations where the civic culture already exists. But this is not the problem of the new nations. If a civic culture is to be created in these nations, it must be newly created. How can this be done? Such a question takes us well beyond the scope of our data, yet the characteristics of the civic culture and the political histories of the nations in which it has developed suggest two points. First, the civic culture emerged in the West as a result of a gradual political development—relatively crisis-free, untroubled, and unforced. Second, it developed by fusion: new patterns of attitudes did not replace old ones, but merged with them.

The reasons why this pattern of historical development facilitated the emergence of a civic culture are clear. It is a political culture of moderation. In it there is awareness of political issues, yet such issues are not the most salient for the ordinary man; there is involvement in politics, but the involvement is not intense. These political attitudes can only appear, one can argue, where political development has been relatively untroubled; where the stakes of politics are high enough to involve more and more people in the political process, but not so high as to force them to enter into politics as if into a battle to protect their interests from dangerous adversaries.

Less obvious, but also implied by the nature of the civic culture, are the reasons why it developed by fusion. For it is a mixed culture, combining parochial, subject, and participant orientations. Its development must be one in which the newer orientations to political participation merge with the older two orientations but do not replace them.

There are, as we have seen, two aspects to this fusion. On the one hand, the orientations associated with the diffuse patterns of traditional authority are not completely replaced by the newer, more differentiated patterns of political orientation. And second, the more active role of participant does not replace the more passive roles of parochial and the subject. The result is the type of civic culture found in the United States and Britain, where the political system is permeated by diffuse and general social values. For this permeation to continue, the development of a modern polity, with its functional, specific political units and its structured form of political competition, must not take place in a way that will shake the original community. These older orientations must be carried on into the modern system.

Similarly, the development of political democracy, with the spread of opportunities for the ordinary man to participate in the political decision-making process, cannot completely destroy the subject orientation to politics if there is to be a civic culture. The new way of making political decisions through participation of citizens does not so much replace the old mode of governmental operations as supplement it. In this way the blend of activity and passivity that characterizes the civic culture can be created.

THE FUTURE OF THE CIVIC CULTURE

This gradual, fusional growth of the civic culture has generally occurred in a political system whose problems have been spread over time. A variety of new groups have wanted entry into full participation, but not all groups at once. Major social issues have had to be resolved, but at different times. This gradualness of political change characterizes British and, to a lesser extent, American political history. The problem in the new nations of the world is that such gradualness is not possible. There is great demand for participation in politics from many who were only recently parochials. Tremendous problems of social change must be faced all at once. And what may be most crucial: the very acts of creating national boundaries and national identity must go on at the same time. A slow political development may foster a civic culture, but what the new nations of the world lack is the time for this gradual development.

These new nations are seeking to accomplish in a brief period of time what took centuries to consummate in the West. Is it possible to find substitutes for this gradual and fusional process of political change? There is no clear answer to this question, and one can only speculate. If our study has taught us anything, it is that there is no simple formula for the development of a political culture conducive to the maintenance of democracy. However, several conclusions do emerge that have a bearing on this problem.

The most obvious substitute for time would be education. Our data have shown education to be the most important determinant of political attitudes; and it is also the most manipulatable. The great advantage of education is that skills that may take years to develop for the first time can be passed on much more easily once there are some who possess them. Education, as our data have shown, can develop a number of the major components of the civic culture. It can train individuals in the skills of political participation. They can be taught how to gather information; they can be brought into contact with the mass media; they can learn the formal structure of politics, as well as the importance of governmental and political institutions. And it is possible to communicate through education the explicit norms of democratic participation and responsibility.

But our data also show that education can create only some of the components of the civic culture. The schools can teach the cognitive skills connected with participation, but can they teach the underlying social attitudes that are an important component of the civic culture? Can education teach social trust and confidence? Can it foster the permeation of the political process by these social attitudes? And can the curious mixture of activity and passivity, involvement and indifference, of parochial, subject, and participant orientations be communicated through formal education? Our analysis of the relationship between the socialization processes and the creation of a civic culture suggests that formal education may not adequately substitute for time in the creation of these other components of the civic culture.

One way of supplementing formal education might be to develop other channels of political socialization. As was suggested above, the very existence of a large number of channels of political socialization fosters the inculcation of the mixed pattern of attitudes of the civic culture. It increases the variety of political orientations that can be transmitted. More important, experience with a multitude of socializing agencies can train the individual to deal with varied roles at the same time — to schedule and balance his political orientations. And this ability to handle numerous roles is a major component of the civic culture. Some important socializing agencies are the family, the work place, and voluntary associations. Perhaps as these institutions change and develop in the new nations, the channels of socialization for the civic culture will broaden. As the family becomes more participant and open to the political process — and our data suggest that this is a function of modernization — new opportunities to foster civic attitudes may develop. Similarly, occupational changes that accompany industrialization, as well as the development of a structure of voluntary associations, may increase the channels of socialization.

But even the opening of these new channels may not be enough for the development of a civic culture. Such channels may foster attitudes toward participation, but their importance in the creation of social trust and affective commitment to the system is more questionable. If these socializing agencies are in a fragmented political system, for example, the affect developed might be one of alienation, and the interpersonal trust might not be translatable into politically relevant trust. What is required is a process by which individuals can come to develop a sense of common political identity; an identity that implies common affective commitment to the political system, as well as a sense of identity with one's fellow citizens. Participation and cognitive skills are not enough to create a political community in which one trusts and can cooperate politically with one's fellow citizens, and in which one's attachment to the political system is deep and affective.

The problem, then, is to develop, along with the participation skills that schools and other socializing agencies can foster, affective commitment to the political system and a sense of political community. How this might come about is suggested if we consider for a moment the patterns of political culture in Germany and Mexico, two nations that are particularly relevant here. In Germany we find a high level of political cognition. What is missing is system affect and a sense of ability to cooperate with one's fellow citizens. In Mexico we find the educational and cognitive components weaker, but there is system affect and a highly developed sense of identity as Mexicans. And this sense of identity is accompanied by a sense of ability to cooperate politically — or at least the aspiration for such cooperation. Mexico lacks the developed educational system that produces the high levels of cognitive political skills in Germany, but it has what Germany lacks to produce a high level of system affect. Mexico has had a symbolic, unifying event: the Mexican Revolution. This revolution, as we have argued, is the crucial event in the development of the Mexican political culture, for it created a sense of national identity and a commitment to the political system that permeates almost all strata of the society.

If a new nation is to create a civic culture, it needs both the unifying symbols and system affect that the Mexican Revolution has provided, as well as the cognitive skills that exist in Germany. There must be a symbolic event, or a symbolic, charismatic leader, or some other means of creating commitment and unity at the symbolic level. But also important are expanding educational opportunity, experiences in industrial contexts, and exposure to the media of communication, to political parties, and voluntary associations. Governmental performance, too, has a crucial effect on the growth of a civic culture. As the German and Mexican cases illustrate, the development of stable political commitment may hinge upon the ability of the political system, especially in its formative stages, to produce output that satisfies the expectations of the members of the system. Only in this way can a stable and balanced commitment to the system be created and maintained.

Stated in these terms, the difficulties confronting efforts to create effective democratic processes and the orientations necessary to sustain them in the developing areas may appear to be insurmountable. What seems to be called for is the simultaneous development of a sense of national identity, subject and participant competence, social trust, and civic cooperaiveness. The resources available to the elites of the new nations are scarce, and there are limits on the capacity of these societies to assimilate these resources rapidly and effectively. Other goals compete for the same resources. We cannot properly sit in judgment of those leaders who concentrate their resources on the development of social overhead capital, industrialization, and agricultural improvement, and who suppress disruptive movements or fail to cultivate democratic tendencies. Nor can we properly condemn those who, when confronted with the enormous range and pressure of the problems of modernization, are unable to make the necessary painful choices and thus permit their societies and political processes to drift into chaos. Few Western statesmen have ever been called upon to cope with such a range of issues and choices all at once.

What our study enables us to argue is that *any* approach to modernization has within it some of the seeds of the civic culture. Any set of modernizing priorities will place heavy stress on education; and rising levels of education will create some of the components of a civic culture. Thus an imaginative approach to education may serve to increase its civic dividends. The probability is also high that any approach to modernization will tend to enlarge the urban–industrial sector of the society. And we know that the urban–industrial family and occupations have within them civic potentialities. Broadly speaking, we can say that these core processes of modernization — education and industrialization — create a democratic opportunity; the problem then becomes, what *other* investments of energy, resources, and imagination can consolidate these tendencies and potentialities, and what are their relative costs?

The answers to these questions are not readily available. It is only in recent decades that political science has turned its attention to a realistic and serious analysis of the nature of democratic and other types of political process. We are only beginning to develop a theory of political systems and political change that might be of use to democratic statesmen in the new nations. What we have done in this book is to spell out methodically the mixture of attitudes that support a democratic system. If it can create a more sober and informed appreciation of the nature and complexity of the problems of democratization, it will have served its purpose.

Index